# Meeting the Standards in Using ICT for Secondary Teaching

Steve Kennewell

RoutledgeFalmer
Taylor & Francis Group

LONDON AND NEW YORK

First published 2004
by RoutledgeFalmer
11 New Fetter Lane, London EC4P 4EE

Simultaneously published in the USA and Canada
by RoutledgeFalmer
29 West 35th Street, New York, NY 10001

*RoutledgeFalmer is an imprint of the Taylor & Francis Group*

© 2004 Steve Kennewell

Typeset in Bembo by Graphicraft Limited, Hong Kong
Printed and bound in Great Britain by Bell & Bain Ltd, Glasgow

*British Library Cataloguing in Publication Data*
A catalogue record for this book is available from the British Library

*Library of Congress Cataloging in Publication Data*
A catalog record for this book has been requested

ISBN 0-415-24987-2

# Meeting the Standards in Using ICT for Secondary Teaching

This book explains how Information and Communications Technology (ICT) has the potential to make a real improvement to teaching and learning across the curriculum in secondary schools. It illustrates a wide variety of ways in which ICT can be used to enhance learning, offering a fresh burst of inspiration for the busy secondary school teacher.

The author takes a structured approach, ensuring that the reader is guided progressively through all the material in order to achieve the required standards for achieving Qualified Teacher Status, and also to continue their development in ICT to an advanced level. This book usefully:

- analyses all the common ICT tools and explains how teachers of each subject in the National Curriculum can exploit these tools for effective learning;
- explores how pupils learn with ICT, how their skills develop, and how these skills can aid their learning;
- provides a framework for planning, analysing and evaluating teaching with ICT;
- offers a range of innovative tasks, resources and methods of assessment.

*Meeting the Standards in Using ICT for Secondary Teaching* represents a major step forward in the professional litera                                    g and will be a must-buy textbook for                                     and practising teachers in all subjects a

**Steve Kennewell** is a fo                                    is now Lecturer in Education at the Uni                                    r specialist ICT teachers and supporting the use of ICT in teaching secondary subjects.

**Meeting the Standards Series**

*Series Editor*:
Lynn D. Newton, School of Education, University of Durham, Leazes Road, Durham, DH1 1TA

# Contents

# Illustrations

## TABLES

## FIGURES

# Series Editor's Preface

This book has been prepared for students training to be secondary school teachers who face the challenge of meeting the many requirements in Information and Communications Technology (ICT) specified in the government's Circular 02/02, *Qualifying to Teach: Professional Standards for Qualified Teacher Status* (DfES/TTA, 2002). The book forms part of a series of publications that sets out to guide trainees on initial teacher training programmes, both primary and secondary, through the complex package of subject requirements they will be expected to meet before they can be awarded Qualified Teacher Status.

Why is there a need for such a series? Teaching has always been a demanding profession, requiring of its members enthusiasm, dedication and commitment. In addition, it is common sense that teachers need to know not only what they teach but also how to teach it most effectively. Current trends in education highlight the raising of standards (particularly in the areas of literacy and numeracy), the use of new technologies across the curriculum and the development of key skills for lifelong learning. These run the requirements of the National Curriculum, the National Strategies, PSHE and Citizenship work, National Curriculum Assessment Tests (NCATs), interim tasks, GCSE examinations, new post-16 examination structures, BTEC qualifications. . . . The list seems endless. Such demands increase the pressure on teachers generally and trainee teachers in particular.

At the primary school level, since the introduction of the National Curriculum there is an even greater emphasis now than ever before on teachers' own subject knowledge and their ability to apply that knowledge in the classroom. Trainees have to become Jacks and Jills of all trades – developing the competence and confidence to plan, manage, monitor and assess all areas of the National Curriculum plus religious education. The increasing complexity of the primary curriculum and ever more demanding societal expectations make it very difficult for trainees and their mentors (be they tutors in the training institutions or teachers in schools) to cover everything that is necessary in what feels like a very short space of time. Four of the books in this series are aimed specifically at the trainee primary teacher and those who are helping to train them:

- *Meeting the Standards in . . . Primary English*
- *Meeting the Standards in . . . Primary Mathematics*
- *Meeting the Standards in . . . Primary Science*
- *Meeting the Standards in . . . Primary Information and Communications Technology*

For those training to be secondary school teachers, the pressures are just as great. They will probably bring with them knowledge and expertise in their specialist subject, taken to degree level at least. However, content studied to degree level in universities is unlikely to match closely the needs of the National Curriculum. A degree in medieval English, applied mathematics or biochemistry will not be sufficient in itself to enable a secondary trainee to walk into a classroom of 13 or 16 year olds and teach English, mathematics or science. Each subject at school level is likely to be broader. For example, science must include physics, chemistry, biology, astronomy, and aspects of geology. In addition there is the subject application – the 'how to teach it' dimension. Furthermore, secondary school teachers are often expected to be able to offer more than one subject and also use ICT across the curriculum as well as as a subject in its own right. Thus, four of the books are aimed specifically at the secondary level:

- *Meeting the Standards in . . . Secondary English*
- *Meeting the Standards in . . . Secondary Mathematics*
- *Meeting the Standards in . . . Secondary Science*
- *Meeting the Standards in . . . Secondary Information and Communications Technology*

All of the books deal with the specific issues that underpin the relevant Teacher Training Agency requirements identified in Circular 02/02. The very nature of the subject areas covered and the teaching phases focused upon means that each book will, of necessity, be presented in different ways. However, each will cover the relevant areas of:

- subject knowledge – an overview of what to teach, the key ideas under-pinning the relevant subject knowledge that the trainees need to know and understand in order to interpret the National Curriculum requirements for that subject;

- subject application – an overview of how to interpret the subject knowledge so as to design appropriate learning experiences for pupils, organize and manage those experiences and monitor pupils' progress within them.

The former is not presented in the form of a textbook. There are plenty of good quality GCSE and A-level textbooks on the market for those who feel the need to acquire that level of knowledge. Rather, the subject knowledge is related to identifying what is needed for the trainee to take the National Curriculum for the subject and translate it into a meaningful package for teaching and learning. In most of the books in the series, the latter is structured in such a way as to identify the generic skills of planning, organizing, managing, monitoring and assessing the teaching and learning. The content is related to the specific requirements of Circular 02/02. The trainee's continuing professional development needs are also considered.

The purpose of the series is to give practical guidance and support to trainee teachers, in particular focusing on what to do and how to do it. Throughout each book there are suggested tasks and activities that can be completed in the training institution, in school or independently at home. They serve to elicit and support the trainee's development of skills, knowledge and understanding needed to become an effective teacher.

*Professor Lynn Newton*
*University of Durham*
*March 2004*

# Introduction

## The purpose of the book

This book is intended to provide a helpful introduction to the effective use of ICT in teaching all the main subjects at secondary level. It goes beyond the introductory level concerning the planning and analysis of teaching situations, and teachers already experienced in the use of ICT in teaching will find much of value in this book.

Good teachers develop tacit knowledge from a range of experiences of using ICT in the classroom. I have analysed a wide range of case studies of effective practice, and attempted to abstract general principles. I have presented these, together with illustrative examples, in a way that should help new teachers to understand something of the complex relationships involved in the effective use of ICT in teaching and learning. Trainee teachers should be able to use this understanding in order to plan for themselves, rather than merely copying their mentors. New teachers will still make mistakes, of course, but the principles set out in this book provide a basis for evaluating their own practice and discussing how to improve.

The principles, practical advice and examples of practice set out in the book are drawn from published research and professional advice, and from observations and reflection on many lessons which I have taught or observed. I would like to take this opportunity to thank the many teachers and students who have given me opportunities to observe and analyse their practice.

The field of ICT in subject teaching is still an immature one in educational research and, furthermore, many of the relevant published studies are subject specific in nature. Consequently, I have often drawn on general principles of effective teaching together with anecdotal evidence about ICT's impact in order to make tentative generalisations. Nevertheless, I hope that the ideas and suggestions provided will guide readers in the planning, implementation and evaluation of lessons that are rewarding for themselves and their pupils, and towards other effective professional activities.

The illustrative examples of ICT in practice draw on published sources as far as possible, so that readers can follow them up in greater detail and investigate the specialist subject issues that I have glossed over. I have provided references which are designed to be accessible and helpful, although they may not be primary sources. The examples do not always showcase the newest technology, because I have focused on applications for which the pedagogical value is well established and clearly analysed. I have selected material so as to represent a wide range of different ICT resources and teaching approaches, and they do not necessarily represent the best possible use in particular subjects. The scope of the book is not designed to be comprehensive concerning the teaching of particular subjects, but it fully covers the current standards for QTS relating to ICT in England, as well as the previous, more detailed specification (4/98 Annex B). Indeed, it goes well beyond the 1998 standards, in order to reflect the higher expectations of the use of ICT which comes with the increase in school resources and in trainee teachers' ICT skills since that time.

There is no reference in the book to particular brands of hardware or software, and no step-by-step instructions on how to carry out particular techniques. Such material can easily be found elsewhere in a form which is regularly updated and tailored for different brands of software and hardware. Furthermore, I have not attempted to include details of basic concepts and skills of operating PCs and networks such as logging on, file management and window manipulation, as I assume that readers can easily access these ideas from other sources.

## How to use the book

The book is structured so as to parallel the way in which your skills in ICT for subject teaching should develop in most courses of initial teacher training. Chapters 1, 2 and 3 provide an introduction to the field and help you to develop your own knowledge, skills and understanding in ICT. Chapters 4, 5 and 6 are concerned with observation and analysis of the use of ICT in subject teaching. Chapters 7, 8 and 9 are concerned with applying ICT effectively in practical teaching. Chapters 10, 11 and 12 take you further into wider professional issues concerning ICT in teaching. A series of tasks are included for you to try.

This book is not intended to be read from cover to cover. It is designed to build your abilities progressively, however, and material in later chapters will refer to ideas and examples introduced earlier. Whilst you may wish to read chapters out of sequence in order to match the content of your course and the expectations of your tutors/mentors, it is important to follow any cross-references in order to make the most of the book.

Much of the content may be covered within your institution's course, and the book should be used to complement the practical experiences you will gain. It will help you to reflect on your experiences, consolidate your understanding and broaden your range of ideas. The book will have value for reference on particular topics, and it will be useful to skim the book quickly in order to pick out sections which you need to supplement your course provision. The examples provided are all designed to be well established and relatively easy to implement, rather than cutting-edge ideas. They will still include some which are unfamiliar in your schools, however, and should provide you with helpful ideas for your own practice.

Of course, a book like this should really be written for use in electronic form, but within the limitations of the print medium, the ideas are presented using both pictorial and written form as far as possible in order to cater for different learning styles. Whatever your preference for how information is presented, it is important to process the ideas rather than passively absorbing them. Tasks are suggested throughout the book to help you to improve your understanding and implement ideas in practice. For some of these, possible solutions are suggested in Appendix C; this information is an essential part of the text and it is important to try those questions and check the suggested answers. Bear in mind, however, that there are no 'right' answers when it comes to teaching – the best solution to a teaching challenge depends on many factors, including school policies, resources available, the abilities of your pupils, and your own personality. With the knowledge you gain from this book, you should be able to make the best of the opportunities that you meet. I wish you every success with your use of ICT in subject teaching.

# 1 ICT in Secondary Education

In this first chapter, you are introduced to the role of ICT (Information and Communication Technology) as a tool for teachers and pupils as well as a subject of study. You are provided with examples of the use of ICT, by teachers and pupils, as a resource for teaching, learning, assessment and management. An outline explanation of the standards for qualified teacher status in the UK is given, and you will examine the place of ICT in both the knowledge and the skills required to meet those standards. Guidance on how to use this book is provided, together with other higher education (HE) sessions and school-based activities, in order to reach and surpass the standards for qualified teacher status.

## What is ICT?

The term ICT covers all aspects of computers, networks (including the Internet) and certain other devices with information storage and processing capacity such as calculators, mobile phones and automatic control devices. The common factors here are that the devices process, store or communicate information, and that they are digital – that is, they handle information by representing it in terms of discrete symbols. This gives them massive information handling power in relation to their size and energy consumed, compared with older analogue technologies such as radio and TV, audio and video recording, and traditional telephones. The term has also been used (TTA, 1998) to cover these older media, and the distinction between computing and other resources is becoming blurred as digital technology increasingly pervades our lives. The important thing is what the technology can do, not how it works, but there are a number of general concepts concerning digital technology that you will need to understand in order to use ICT most effectively in teaching your subject. Chapters 2 and 3 explore these in some detail, and Chapter 12 considers some implications of future technology, whilst the rest of this guide focuses on the use of ICT in teaching.

## ICT resources

ICT resources can be broadly classified as:

- **hardware** – the equipment, such as a PC or interactive whiteboard;
- **software** – the stored instructions which enable the hardware to operate automatically, together with the information that it stores and processes, such as a word processing program and the documents produced using it;
- **media** – the materials that carry data and programs, such as floppy or hard disks;
- **services** – combinations of hardware, software and human resources that enable users to achieve more than they could with hardware and software alone, such as the Internet.

---

**Task 1.1**    Table 1.1 shows some ICT resources which are relevant to education. Some of them will be very familiar, others may be less so. For each one, first check that you know what it does (or find out what it does – you do not need to know how it works!) and then classify it as hardware, software, media or a service. You should refer to a glossary, either in book form or on the web, and for more detail about its use in education, see guides such as those from Becta's ICT Advice website (see *Further reading* at the end of this chapter).

Suggested answers are provided in Appendix C as a check.

---

The resources listed in Table 1.1 can be used in three main ways as tools for teaching and learning:

- teacher use in preparation, assessment or professional development;
- teacher use with a class;
- pupil use in the classroom, either to find information or represent their ideas.

The resources will not all be relevant to every subject; process control, for instance, will probably only be relevant to science and technology teachers. Some will only be used in one of the ways listed above: MIS, for instance will usually only be used by the teacher, out of sight of the pupils.

## Case studies on using ICT

Here are some examples of how ICT resources may be used for different purposes related to education. At this stage, the focus will be on the technology and considering what role it might take in teaching and learning. It will be valuable, therefore, to read all these examples carefully and consider what is being achieved by using

**Table 1.1** Types of ICT resource

| Resource | Type |
|---|---|
| CAD (computer-aided design) | |
| Calculator | |
| CD-ROM | |
| Data logging | |
| Database | |
| Desktop PC | |
| Digital camera | |
| Digital video | |
| DTP (desktop publishing) | |
| E-commerce | |
| E-mail | |
| Encyclopaedia | |
| Graphic organiser | |
| Internet | |
| Intranet | |
| Laptop PC | |
| MIS (management information system) | |
| Mobile phone | |
| PDA (personal data assistant) | |
| Playstations | |
| Process control | |
| SMS (text messaging) | |
| Spreadsheet | |
| Video games | |
| VLE (virtual learning environment) | |
| WWW (World Wide Web) | |

**Task 1.2** Which of the resources listed in Table 1.1 do you use regularly? Which have you used occasionally?

Think back to your own schooling. Did you or your teachers use ICT for any aspects of education? If so, how was it used? Do you think it helped?

How is ICT used in your current course for each of the purposes above? How does it help?

Consider the possible ways in which you may use ICT in teaching. Which resources do you think that you will need to become familiar with for teaching?

Are there other ICT resources that you have used in your education or in employment that you think would be useful in schools?

ICT rather than other ways of approaching the teaching. As your pedagogical thinking develops, you will need to switch your focus from the technology itself to the teaching of your specialist subjects, and consider how pupils' learning may be supported by ICT.

## Example 1.1

The Internet was selected by an English teacher to help pupils prepare for a debate on the topic of capital punishment. It enabled pupils to work in small groups, using books and bookmarked websites on the WWW through networked PCs in the Resource Centre, to find information and opinions from a wide range of sources, both from the UK and from countries which have the death penalty. It also enabled each group to send a summary of their arguments by e-mail to other pupils who were acting as speech editors in preparation for the formal debate (TTA, 1999a).

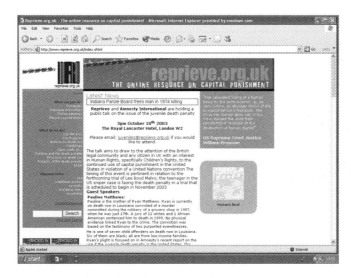

**Figure 1.1**  Accessing views on capital punishment from the World Wide Web: http://www.reprieve.org.uk/ copyright Reprive 2003

## Example 1.2

A spreadsheet program was selected by a science teacher to help pupils produce graphs from prepared data in order to identify relationships between the properties of the planets in the solar system. The topic was introduced by showing animated images from a CD-ROM to the whole class and asking questions to focus pupils' attention on the relative position and movement of planets. Pupils were then required to produce the graphs and use them, together with printed information and the content of selected websites, to produce reports of their findings (TTA, 1999a).

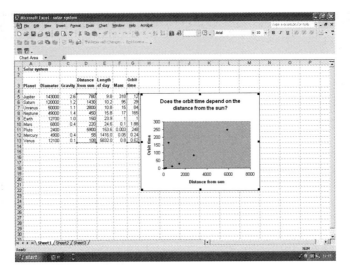

**Figure 1.2**   Spreadsheet showing graph of solar system data

## Example 1.3

A presentation program (such as PowerPoint) was selected by an RE teacher to help pupils to work in small groups preparing a talk to the class on the forms and places of worship of different faiths. Pupils used visits to places of worship and talks with representatives of faiths in order to carry out research. This was supplemented by accessing websites (though search engine or bookmark) and CD-ROM, and by e-mailing information services of different faiths in order to ask detailed questions. The presentation program enabled pupils to use the digital videos and images they had taken on visits or scanned from other sources to illustrate the points made in their talks (TTA, 1999a).

## Example 1.4

A dynamic geometry program was selected by a mathematics teacher to help pupils develop their understanding of the angle properties of parallel lines and triangles.

The teacher was able to demonstrate certain effects and techniques using the software with an interactive whiteboard, and as the image was manipulated, the teacher asked pupils questions to focus their attention on what was changing and what was not. The pupils were then able to use the software in pairs in the ICT room to investigate the relationships between angles made by a line crossing two parallel lines, to make conjectures and test them out with instant feedback (TTA, 1999a).

## Example 1.5

A laptop computer linked to a data projector was selected by a geography teacher to present video clips to a class during an investigation of whether there is a North/

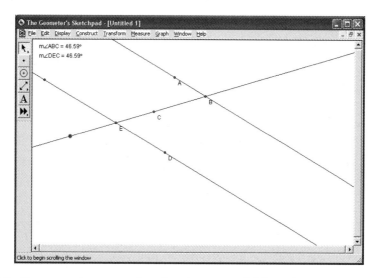

**Figure 1.3** Demonstrating properties of angles on parallel lines dynamically

South divide in Italy. The teacher had filmed a number of key aspects of each area, and transferred the material to her laptop and used video editing software in order to divide it into short clips, each of which illustrated a particular point she wanted pupils to note. She played a number of clips, first without sound in order to focus their attention on what they could see, and then with sound. She was able to ask pupils questions and, depending on their answers, show appropriate clips in order to help pupils to develop their understanding. She encouraged pupils to formulate their own questions and replayed particular clips to help with responses. She used a word processing program, using a large, clear typeface, to record key points as they arose. She switched the display between the video and the document frequently, and developed a long list of ideas that was stored and retrieved for later discussion. The pupils were then required to make summary notes for themselves about what they had learned. This was followed up by a task where pupils worked in pairs on networked PCs, using mapping software to plot the distribution of different social and economic factors across Italy. They were able to draw conclusions about differences between North and South by visually examining the map shading for general patterns concerning population, employment, car ownership, etc. Printouts of each pair's map were displayed on the wall and the conclusions discussed. Pupils then extended their own notes about their learning (based on TTA, 1999b).

## Example 1.6

An Integrated Learning System (ILS) is being used by a specialist teacher of pupils with Special Educational Needs (SEN). The ILS presents information and instructions to pupils (visually on screen and aurally through headphones), sets them tasks, accepts their responses, and, depending on their answers, moves them on to more difficult material or takes them back to further explanation and practice. The teacher is able to access detailed diagnostic reports on each pupil, enabling him to intervene and discuss a point with which the learner is struggling or give praise and set more challenging tasks if the learner is finding the work simple (Underwood and Brown, 1997). There are four computers dedicated to this software, located in a resource base specifically for SEN. Pupils are allocated time for extra help with the basic skills of literacy and numeracy that they need in order to follow the standard curriculum. Pupils use the ILS individually for 15 minutes at a time, usually without teacher intervention, so that the teacher can give more attention to other pupils in a demanding group of children with learning and/or behavioural difficulties.

## Example 1.7

A database management system is being used by a modern foreign languages (MFL) teacher to help with the administration of attainment records for pupils. Every teacher in the school is able to access the database in their classroom when pupils are not present and type in the results of regular assessments of pupils' attainment in their subject together with their judgements of the effort that pupils are exerting. Teachers are able to produce graphs showing the progress of each pupil in their subject, and then compare the overall performance of their class with the results which would be expected on the basis of their previous attainment. Form tutors can chart the performance of their pupils in different subjects, in order to identify areas for potential improvement.

## Example 1.8

E-mail is being used by a design and technology (D&T) teacher to take part in a computer conference with a group of colleagues in other schools around the country. They are piloting a new short GCSE course and need to develop their knowledge of the subject matter and share ideas about teaching materials and project briefs for students. The group is coordinated by an officer from the examination board, and includes the Chief Examiner and an LEA adviser who are experts in the field. Members for the group can send e-mails to a single address, and the exam board server automatically distributes them to members of the group. The teacher can submit a question, and responses can be made by the 'experts' and by other members of the group who have suggestions. The teacher can also respond to questions and follow up points made by anyone in the group. All previous e-mails are available for review, stored and displayed so that it is clear which previous messages are relevant.

## Example 1.9

This example returns to the WWW, but this time to consider its use in planning and preparation. A history teacher is looking for a new approach for introducing the Russian Revolution to a GCSE group, so that pupils gain a better understanding of the conditions in Russia at the time and the relationships amongst the key players. The teacher thinks that ICT may be able to help, and she accesses the Teachers'

Resource Exchange, one of the government's websites that provides support for teachers. The teacher is able to specify the subject, age range and type of resource, and finds that another teacher has contributed a simulation of the Russian Revolution. This is not a simulation program (see Chapter 3), but a role play and decision-making exercise in which character briefings and event scenarios are provided through the web. The teacher decides that it is just the sort of activity that she was looking for, but the web material is presented as rather dense text. The teacher then searches for some images to illustrate the characters and issues which are contained in the scenarios, so that those pupils who are more visually oriented will be more engaged with the material (see Chapter 5).

**Figure 1.4**  Example of contribution to Teacher Resource Exchange: copyright Becta 2003
http://tre.ngtl.gov.uk

---

**Task 1.3**    Find out through your subject mentor and senior mentor what ICT resources you will have access to in school:

- for professional use (for example, in staff room or departmental workroom);
- for teaching (in subject classroom or school ICT rooms).

Find about also about booking arrangements and technical support.

---

## ICT as a key skill and as a specialist subject

Although you are probably learning to teach a subject other than ICT, it will be helpful to gain some understanding of the background to specialist ICT curriculum and teaching.

The original National Curriculum (NC) in England and Wales included an attainment target and programmes of study for IT (as it was then) which included the following strands:

> *Developing ideas and communicating information* includes the use of word processing to draft and re-draft written work; the use of DTP for presenting ideas attractively and effectively; the use of graphics in design; e-mail communication to distant locations.
>
> *Handling information* includes interrogating databases to find numbers and lists of items satisfying particular conditions; creating and editing databases in order to store and retrieve information; analysing and displaying stored data in various ways including graphs and charts.
>
> *Modelling* includes exploring simulations and solving adventure games; creating stored relationships between variables using spreadsheets and programming languages such as Logo.
>
> (Kennewell *et al.*, 2003: 19, based on NCC, 1990: C4)

A growing awareness of applications and effects of ICT within and beyond pupils' experience was also expected.

Since 2000, the National Curriculum for ICT (as the subject is now called) in England has been specified slightly differently, covering the following themes:

- finding things out;
- developing ideas and making things happen;
- exchanging and sharing information;
- reviewing, modifying and evaluating work as it progresses.

(DfEE/QCA, 1999)

This is shown in more detail in Appendix B.

In Wales, a similar structure to the original has been maintained; however, the expected outcomes as set out in the levels of attainment are broadly similar to those in England.

The National Guidelines for ICT in 5–14 Education in Scotland specifies slightly different strands:

- using the technology;
- creating and presenting;
- collecting and analysing;
- searching and researching;
- communicating and collaborating;
- developing informed attitudes.

(Scottish Executive, 2000)

In Northern Ireland, the 11–14 curriculum proposals include the ICT requirement within a Skills and Capabilities Framework (CCEA, 2003). Its main headings are:

- managing and communicating information
- investigating and problem solving.

Despite the differences in how the ideas are presented in different nations, there is a high degree of agreement about what is important in ICT knowledge, skills and understanding. The teaching of this subject matter was originally intended to permeate the rest of the curriculum as far as possible. It was felt that discrete lessons tended to focus on the technology and how to operate it at the expense of understanding a range of situations to which it could be applied. Schools found it difficult to achieve a balance, however, and there was a lack of focus on general understanding of ICT when teachers of other subjects taught what they needed to achieve their subject objectives. Criticisms by the inspection body Ofsted (Goldstein, 1997) led many schools to introduce specialist lessons in ICT, although, ironically, these were often taught by teachers of other subjects because of the shortage of ICT specialist teachers. There have been two UK government responses to this problem. One is to set up more teacher training courses for ICT specialists (see Kennewell *et al.*, 2003); the other is to introduce the National Strategy for ICT at KS3 (DfES, 2002a). It is important for all teachers to be familiar with the ideas taught in the NC for ICT, and the content and approach will be discussed further in Chapter 6.

Beyond the age of 14, ICT remains a compulsory subject in England, but not so in Wales. In any case, at this age the study of ICT tends to be either as a key skill taught within other subjects, or a specialist course leading to a public examination. These courses may be specifically vocational (such as the Applied GCSE and GNVQ in ICT) or more general in nature, such as the GCSE and A-level in ICT or A-level in computing.

The effective teaching of ICT, whether through special lessons in ICT or through the use of ICT in other subjects, should help pupils to develop:

- positive attitudes to the use of ICT;
- confidence in their own abilities to use ICT to solve problems;
- a disposition to apply ICT in relevant situations and critically evaluate its effect;
- personal autonomy in their use of ICT for learning and problem solving.

(Tanner, 2003: 7)

In most schools, you will find an ICT department with a Head and a team of specialist teachers. These colleagues may have a role of helping teachers to use ICT in other subjects as well as teaching their own courses. There may alternatively be a separate ICT coordinator for the whole school, with a leadership role in promoting the development of ICT skills, resources and effective use in the curriculum. Chapter 11 will consider this role in more detail.

## Why is ICT important in education?

*[handwritten note: Link to why do and need ICT]*

ICT is an important part of the modern world, and many aspects of our lives now depend upon it. Its value in supporting effective activity in industry, commerce and the home was noted in the Stevenson (1997) report, which concluded that it was essential for education to incorporate ICT into aspects of activity, even though it had not been established that use of ICT produced improvements in attainment. It was thus an act of faith when the UK government invested large sums in the ICT infrastructure which was referred to as the National Grid for Learning (NGfL) and in the training for serving teachers through the National Opportunity Fund (NOF).

Since then, the evidence of a general impact of ICT on learning has been growing (see, for example, Becta (2002a); Knowsley LEA (2003)). There is much evidence that well thought out applications of ICT in teaching and learning can bring about a variety of benefits for learners (NCET, 1994). Bransford *et al.* (1999: 195) identify five particular ways of using ICT that research suggests are likely to be fruitful:

- bringing exciting curricula based on real-world problems into the classroom;
- providing scaffolds and tools to enhance learning;
- giving students and teachers more opportunities for feedback, reflection and revision;
- building local and global communities that include teachers, administrators, students, parents, practising scientists, and other interested people;
- expanding opportunities for teacher learning.

All these themes will be developed in subsequent chapters.

There are unique features of digital media that make new approaches to traditional activities possible and offer opportunities for new ways of teaching and learning. It is clear that children are using ICT from the earliest possible age, and that knowing *with* ICT as well as knowing *about* ICT is not only essential but also relatively easy for pupils (Kennewell *et al.*, 2000). It may still take some time for the benefits to be demonstrated in terms of attainment, because:

- attainment is currently measured in ways which correspond to traditional teaching and learning approaches;
- although teachers generally believe that ICT has the potential to improve learning, the extent to which ICT is used in the classroom is still very limited for most subjects;
- the ways in which teachers use ICT to improve learning are fundamentally different from the ways in which it is used to improve productivity in offices and factories;
- as with all new initiatives, teachers respond by adapting the new ideas and resources to their existing practice, rather than changing their practices to exploit the new ideas.

> **Task 1.4**  Identify a task that professionals in your subject (research or application) carry out routinely using ICT.
>
> How would it have been done in the days before widespread ICT?
>
> What difference has ICT made to the task?
>
> What are the implications for other aspects of the work?

If you consider the examples set out earlier in this chapter, you can identify a number of aspects that are particularly important in their implications for teaching and learning generally. ICT helps learners to:

- access a wide range of up-to-date information sources from within and beyond the school;
- process information and develop high quality reports;
- produce dynamic images to represent relationships;
- hypothesise and test ideas for themselves;
- engage in activities similar to those carried out by professionals and academics in the subject;
- work together in teams;
- work independently of their teacher.

ICT also helps teachers to:

- access a wide range of up-to-date information sources from within and beyond the school;
- prepare high quality material for pupils to see as a class and to interact with individually;
- organise a variety of resources in advance of a lesson that can be accessed easily and rapidly for class use;
- focus pupils' attention on key concepts;
- monitor pupils' progress on tasks;
- analyse pupils' attainment and set targets for learning;
- collaborate with colleagues in other schools and at times of their choice.

(Kennewell and Beauchamp, 2003)

## What do you need to know about ICT in teaching your subject?

In brief, you need to know how to use ICT effectively in every aspect of teaching. This involves having sufficient ICT skills to be able to decide when it will be beneficial to use ICT, and when it will not; and if it is, what resources and teaching strategies will be appropriate. This is not a simple matter, of course, and in any case there are no definitive right answers. What is most effective depends on the resources available, your skills in using ICT, your experience in the classroom, your subject, your pupils and the school setting in which you are working.

ICT skills are important, but they are not enough on their own. What matters most is your teaching skills and your use of ICT should develop in parallel with your technical capability. The standards to be met in order to qualify as a teacher reflect this. In England, there are statutory requirements which form the basis for inspection of the ICT component of initial teacher training (ITT) courses. They are deliberately brief – the previous version was complex in structure and difficult to manage – but supplementary guidance (see Appendix A) has been issued to provide more detail. Table 1.2 lists the four Standards (TTA, 2002) applying in England, for which either the standard itself or the guidance refers to ICT.

**Table 1.2**   Extracts from *Qualifying to Teach: Professional Standards for Qualified Teacher Status and Requirements for Initial Teacher Training* (TTA, 2002)

Those awarded Qualified Teacher Status must demonstrate that:

- They have a secure knowledge and understanding of the subject(s) they are trained to teach. For those qualifying to teach secondary pupils this knowledge and understanding should be at a standard equivalent to degree level.
- They know how to use ICT effectively, both to teach their subject and to support their wider professional role.
- They teach clearly structured lessons or sequences of work which interest and motivate pupils and which:

  - make learning objectives clear to pupils
  - employ interactive teaching methods and collaborative group work
  - promote active and independent learning that enables pupils to think for themselves, and to plan and manage their own learning.

- They use ICT effectively in their teaching.

## Why is this knowledge necessary?

The potential benefits of ICT have not influenced teaching and learning to the extent that might be expected from the influence of ICT in other walks of life (Stevenson, 1997). This has highlighted the importance of teachers and others involved in education gaining the knowledge needed to use ICT appropriately so as to exploit the skills which pupils are gaining in ICT for the purpose of learning other subjects.

The role of the teacher is changing (Cornu, 2003), and the teacher no longer needs to be the main source of knowledge in the classroom. With ICT, it is possible for children to learn at different times, in different places, without direct supervision by an expert teacher. ICT can facilitate autonomous learning for pupils (Somekh and Davies, 1991), and it is expected that allowing pupils greater autonomy in their work will help them to develop learning skills, which will serve them well during formal education and beyond. But this does not remove the need for an expert teacher to be at the heart of learning activity; learners need a combination of stimulation, structure, guidance and feedback and it is hard for a machine to judge when to inspire, when to encourage, when to support, and when to intervene. The teacher's role as a manager of learning – setting targets, advising on pathways and validating knowledge – is still important, and arguably more so than in traditional educational methods. The difference now is that the teacher must know how to use ICT in teaching and how to help learners use ICT in learning.

## What do you know at present?

Appendix D provides a checklist of basic ICT skills and pedagogical skills with ICT. You and your tutors can use it at a number of stages during your pre-service course and during your early professional development if appropriate. You should aim to become confident and competent in all aspects as soon is as realistic. You should certainly be rating all aspects at least 2 by the end of your pre-service course.

For some subjects, there are extra items which you should add to this general list, and Chapter 5 will help you identify these.

| **Task 1.5** | Complete the self-assessment in Appendix D up to Question 5. |
|---|---|

## How should you develop your knowledge?

In any course of preparation for teaching, whether based in HE or in school, you should be provided with requirements and opportunities to develop your knowledge and skills systematically. This programme may be based on a separate course or module, or it may be integrated into your subject teaching development work. It may be directly taught, or may be based on self-study materials. It is important that you plan to make the most of the opportunities offered. During taught sessions, you should not merely aim to achieve the tasks set, but also consider how you can transfer the skills used in the session to other tasks you might have in future, and what other skills you may need to acquire. You should discuss the methods you use to achieve tasks with your fellow student teachers and with your tutor, to ensure that you develop more efficient ways of solving problems using ICT. It follows that, if you have greater knowledge than your colleagues or your tutor, you should be prepared to help them when appropriate as well. If you have self-study material available, it makes sense to use it while you can. However, it may not be advisable to go through a unit in isolation if you will not have the opportunity to apply the techniques fairly soon afterwards.

There are three stages in learning a new piece of software. The first is to become familiar with the process that the software is designed to help carry out, and with the type of techniques that it provides, so that you can judge when it is appropriate to use it. The second stage involves choosing and using techniques in order to complete a task. This can be left until you need to use it for a real purpose, as this may be the best time to learn the techniques in detail. The first job that you do with the software may be slow to complete and the outcome may be imperfect, but the skills will have a meaningful context and will be more easily remembered. The third stage is to reflect on what you have done, how it could have been improved, and what else you might be able to achieve with the new skills. This will help to ensure that your skills can be utilised in different types of situation. If, for example, you can use a pupil records database to search for pupils living in a particular locality, consider how you might be able to use database search techniques in your subject teaching to help pupils undertake research into a particular issue.

You also need to develop your teaching to incorporate ICT. Your HE or school-based preparation programme should provide ideas about how ICT can best be used in teaching your subject, with demonstration of practices and examples of activities for you to try. The programme should also provide opportunities to discuss issues of planning, preparation, class management and assessment associated with using ICT. But your own teaching skills with ICT cannot be achieved purely by study in HE or at home, and it may be best to use ICT in the classroom at an early stage if possible rather than trying to add it on to your practice later. As with most aspects of teaching, the keys to success are confident knowledge of the subject matter and carefully considered preparation. You cannot be expected to know exactly how to operate every option in a complex software package, but you should be clear about the general principles of its operation, the main techniques that you expect pupils to use, the level of skill that the pupils are expected to have, and the school's policies in relation to developing their skills.

Your opportunities in HE and school may be limited, however, particularly if you are pursuing a one-year course. This book is designed to supplement the skills development programme and subject-specific activities provided in your course of initial teacher training. It will provide extra examples, raise further issues, and offer additional advice. It will also provide a good foundation for early professional development, with Chapters 11 and 12 looking forward to the future.

## Further reading

Becta ICT Advice website http://www.ictadvice.org.uk

BCS (2002) *A glossary of computing terms* (10th edition), Harlow: Addison Wesley

Collin, S. (2002) *Dictionary of information technology* (3rd edition), London: Peter Collin Publishing

*Free on-line dictionary of computing.* Online at http://wombat.doc.ic.ac.uk/foldoc/index.html

# 2 The Nature of ICT and its Potential Contribution to Teaching and Learning

In Chapter 1, you were introduced to a variety of issues concerning ICT in education, and we will now consider some of these in more depth. In this chapter, you will continue to focus on ICT itself and consider critically the reasons for using ICT in education. In order to analyse the ways in which ICT can help in the classroom, you are provided with in-depth explanations of the features of ICT that are listed in the TTA guidance documents, with examples using a range of up-to-date educational technology to help to develop your understanding of the principles and characteristic features of ICT.

## What are the features of ICT that contribute to education?

Certain features have been suggested as those that best characterise what it is about ICT that can help with teaching and learning:

a.  **speed and automatic functions** – the feature of ICT which enables routine tasks to be completed and repeated quickly, enabling teachers to demonstrate, explore or explain aspects of their subject, and allowing pupils to concentrate on thinking and on tasks such as analysing and looking for patterns within data, asking questions and looking for answers, and explaining and presenting results.

b.  **capacity and range** – the ability of ICT to access and to handle large amounts of information; change timescales, or remove barriers of distance; give teachers and pupils access to historical, recent and immediate information and control over situations which would normally be outside their everyday experience.

c.  **provisionality** – the feature of ICT which allows information to be changed easily and enables alternatives to be explored readily.

    **d.**   **interactivity** – the function of ICT which enables rapid and dynamic feedback and response . . .

                       (TTA, 1998: 4 and 14–15)

There are some other implications of these features of which you need to be aware at this stage.

**Speed and automation**: as well as the carrying out of routine tasks quickly, it is worth noting the immediacy with which material, particularly images and video, can be retrieved for display by individual pupils and by the teacher in front of the whole class (Trend et al., 1999). This feature alone can often justify the use of ICT in a lesson.

**Capacity and range**: the sheer amount of information that can be stored by individual teachers and pupils is a significant factor; this is of tremendous value as long as it is organised effectively for later identification and retrieval. The range feature includes three terms for the age of the material:

- historical – archived data and old documents which have been digitised can be viewed;
- recent – ephemeral documents and up-to-date versions of changing documents can be obtained;
- immediate – continually changing data can be accessed in 'real time'.

None of these types of material can easily be obtained in other ways for learning activity in the classroom.

**Provisionality and interactivity**: these features work together to achieve the most important effects for learning: pupils can try out ideas, gain feedback immediately

---

**Task 2.1**    In order to check your understanding of these ideas, consider the features:

- speed
- automation
- capacity
- range
- provisionality
- interactivity.

Which of these apply to each of the following?

1  Mobile phone with voice and text messaging (ordinary telephone)
2  Simple calculator (pencil and paper)
3  Notebook PC (briefcase)
4  Video-conferencing (face-to-face meeting)
5  Digital camera (film camera)
6  Automated Teller Machine or ATM (bank cashier)
7  E-mail (postal service)
8  Playstation (playground)

Suggested answers are given in Appendix C as a check.

from the screen or sound, and then change their original input rather than starting from scratch.

These features are at the heart of ICT's <u>impact on teaching and learning</u>, and you will explore their influence in some detail throughout the book. New technologies are emerging all the time, and current technologies becoming smaller, quicker and more powerful. Consequently, our perception of the possibilities and implications for teaching and learning is continually changing; Chapter 12 will consider how you might attempt to keep up with these developments.

Certain technologies have proved particularly valuable in education. It is worth examining what combinations of the features they demonstrate, and whether there are other features which add further value to these particular forms of technology. As well as the features identified by TTA, it seems that there are at least five other useful features that distinguish ICT from traditional media, and which cannot be represented in terms of the others.

- **Clarity**: text and images can be produced, combined and reproduced with a degree of clarity that is hard to achieve in other ways, for example: choice of neat or artistic fonts; enlarged sizes of text and images; overlaying of annotation; 3-D rendering, graphing of data.
- **Authenticity**: ICT is a professional tool in many fields of life and enables users to engage in realistic tasks and to achieve effects that appear far more professional than can be accomplished with tools traditionally used in education.
- **Focusability**: menu structures and search tools in various forms allow rapid narrowing down of information requirements; also selected parts of images can easily be identified and enlarged to focus attention and facilitate analysis.
- **Multimodality**: information can easily be changed to communicate through multiple senses: sight, hearing, movement.
- **Availability**: the user can choose when and where to use ICT services, without being dependent on the availability of the provider.

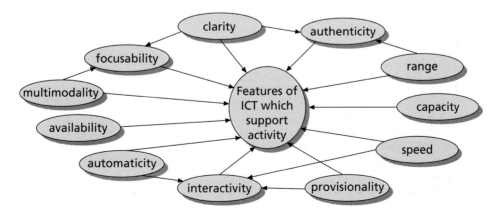

**Figure 2.1** Features of ICT which support activity

**Table 2.1**   Features of ICT resources

| Resource | Principal TTA features | Other principal features |
|---|---|---|
| Word processing/DTP | Provisionality | Clarity and authenticity |
| Presentation | Provisionality | Clarity plus multimodality |
| Web | Range, capacity, interactivity | Authenticity, focusability, availability |
| Digital images and video | Provisionality, capacity | Focusability |
| Data logging | Automation and speed | Authenticity |
| Spreadsheets | Provisionality, automation, interactivity | Authenticity |

You may well be able to identify more as you gain experience and reflect on the use of ICT.

Chapter 3 will consider examples of these features in terms of the software that exploits them and Chapter 4 will consider their application in teaching.

| **Task 2.2** | In contrast to networked and laptop PCs, little direct educational benefit has been gained from the mobile phone. Can you explain this in terms of features you noted for mobile phones in Task 2.1? Do mobile phones have other features which limit their value in education? Do you think that this will change? |
|---|---|

## How can these features assist with educational activities?

There are two main reasons for the current drive to integrate the use of ICT into all subject teaching:

- ICT permeates most other aspects of life – from the supermarket and petrol station to the hospital operating theatre and aircraft autopilot – and it would be perverse to exclude it from education (Stevenson, 1997);
- detailed studies of particular uses of ICT have identified features that support approaches to teaching and learning which should, in the long run, be more effective. ICT:
  — can be a non-threatening environment for learning;
  — has the flexibility to meet the individual needs and abilities of each pupil;
  — allows pupils to reflect on what they have written and to change it easily;
  — gives pupils immediate access to richer source materials;
  — can present information in new ways which can help pupils to concentrate on its interpretation and use;

— removes the chore of processing data manually and frees pupils to concentrate on its interpretation and use;

— gives pupils the power to try out different ideas and take risks;

— offers potential for effective group working.

(NCET, 1994)

> **Task 2.3**    Which of the features do you think will be of most value in the teaching and learning of your subject?

When you observe pupils using ICT, rather than traditional methods, you usually notice a higher level of motivation, a more intense engagement with the activity, and a greater willingness to explore ideas and to persevere in the face of challenge. If exploited effectively, these factors can produce worthwhile improvements in learning through the perception by pupils that events are under their personal control and a belief that greater effort will lead to an improved outcome (Cox, 1999).

In order to plan how best to apply these research findings, you need to understand first how the features of ICT generate the motivation and engagement. This is best explained by examining how three of the features – speed, provisionality and interactivity – work together to provide feedback on activity to the learner and facilitate improvement of work. In a traditional classroom, how long do pupils have to wait for their efforts to be checked by a teacher? They may put their hand up in class and wait for attention, they may be dealt with in strict rotation and have to await their turn, or they may hand work in at the end of the lesson and have it returned with comments the following day or the following week. This is unhelpful to pupils who are unsure of their ideas and are keen to gain confirmation that they have acquired the skills and understanding to the teacher's satisfaction.

With the speed of ICT, however, the pupil gains a response immediately. The response will not be the same as a teacher would provide, but it is often enough to enable the pupil to continue with confidence. Because ICT is interactive, a visual display or sound will be produced when the pupil chooses an option in a quiz, enters some data into a spreadsheet or types a word in a passage of text. Furthermore, if the pupil realises that they have made a mistake – in a spelling, in the response to a multiple choice question, or in a calculation – they can easily correct it because of the provisional nature of ICT storage.

Other features of ICT can help as well. For many learners, routine tasks such as writing and calculating are difficult and daunting. Consequently, they find it hard to focus on the more specific ideas that you are trying to teach. The basic skills form barriers to learning rather than supporting it. The automatic features of ICT can carry out such routine tasks for pupils: through voice input and clicking on menu options they can avoid the laborious entry of text; with a spreadsheet they can quickly produce a graph which would have taken most of the lesson previously. They will often gain in accuracy, too. Many pupils are reluctant to write because the appearance of their text on the page is untidy and difficult to read: for these pupils, typing into a word processor can make a significant difference to the extent and quality of their writing (NCET, 1994). Spellcheckers provide further assistance with accuracy of writing, if used sensibly. Graphs generated by computer or calculator may be limited in their accuracy because of screen or printer resolution, but they will at least have the scales correctly represented and points plotted in the correct places! The learner can then focus on whether the type of graph selected correctly represents the data.

This combination of features is very powerful and promotes a continued engagement with the activity – learners will persevere longer with ICT tasks (NCET, 1994). You also need to understand how the motivation and engagement can be harnessed to stimulate the learning that you are trying to achieve. This will be considered in Chapter 6.

| Task 2.4 | Analyse the examples of activities in Chapter 1 in terms of the features used. | | | | | | | | |
|---|---|---|---|---|---|---|---|---|---|
| | 1.1 | 1.2 | 1.3 | 1.4 | 1.5 | 1.6 | 1.7 | 1.8 | 1.9 |
| Capacity | | | | | | | | | |
| Range | | | | | | | | | |
| Speed | | | | | | | | | |
| Automation | | | | | | | | | |
| Provisionality | | | | | | | | | |
| Interactivity | | | | | | | | | |
| Clarity | | | | | | | | | |
| Authenticity | | | | | | | | | |
| Focusability | | | | | | | | | |
| Multimodality | | | | | | | | | |
| Availability | | | | | | | | | |
| Suggested answers are given in Appendix C as a check. | | | | | | | | | |

In order to make the most of the features of ICT there may be a need for fundamental changes in teaching approach compared with traditional methods. ICT supports a shift from an *instructive* mode to a *constructive* mode of classroom activity. In instructive mode, the primary function of the ICT is to convey knowledge, skills and understanding in a direct way. It supplements, or even replaces, the teacher's role in instructing, demonstrating and explaining points to the learner. It may be used in this way by the teacher (with the whole class or a small group) or by the learner (working independently or in a group, at school or at home). When used by the teacher, the material may be acquired commercially or from other teachers, it may be prepared in advance by the teacher personally, or it may be created on the spot according to the learners' responses to questions.

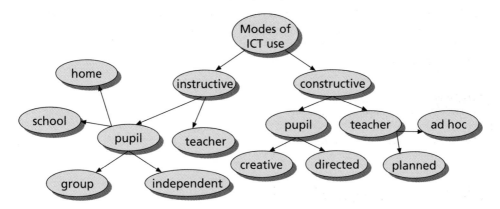

**Figure 2.2**   Modes of ICT use

● In constructive mode, the primary function of ICT is to help to complete a task that produces an outcome, such that learning results from the thinking carried out by learners in order to achieve the task outcome. Again, this can be carried out by the teacher or by the learners. When using this mode, the teacher will be asking pupils for suggestions on how to proceed, and explanations, so that the whole class or group feels involved in achieving the result. The strategy may be planned carefully in advance, or it may occur on the spur of the moment. Learners using ICT construct-ively may be set a specific outcome to achieve (directed) or they may use their own interests and imagination to generate ideas for the outcome (creative).

For instance, Example 1.1 in Chapter 1 (see p. 7) shows the use of constructive mode. The pupils are collecting material and producing scripts in preparation for a debate, and this debate is the overall task outcome. However, the teacher intends that they learn something from the process of preparing and debating, particularly:

● identifying and validating information sources;
● seeking evidence for both sides of an argument;
● evaluating arguments;
● written and oral communication skills;
● working together in teams.

The ICT resources do not teach any of these matters directly; what ICT does is to support pupils' work in the task in such a way that the teacher can more effectively address the learning objectives than if traditional information sources and media were used.

Example 1.2 in Chapter 1 (see p. 7) shows the use of the instructive mode initially. The teacher presents key points about the position and motion of the planets with the aid of software which displays dynamic 3-D images in a way which the teacher could not produce using diagrams or physical models. This is followed up by a switch to constructive mode, where the pupils are required to produce graphs from prepared data using a spreadsheet program. This does not show them the relationships directly, but helps them to formulate the ideas for themselves much more quickly and efficiently than if they were to plot graphs laboriously, and possibly incorrectly, on paper.

---

**Task 2.5**    Consider Example 1.5 in Chapter 1. What mode of ICT use was involved in each stage of the work? How did the different modes of ICT use contribute to pupils' learning?

Suggested answers are given in Appendix C.

---

## When is it appropriate to use ICT?

You have considered how ICT impacts upon motivation and engagement. In many cases, this may be enough justification to use ICT, because of the potential impact on the quality of pupils' experience and the depth of their learning. There are other ways in which using ICT can improve matters in the classroom, however.

1   *Improve efficiency and pace.* An otherwise good lesson can be spoilt by minor delays while resources are assembled, records are checked/completed, home-work collected and important but irrelevant questions from pupils dealt with. ICT enables more effective collation of materials, speedier record keeping, automated submission of homework and greater opportunity for pupils to solve minor problems themselves. Chapter 9 will consider how you can best achieve the goal of efficiency and pace.

2   *Provide resources and structure to support learning independently of the teacher.* If you are to prepare pupils for a future characterised by lifelong learning, it is important that they gain early experience of independent study. However, young learners generally need help in making choices concerning content and methods, and ICT can provide a varying degree of structure to their learning strategies and resources to support their learning without requiring the immediate presence of a teacher. The teacher will still be needed as part of a team providing the structure and resources, but learners can work at their choice of time and place.

3   *Provide experiences for learners which it would be hard to achieve in other ways.* Because of the information handling and presentation tools which ICT pro-vides, it is possible to set more authentic tasks. Where it is not possible to provide realistic situations, in dangerous or expensive science experiments, for instance, simulations can be used to enable pupils to gain a surrogate

experience. It is also possible for pupils to communicate with teachers and other pupils over a large distance, through the WWW, e-mail or video-conferencing. This enables them to study minority subjects even in remote areas.

4   *Improve the quality of task outcomes for pupils.* As well as the impact on motivation, the achievement of well-presented and effectively constructed pieces of work is a worthwhile objective in itself, particularly for examination coursework which may be evaluated externally. The provisionality of ICT enables pupils to undertake several stages of redrafting and reconstructing their work. This needs to be managed carefully to ensure that a finished product is achieved in a reasonable amount of time, and that changes are worthwhile rather than superficial. The colour of the border round the title page of GCSE coursework is not as important as many pupils seem to think!

5   *Make higher level of challenge feasible.* Many tasks expected of pupils are mundane and require little conscious thought on the part of pupils. One reason why teachers may do this is that they feel anything more difficult will cause pupils to give up and then misbehave. ICT helps to overcome this problem because pupils can usually find a way to proceed with a difficult task merely by clicking something on the screen, seeing what happens, and then changing what they have done as a result of the feedback they receive on screen. They do not have the same fear of the teacher telling them they have done the wrong thing, which often inhibits their experimentation during non-ICT tasks. They also pick up easily what their more successful classmates have done to achieve success – and this is not 'copying' in the traditional sense, because the pupil who observes someone else still has to carry out the procedure themselves and is thus starting to learn how to do it independently. The implication for the teacher is the need for clear instructions concerning what is expected of the pupils, and then giving them a chance to try to achieve it for themselves.

6   *Encourage reflection.* Achievement of the outcome of a well-planned task will usually mean that pupils have engaged in the sort of thinking about the subject matter which helps them understand the concepts and remember the facts and procedures. But if they are subsequently expected to think back over the work, not only to recall what they did but why they did it, their retention is likely to be better and their understanding significantly improved. This process of reflection can be achieved in many ways – questioning, discussion, summarising, explaining to others – and you are no doubt familiar with the process from your own learning. Reflective activity, too, can be aided by ICT. This is seen in the way that the communication and processing of information is achieved very rapidly, so that the results can be discussed before pupils' attention and interest start to wane. Another way in which ICT supports reflection is through specific tools such as concept mapping software. Chapter 3 will explain some of the tools available and Chapter 7 will consider the process of reflection further.

7   *Facilitate differentiation.* Your pupils will vary widely in their capacity for learning and in the ways in which they learn best. Chapter 5 will consider these issues in detail, but it is worth noting at this stage how the feature of

provisionality helps the teacher to provide a range of different versions of resources covering the same topic, each one designed to provide support for the needs of particular groups of learners. You can vary the size and style of print in documents, the difficulty of language used in work sheets, the use of images and sounds in presentations, the amount of detail and depth provided in information sources, and the amount of structure provided in tasks to be completed by pupils. Chapter 9 will consider this further.

---

**Task 2.6**    Consider a lesson where you have used ICT yourself with a class or where you have seen another teacher using ICT with a class.

Was ICT used in instructive mode, constructive mode, or both?
What do you think the teacher wanted the pupils to learn?
Use the ideas introduced in this section to analyse how ICT contributed to their learning.

*Note*: Be careful how you approach any observation of teachers. Make it clear that the purpose of the observation is to learn about the use of ICT. Be professional; do not make comments on the effectiveness of the teaching or use of ICT unless asked, and then focus on only positive aspects. Remember, too, that experienced teachers often make complex classroom management look simple and straightforward. They have the advantage of knowing the pupils well and taking this into account when planning and preparing their lessons. Consider how this experience is used in the ICT setting.

---

It is valuable to note pupils' opinions concerning teaching and learning, and secondary school pupils say that they gain most from ICT in activities involving *finding information* and *presenting information*, with quite a lot of help from ICT in *planning, writing* and *improving of work*, in *spelling*, and in *using diagrams, graphs* and *tables* (Becta, 2002b).


## Further reading

Impact2 project reports:

Becta (2002) *The impact of ICT on pupil learning and attainment*, Coventry: Becta

Becta (2002) *Pupils' and teachers' perceptions of ICT in the home, school and community*, Coventry: Becta

Becta (2002) *Learning at home and school: case studies*, Coventry: Becta

Poole, P. (1998) *Talking about ICT in subject teaching*, Canterbury: Canterbury Christchurch University College

Trend, R., Davis, N. and Loveless, A. (1999) *Information and communications technology*, London: Letts Educational

# 3  ICT Tools and Concepts

For each of the principal ICT tools used in education, this chapter explains features provided by the tool, together with the key processes and concepts involved in using them effectively. It illustrates how you can use them in teaching, learning and administration, but does not attempt to give detailed guidance on techniques for operating particular packages. You are provided with practical tasks, involving the production of realistic resources, following which you are asked to reflect in a structured way on what you have learned in carrying out those tasks.

## What can you do with word processing?

A word processing program is primarily designed for producing an effectively presented, text-based document. This process involves entering text in draft form (usually through a keyboard, or a microphone plus voice-recognition software), then reviewing and editing the content to ensure that the intended meaning is complete, correct and in language appropriate for the intended readership, and finally improving the presentation to ensure that it is easy to read, any structuring into sections is clear, tables are clearly set out, and that appropriate emphasis is given to headings and key words in the text. Other objects such as images (clipart, digital photographs or images scanned from other sources with permission), diagrams and graphs may be incorporated. If a complex page layout is required, however, or if graphics are to be the main feature of the page, then a DTP program will usually be a more effective tool.

In order to carry out this process, a variety of techniques are likely to be available in any word processing program.

**Outlining**: when developing a structured document, the process can start by listing main points, then breaking these down further before converting these automatically into headings and subheadings.

**Format text – size, face, font**: any selected piece of text can have its appearance changed.

**Format layout – spacing, indentation, justification**: any selected paragraph or section can be changed in line spacing, left/right indented, centred, or lined up to the margin on the right.

**Bullets/numbering**: numbered or bulleted lists can be created.

**Word art**: produces fancy styles for small pieces of text such as headings.

**Insert clipart, pictures, shapes, charts, diagrams, files, bookmarks, text boxes**: various options for incorporating resource material supplied with the word processing program or material prepared in another program.

**Picture tools**: allow images to be manipulated and the way text flows around them to be controlled.

**Drawing tools**: include standard shapes, arrows, text boxes and other features for drawing and editing diagrams.

**Tables and borders**: a tabulated layout can be specified, either in terms of a simple grid of any size, or by drawing out precise borderlines; any borderlines can be made invisible on printing or varied in thickness.

**Columns**: multiple columns can be used, with text flowing between them when edited, but this effect may be handled more easily with tables for most purposes.

**Borders/boxes**: horizontal lines or boxes can be placed around particular paragraphs.

**Insert symbol**: characters not on the keyboard can be included; note that common ones (such as accented characters) may be obtained by combinations of keys (shortcuts).

**Headers and footers**: short pieces of text which appear at the top or bottom of every page for identification, commonly used for the author's name.

**Insert page numbers, date/time**: these appear in the same way as headers/footers, but are updated automatically.

**Spelling and grammar check**: words are compared with a stored dictionary and any discrepancies highlighted with suggested corrections; similarly, sentence construction is analysed and departures from standard grammar and style are indicated.

**Search/replace**: all occurrences in a document of a particular word or phrase can be found and, if required, replaced with another particular word or phrase.

**Thesaurus**: suggested synonyms for any word can be found.

**Wordcount**: counts the number of words in the document or section of it.

**Reviewing/track changes**: amendments and deletions are shown on the screen, with an indication of when and by whom changes were made.

**Annotation**: comments can be added to the text by a number of different people without them forming part of the document itself.

**Language**: if the appropriate language dictionary is available, non-English text can be checked against a dictionary in the correct language.

## What are the concepts involved?

In order to use word processing effectively, you need to understand that a document is a stored file of characters together with formatting tags which control how it

**Figure 3.1**   Word processing effects – showing changes made to document

appears on the printed page and on the screen. This allows the file to be transferred easily to different resources without affecting the appearance of the text. The typing position is indicated by the cursor, which can be moved within existing text using the separate mouse-controlled pointer. It automatically adjusts to start a new line when required, without splitting words in general. The same applies at the end of a page (not the bottom of the screen, as the text scrolls up automatically for you to see the section into which you are typing). White space will appear on the page wherever there are no characters, including outside where the margins are set, at the end of a line where the Enter key has been pressed (this is the usual way of creating blank lines), below a forced page break on a particular page, and below the last line on which you have typed anything.

## Why is word processing effective in education?

Writing is effectively presented, though subject to the constraints of the author's literacy skills, and it is easily changed. Word processing aids collaborative work, both between teacher/pupil and between pupils. For example, the teacher can provide an outline structure or 'writing frame' (Deadman, 2003) to which the pupil can work, and can annotate a draft text to which the pupil can respond. Each pupil in a group can work on a separate part of the task, and then combine the text.

Pupils can use spellcheck facilities to obtain guidance on where they may have made errors and what the correct spelling may be. They need to be aware that any word not stored in the computer's 'dictionary' will be indicated as incorrect, and that they will need to check names and non-English words themselves. They also need to be aware that some spellings may be valid words, but not the spelling they need in the context (for example, 'there' and 'their' or even 'no' and 'know'), and that suggested alternative spellings need to be considered carefully in order to choose the word required. The correct word may not be suggested at all if the spelling is very different, particularly at the beginning of a word (for example, 'acur' for 'occur').

Electronic or on-line work sheets can be produced, so that the advantages of good presentation and easy amendment by the learner are combined with the traditional strengths of structured information and questioning from the teacher. A variety of visual cues can be employed. Text completion exercises, such as cloze procedure, can be implemented easily. Furthermore, links can be added to other electronic resources in order to give learners options concerning the resources they use, the problems they attempt and the help they access (see What can you do with web creation below).

---

**Task 3.1**    Use a word processing program to produce a template for your lesson plans which will be helpful to you and to your tutors.

What features/techniques did you use?

Does it provide a good sectional layout into which your lesson details can be inserted?

Is it straightforward to insert details which may vary in length?

Improve your template if you find that there are disadvantages at any time to its design.

---

## What can you do with desktop publishing (DTP)?

Although very similar to producing a document, the process of producing an effective publication using DTP has some important differences. The first stage is to decide on the format, such as single page, bookfold, or poster, then decide on the page layout. If there are several pages, you need to consider the style to be adopted through the publication. Assemble all the content in draft form using the most suitable programs – WP for text, graphics for drawings, etc. Finally, arrange the material on the page(s) using the intended layout and edit it appropriately. In practice, most DTP packages include many of the tools associated with other software such as text editing and formatting, drawing, image manipulation and for a simple publication you may not need to prepare material using more specialised software first.

In order to carry out this process, a number of techniques are likely to be available in addition to those in WP and other programs.

**Master page**: allows features which will appear on every page to be laid out on a single page which is then provided as a 'background' on each page created.

**Templates**: in the commercial world, there are many standard types of publication such as letterheads, three-part brochures, advertising flyers and newsletters; a variety of prepared designs and formats for these may be provided.

**Rulers and guides**: various features to help control precisely where the features of the page are positioned.

**Frames**: each object, including text, is placed in a specified area of the page known as a frame which must be created first; in the case of text, frames can be linked so that text automatically flows between them when entering and editing.

**Manipulation of frames**: control over the position, size and orientation of frames is flexible so that text can be rotated, for example.

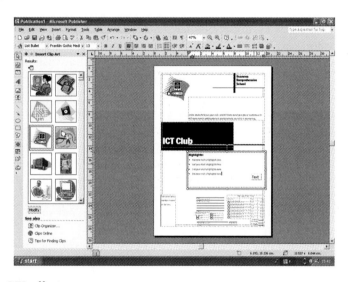

**Figure 3.2**  DTP effects

## What are the concepts involved?

The nature of a publication is different from a document, as it is made up of pages each of which has a set of frames at specified positions; the text content of each frame is normally a separate item. A publication has a format (such as book, poster, business card, etc.); a style or design (involving particular shapes, symbols, colours, lines, etc. used throughout the publication); and each page has a layout (the structure of headings, images, blocks of text, etc.).

## Why is desktop publishing effective in education?

One feature of DTP is the authenticity of the results, and if a professional look is required it will usually have advantages over a WP program. The standard formats and designs provide a structure that can encourage pupils to contribute high quality content. It is easy to incorporate text and images from various sources, and this supports collaborative work.

> **Task 3.2**    Produce a brochure to 'sell' your subject to pupils and their parents when they are choosing examination course options. Include text and images in an attractive layout to represent what is distinctive and interesting about the subject in an immediate, visual form.

## What can you do with multimedia presentation?

The process of producing a presentation involves placing text, images, video and audio objects onto an animated sequence of screen-shaped slides for subsequent display to an audience (usually in magnified form), either pre-timed or under the control of the presenter. It is similar to that of producing a publication, in that there is value in advance planning and preparation of component materials if you want to produce an effective presentation efficiently. You can plan a multimedia presentation using a *storyboard*, which describes the content of each slide and shows the structure of links between them. However, it has similarities to WP in that it is easy to draft ideas quickly to help organise and share information; the advantage of a presentation program is in the structure provided in terms of short sections of information and the bullet point format provided by default. Note that the bulleted list format should be used more sparingly in professional presentations. Also, the effects available for animating objects on the screen can be distracting for the audience, and should be used only when there is a valid purpose.

In order to carry out this process, a number of techniques are likely to be available in addition to those in WP and other programs.

**Slide format**: each new slide can have a different format, with a choice of particular layouts of objects such as text, bulleted list, image, or blank ready for objects to be inserted.

**Master slide**: a similar idea to the master page in DTP.

**Views**: choose whether to see small versions (thumbnails) of all the slides, a list of the slides in text format, a complete slide with notes, or to view the slide show itself.

**Insert movies and sounds**: as well as text and images, video and audio objects can be added to a slide; these can be triggered automatically when the slide appears in the show, or under the presenter's control.

**Add notes**: separate from the slide which will be seen by the audience, the author can create notes to be printed (alternatively, the author can use a microphone to record a narration to go with each slide in the show).

**Timing**: the show can be set to play with each slide/object given a specified timing for display, or can be under the control of the presenter's mouse clicks.

**Transitions and animation**: various effects can be specified concerning transition (how one slide leaves and the next arrives on the screen) and animation (the way in which objects appear on the screen).

**Action buttons**: an object can be set to trigger another event when clicked, such as jumping to another slide in the set or to an item outside the presentation such as a web page.

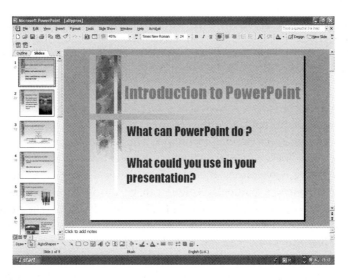

**Figure 3.3** Multimedia presentation effects

## What are the concepts involved?

The nature of a presentation is different from a document, with each slide a separate unit and objects positioned on it. There is no continuity of text across slides, and only one section of the whole presentation is seen at any time, with each object being revealed under one person's control. The ideas of transition and animation are therefore important in designing a presentation and do not have equivalents in the printed form.

## Why is multimedia presentation effective in education?

For the teacher, presentations have tremendous value in supplementing and supporting an oral presentation by showing visually the structuring of ideas in a more effective way than is usually possible with traditional board and OHP. The position, timing and animation of the appearance of pieces of text, images and diagrams can help with emphasis of points and the focusing of pupils' attention on key issues and relationships.

Furthermore, the slide and bullet point structure can aid the author's identification, development and sequencing of the points to be made. This is valuable for teachers who find they can use a presentation to help plan a coherent lesson and manage it more effectively (Kennewell and Beauchamp, 2003). It is even more valuable for pupils to use for presenting their ideas, as they do not usually have the higher order planning and monitoring skills required to structure their thinking effectively. It not only helps them present to a class, it can help them to turn their ideas into a written report and forms an important tool for reflection (see Chapter 5).

| Task 3.3 | Produce a presentation about yourself, suitable to introduce yourself to a school where you are going to be placed. Include images and, if possible, a piece of video. |
|---|---|

## What can you do with image capture/manipulation and drawing tools?

This field covers a number of processes, including digital photography, scanning, photo editing, digital video recording, video editing, graphics programs and CAD. For details of these processes, you will need to refer to more specialised books, but some of the more important are listed below.

For photo editing the following techniques are available.

**Cropping**: any block within a picture can be selected and the rest of the picture removed to create a new image.

**Changing colours**: a particular colour can be changed to another throughout; particular areas can be changed to a background colour with the effect of 'removing' an item in the original picture.

**Rotation/flip**: the image can be rotated or reflected.

For movie making the techniques given below may be employed.

**Clip creation**: splitting a piece of continuous video/audio recording into short pieces, together with stills if required.

**Movie creation**: combining several clips into a continuous sequence.

**Storyboard**: the means of specifying the sequencing of clips.

**Timeline**: the means of specifying the timing of clips.

**Trimming**: specifying the start point and end point for the viewing of each clip.

For vector graphics programs a variety of techniques are available.

**Order**: objects can overlap, and this allows you to specify which is at the 'front' and 'back'.

**Group**: a number of separate objects can be grouped together to form a single object.

**Rotation/reflection**: as for photo editing.

**Standard lines/shapes/symbols**: objects can be created from a library of predefined features.

**Line and fill colour/style**: the colour and solidity of outlines and filled shapes can be selected.

**Text**: text can be added to a drawing, in a variety of colours and effects.

Pixel graphics programs will have more limited features.

## What are the concepts involved?

An image is made up of a large number of small dots called pixels, each of which has the property of colour. A pixel graphics program stores information about pixels and can only manipulate individual pixels, a selected area of the screen, or colour properties; a vector graphics program stores instructions concerning the construction of objects, so that complete objects can be manipulated. A movie is made up of a timed sequence of video clips and still images, with audio included or added later.

## Why is image capture/manipulation effective in education?

The main value is in the visual effect, enhanced by the ability to represent a story in a movie, and the ability to tailor images in order to focus on particular features or to change the idea represented.

---

**Task 3.4**  Obtain a photographic image using a digital camera or by scanning. Use photo editing software to 'remove' a particular person or object so that the picture misrepresents the original scene. Use this new image alongside the original in a work sheet where pupils are asked to 'spot the difference' and discuss what would happen in the situation represented by the new image.

---

## What can you do with spreadsheets?

Spreadsheets enable you to represent relationships between numerical variables – to create and explore models of situations where quantities vary. The process is therefore a mathematical one, although it can be applied to a range of subjects. The first stage in creating a spreadsheet model is to identify the independent variables (the inputs to the model) and the dependent variables (the outputs of the model), and specify the relationships between them. The layout of the spreadsheet is based on the grid structure which is intrinsic to such programs, and you need to decide which cells to use for particular variables in order to make the structure clear to users. The initial values of the input variables can then be entered, the text entered to label the values, and the formulas to calculate the output variables. You can then alter the values of the inputs in order to explore the effect on the outputs.

You can also use a model prepared by yourself or someone else for pupils to investigate unknown relationships. They should be taught to do this systematically, changing only one input variable at a time and identifying how it affects the outputs before moving on to do the same with the next input. Most spreadsheet programs provide graphs to help with this process and to help communicate results.

Spreadsheets can also be used at a more basic level, just using their calculating and graphing features on single sets of figures rather than for the full modelling process.

In order to carry out these processes, certain techniques are likely to be available in any spreadsheet program.

**Tables**: with the grid structure already present, setting out a table just involves specifying the borderlines.

**Graphs**: a variety of different business and statistical charts, as well as Cartesian $(x-y)$ graphs, can be produced by selecting a block of data and specifying graph format options.

**Formulas**: a calculated value in a cell can be specified by a mathematical expression (such as $2*B6 + 6$) made up of cell references, numbers and the operations $+$, $-$, $*$ (multiply) and/(divide); if the contents of cell B6 changes, the result will be recalculated automatically.

**Functions**: many predefined functions can be selected in a formula (such as SUM for total and AVG for average).

**Replication**: a formula can be copied into other cells, and the cell references in the formula will adjust to reflect the position of each result cell in relation to one containing the original formula.

**Naming**: a cell can be named and the name used to represent that cell in formulas instead of the cell reference.

**Format**: the number type, colour and size of text or cells and the alignment of cell contents can all be changed.

**Merge cells**: blocks of cells can be combined for layout purposes.

**Protection**: selected cells can have their contents hidden or 'locked' (which means that a password is needed to change them); these features are particularly valuable in the case of formulas which you do not want pupils to see.

**Hide gridlines, row/column refs**: again, for layout purposes, the lines and labels can be hidden.

**Sort**: a selected block of data can be re-ordered according to any particular column, numerically or alphabetically.

**Goal seeking**: if a particular value is required in an output variable, then instead of repeatedly adjusting input variables by trial and error, the spreadsheet can be asked to calculate the input values that will produce the required output.

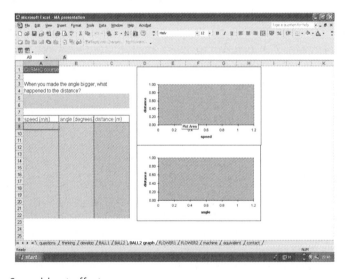

**Figure 3.4**   Spreadsheet effects

## What are the concepts involved?

The idea of a computer model of a situation is more precise than the everyday use of the word model, because it involves the idea that certain relationships are preserved when changes are made. It is as though, with a toy animal, for instance, you could stretch one leg and the other legs, head, etc. would all stretch automatically to keep the same body shape. A spreadsheet is a grid of cells of effectively infinite extent. The idea of a cell, referenced by its row and column, is fundamental to a spreadsheet, and it is the main editable unit which can contain a single piece of text, a number, a formula, or an imported object such as an image. A spreadsheet table thus has more structure than a table created in a word processing program where a cell can only be located from its (provisional) contents. A formula, which specifies a relationship between cells, is the final key concept underlying the creation of a spreadsheet. The idea of a 'what if' investigation must be grasped, too, in order to understand the purpose of creating a spreadsheet model rather than just doing a lot of individual calculations.

## Why is spreadsheet modelling effective in education?

Although this seems a very mathematical and business-oriented program, the educational potential in quantitative subjects is considerable. Spreadsheets enhance the display and analysis of data, enabling pupils to gain rapid and accurate summaries and graphs from raw figures. They enable simulations of situations to be carried out without expensive software; as well as the general task of identifying relationships with the aid of graphs (for instance, the relationship between the number of foxes and rabbits in an area), challenges can be set (such as 'can you keep the number of rabbits in the area below 500?') and the relationships found in attempting this can be discussed afterwards. This process is described as exploratory modelling by Mellar *et al.* (1994). Spreadsheet modelling also enables pupils to represent their conjectures about relationships (such as 'I think that the circumference is always about three times the diameter') and test them out in comparison with actual results. This is described as expressive modelling by Mellar *et al.* (1994). A spreadsheet can serve as an important reflective tool, but for different types of knowledge than a presentation program.

> **Task 3.5**    Obtain a table that shows figures for examination passes in different subjects over the past few years (see www.qca.org.uk/rs/statistics/gcse_results.asp, or obtain data from a school). Enter (or copy) the figures into a spreadsheet program and investigate the trends in different subjects.

## What can you do with databases?

There are two main database processes that have value in education: creation and interrogation. Creating a database first involves deciding on the purpose of storing the data; for example, a database to be used in geography might have the purpose of analysing the economic development in different regions of the world. The next stage is to devise a structure for the information to be stored so as to be clear about what each record contains (in our example, each record might concern a country), and what each section (or field) of data will contain for all the records (in the example, one

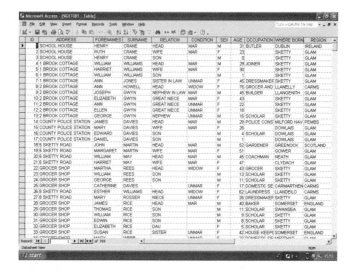

**Figure 3.5** Database table of imaginary criminal records, showing structure

field would be the name of the country, another would be the population). Only then will the database structure be set up, the data collected, and the data entered into the structure to form a table (or set of related tables for a more complex database).

Once a database has been created and checked, or acquired from another source, it can be interrogated, that is queries can be entered in the form of conditions on the fields which limit the selection of data to be displayed. For instance, you could request all countries in Asia with a birth rate of less than 1 per cent per annum and a GDP of more than $5000 per person. Results can be displayed as tables or printed reports formatted in various ways.

Some databases will contain 'volatile' data, which will need to be continually or regularly updated, like our example. Others will not need to be changed, such as a database of properties of metals.

In order to carry out these processes, certain techniques are likely to be available in any database management program.

**Create table**: you will need to give the table a name.

**Specify fields**: you will be required to specify the name, type and length of each field, and you may optionally specify validation rules, for instance only valid dates or only numbers between particular values.

**Enter data**: type in the details for each field of data within successive records; it will be checked and rejected if it does not meet the validation rules.

**Sort**: the data can be re-ordered according to any particular field, numerically or alphabetically.

**Query**: select records for display by specifying criteria on particular fields, combined using the operators AND, OR, NOT; also select fields to be displayed for these records.

**Reporting**: specify the layout of the selected data together with headings, summary values such as a count of records or total of a certain field.

Many of these techniques will be possible within a spreadsheet program, although interrogation facilities will not have the power of a full database query and reporting facility. A spreadsheet will have better statistical and graphing features, however, and it will be valuable to master the technique of transferring data from a database to a spreadsheet and vice versa.

## What are the concepts involved?

The concept of a database is the most difficult of the information structures used with common ICT tools. The familiar table has extra structure, different from that of a spreadsheet in that the user specifies the column headings (field names) and the software uses these throughout. This allows more meaning to be contained within the structure, rather than being left to the user to interpret. Consequently, anyone entering data has to be careful to enter data into correct fields, and must also ensure that all data within a record is concerned with the same subject. The concept of a field is more constrained than that of a column, and that of a record more constrained than that of a row. It is important to ensure that information stored in a database is accurate, and a database program will have validation techniques available, for instance checking that a value entered into a field is within a particular range.

## Why is database management and interrogation effective in education?

The creation of a database structure requires learners to analyse the information that they are recording, which in turn should bring about a greater understanding than merely reading the information. Interrogating and analysing large amounts of data (including pre-prepared) also helps learners to understand the information they are generating, as they have to formulate suitable questions and interpret the results they obtain.

## What can you do with e-mail?

The process of sending and receiving messages using e-mail is quite simple. E-mails are usually quite short, and may be composed whilst connected to the Internet or local network, or they may be composed on a local PC and then sent when a connection is made. They need an address for the recipient, which may be a general Internet e-mail address of the form name@location, where the location is an e-mail service provider and the name is unique for that service provider, or an *alias* which represents the full name for brevity and display purposes. E-mails can be replied to without specifying an address, since the address of the sender of the original e-mail is sent with the message. A subject line can be entered for any e-mail; this enables the recipient to see what the message is about without reading the message. E-mails, both sent and received, can be stored indefinitely although there may be a limit on the total size of storage allowed for this.

In order to carry out these processes, certain techniques are likely to be available in any e-mail program.

**New message**: enables the user to compose a message and enter the recipient's address and the subject of the message.

**Send message**: transmits the message through the Internet or local network.

**Read message**: enables the user to see the contents.

**Copy to**: the user can list other addresses to receive a copy of the message.

**Reply/reply to all/forward**: the user can compose a response to a message received, and send it back to the sender (and, optionally, anyone who was sent a copy of it), or can send it on to other people (ethically, this should have the agreement of the original sender) together with added comments if required.

**Organisation of messages**: sent and received messages can be stored in separate folders according to subject or person.

**Filtering/directing**: criteria on sender or subject can be set to exclude particular messages, redirect them or send them straight to folders.

**Distribution list**: a single alias can be specified to represent a whole group of addresses to which the same message is commonly sent.

**Discussion list (or listserv)**: a message sent to a single e-mail address is redistributed to all members of a group who have requested inclusion and been approved by the 'owner' of the list; this allows discussion amongst the group without each member requiring a copy of the distribution list.

**Conference (newsgroup or bulletin board)**: this is similar in purpose to a discussion list, except that you have to log in to the service especially and the software allows you to access previous messages in the form of 'threads' of discussion.

**Attachment**: other files (such as documents, images, spreadsheets) can be included with the main message, so that the recipient with a suitable program can open them or store them for later access.

**Address book**: enables you to store a list of addresses commonly used for quick access.

**Signature**: enables you to specify lines of text which will appear at the end of each message you send.

**Find by sender/topic/content**: enables you to search your store of sent/received messages for particular people, subject lines or message content by keyword.


## What are the concepts involved?

The main concept is that of a message, comprising an address and some content. It is also helpful to understand the idea of a server, which receives your messages and holds them until you are ready to read them. This means that instead of conversations being *synchronous*, in that the participants are speaking at the same time, they can be *asynchronous*. A sense of audience and etiquette is required; e-mail tends to be an informal medium, and you need to remember who will be reading your e-mail, to be aware that your intended tone may not be as clear as if you are speaking, and that you should not forward messages unless you have an agreement with the sender to do so.

## Why is e-mail effective in education?

The value of e-mail is that it is:

- asynchronous: you do not have to be present to receive it, and you can respond at a time which is convenient to you;
- interactive: you can respond immediately if you are present on receipt;
- worldwide at no extra cost;
- used to send large amounts of information.

Compare these points with ordinary mail, phone and text messaging: e-mail has some advantages over each of the others, as long as you have a PC connected to the Internet.

There are problems associated with pupils using it, however, in that you need to check who the learners are communicating with (see Chapter 11), and whether their messages are appropriate in content and tone.

---

**Task 3.6**     Join a discussion list related to your subject.

---

## What can you do with the World Wide Web?

The main processes involved are browsing and searching as means of finding information. The software that allows you to do this is called a web browser. Browsing involves accessing a particular web page initially, and then clicking on particular parts of the page that constitute links to other pages or other parts of the same page. At each stage, you will read and perhaps remember, note or store the information that you want, before clicking again on a link that appears to be potentially useful. Searching involves using a search engine to specify keywords representing your subject of interest. A single word is likely to generate a large number of suggestions, but you can enter a more sophisticated criterion (using AND, OR and NOT as with a database) or a more specific phrase enclosed in quotation marks. When a list of suitable pages appears, you can click on the ones that seem most relevant and browse. Table 3.1 shows an advice sheet designed for pupils.

In order to carry out these processes, certain techniques are likely to be available in any web browser.

**Hyperlink**: you can click on a particular area of the screen and immediately be shown a linked page.

**URL**: you can type in the web address for a specific page if you know it.

**Search**: a web browser may have a particular search engine built into it, and this option will be displayed as a browser option.

**Change text size**: you can make the text appearing in your browser larger or smaller.

**Table 3.1**  Searching the Internet – adapted from NCET (1998) *Delivering and assessing IT through the curriculum*, p. 86.

---

### Searching the Internet

- An Internet browser is a software application that allows you to search the Internet. Netscape and Microsoft Internet Explorer are common examples.
- Every site on the Internet has an address known as a Uniform Resource Locator (URL). In order to access a site you can enter its URL into the Internet browser; there is a space at the top of the screen for this.
- If you do not know the URL of the site you want, you can use a search engine, which is a software application that will find sites using keywords.
- If there is no search engine available to you, a good example to use is Google. Enter the following URL to access the Google search engine: http://google.co.uk
- Once you have accessed the search engine, type in one or more keywords or phrases to indicate the type of site you wish to find. Most search engines also allow more complex searches; look at the 'help' information provided on the search engine screen for more information about complex searches.
- The search engine will list all the sites which match the keyword(s) you have typed in. Sometimes there will be thousands of these. Usually the first sites listed are the most relevant.
- Read through the list of sites until you find one that sounds interesting. Click on the coloured or highlighted lettering in the site title to access the site. When you have finished, click on the 'back' arrow to return to the search engine.
- Some sites include 'links' that will take you directly to other sites. Links are shown as coloured or highlighted text. Click on the link to move to another site. In this way you can move from site to site without using the search engine or entering a URL. This is sometimes known as 'surfing'.
- Whenever you find a site that you think you would like to visit again, you can 'bookmark' it, adding it to your list of favourite sites. By opening the list of favourites you can go straight to a site you have bookmarked without typing the URL or using the search engine.
- When you find a site with information that you are interested in, you can make notes or print out the contents of the site on your printer. You can also save the site contents to your own computer, using a suitable file name.

---

**Bookmark**: if you want to be able to revisit a particular page quickly, you can store the address in a list for quick access; your list can be subdivided into folders and you can 'import' and 'export' lists between users.

**History**: a list of pages you have recently accessed, stored automatically so that you can easily revisit them.

**Homepage**: the main page of a particular organisation or person that contains links to other parts of their website.

**Cookies**: these are not options for the user, but are techniques used by websites to help speed access or provide them with information about you in future.

**Security options**: you can choose to allow access only to particular sites, to exclude particular sites or content, control the type of cookies you receive or allow unlimited access.

## What are the concepts involved?

The main concept is *hypertext* (or *hypermedia* since it involves images and other objects which may appear on a page). This means that some of the text or images are hyper-linked, that is when the text or image is clicked on, the browser loads up another page specified by the author of the text. This is controlled by a set of codes known as hypertext markup language (HTML). A *web page* is a single hypertext file, and can be as long as the author likes, as the browser can scroll down indefinitely. A *web* is a set of linked web pages and may be just stored on a single PC or local network, whereas a *website* is a web stored on particular computer acting as a server on the WWW. The URL of a web page identifies the server and location at which the page is stored. A portal is a website that contains links to many other websites with a particular purpose or interest in common, such as the National Grid for Learning (NGfL) in the UK. A search engine is a program on a particular website that checks the content of several billion web pages and indexes the material so that it can quickly check which pages best match your keywords.

## Why is the World Wide Web effective in education?

The sheer amount of information and the range of locations and personal contacts that can be accessed very quickly is of immense value in itself, but of particular value is the access that the WWW gives to more authentic and up-to-date sources rather than relying on text book interpretations. The idea of a web quest can be valuable. According to Dodge (1995), a web quest is an 'enquiry-oriented activity in which some or all of the information that learners interact with comes from resources on the Internet . . .'. They involve an introduction, a task, a set of information sources, a description of the process that learners should go through in accomplishing the task, some guidance on how to organise the information acquired, and a conclusion that reminds the learners about what they have learned and perhaps encourages them to extend their enquiry (Dodge, 1995). As you might expect, the best place to obtain examples of web quests and guidance on designing and implementing them is on the WWW (see, for instance, March, 1997).

The hypertext structure of the web provides a greater interactivity than books, although it is hard to see more than one page at a time, and often hard to see even a whole page on one screen and slower learners can easily get 'lost'. The other disadvantages are the large amounts of unsuitable material available, and even relevant information can be hard for learners to interpret, so that they are inclined just to reproduce it rather than interpreting it for themselves. Some of these disadvantages can be overcome by using encyclopaedias on CD-ROM with validated content at a suitable level, rather than the WWW. There are also a number of websites that have been developed especially to provide particular groups of learners with appropriate curriculum content, and for many purposes it will be adequate to require pupils to search only within the chosen website using the specialised search facility provided. Many of these websites are available only on subscription, but the BBC service is freely available and increasingly extensive (see Further reading below).

> **Task 3.7**    Choose a particular topic which you may have to teach. Investigate websites which give advice on teaching the topic, using:
> 1  a search engine such as Google;
> 2  an education portal site such as NGfL;
> 3  a subject association site.
>
> Now find some websites which contain source material on the topic itself, and evaluate them for possible use by pupils in terms of:
> - the suitability of the language and images;
> - the validity of the material.
>
> For those which are appropriate, create a web quest.

## What can you do with web creation?

The process of creating a web is similar in many ways to a multimedia presentation, with hyperlinks rather than slide transition as the main method of allowing user interaction. Once you have created a web, if you want to make it available on the WWW (in which case it will really be available to anyone with an Internet connection across the whole world), you will need to 'publish' or upload it to a web server which will allocate the URLs.

In order to carry out these processes, certain techniques are likely to be available in any web-editing program, in addition to many of those found in word processing, DTP and multimedia presentation programs.

**Hyperlink**: any piece of text or graphic object on a page can be set so that if the reader clicks on it, a new specified web page will be shown (or another section of the same page, or another resource such as a document); this feature is often available in word processing, DTP, multimedia presentation and spreadsheet programs as well.

**Frame**: a frame in a web environment is slightly different from a DTP frame, in that it enables certain content from a page to remain on the screen (such as titles or menus) in one or more frames, while the content from another web page is displayed in another frame.

**Table**: this is the same as a word processing table, but because frames have a new role, the table has a wider application in controlling layout within a web page.

**Form**: a form can be produced for web users to complete in order to send you a response, using the familiar types of dialogue box features.

## What are the concepts involved?

See the section above on web access. In addition, it may be helpful to use the term *web* on its own for a coherent set of linked web pages on an individual PC, and use *website* for a web which is located on a web server and thus available on the Internet. A web may be *linear* in nature, so that the content pages are accessed sequentially, like in a presentation, or *hierarchical*, so that the content pages are accessed in any order from an index page.

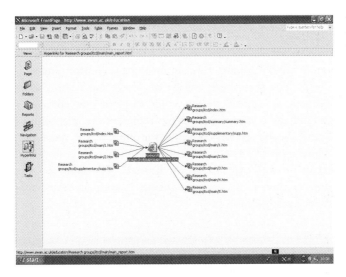

**Figure 3.6**   Using a web editor to show links between pages

## Why is web creation effective in education?

There are two aspects of value to learners. One is the value of the process of producing web pages, which is similar to multimedia presentation but with the additional feature of hierarchical structure which requires learners to analyse and understand the conceptual structure of the material (note also graphic organisers below for an alternative way of achieving this). The other is the ability to publish material on the WWW and hence reach a wider audience of other pupils, parents and the local community; unfortunately, you have no control over who else will see it, and this affects the content which might be appropriate.

For teachers, it has the power to combine text, images, video, and audio in a non-linear sequence under the control of the user, which can be the teacher at the front of a class using it interactively with them, or a single pupil or group working independently – perhaps at home.

| Task 3.8 | Create a web of your own to provide a simple quiz activity for pupils to use. You can do this in various ways: |
|---|---|

- a web-based service for producing simple interactive activities such as *Hot Potatoes*, which is easy to use and goes onto a website automatically, or the *Discovery Channel school website* – see Further reading at the end of the chapter;
- a word processor, DTP or presentation program which creates web pages (easy to use and put onto single PC or school/college network);
- a web-editing program (harder to use but more powerful and can publish to a website easily).

## What can you do with graphic organiser software?

There are a number of similar processes which can be carried out with a graphic organiser, including mind mapping, concept mapping, brainstorming and storyboarding (see Conlon, 2002). The focus here will be on producing a concept map. A graphic organiser enables you to create boxes in which to name concepts, use arrows to link related concepts, and add text to the arrows to represent the relationships. All elements can be edited, and the boxes can be moved around whilst retaining the links and relationships. More extensive notes can be attached to each concept box in order to record thoughts or provide explanation for learners. The graphic representation can be converted into outline format for producing a word processed report, or into a web page for wider publication.

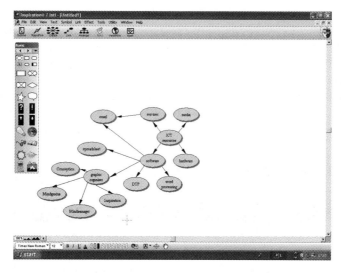

**Figure 3.7**   Graphic organiser effects – a teacher's concept map for ICT in teaching

## What are the concepts involved?

A concept map is 'a hierarchical diagram used to represent a set of concepts, beginning with the most general or most important, and then working down to more specific detail. Key concepts are connected by links that have descriptive words on them explaining the relationship between the concepts' (Inspiration Software Inc., 2002: 20).

## Why is graphic organiser software effective in education?

This type of software is a valuable tool in the classroom for planning, reflection and assessment. It can be used by the teacher with a large display, eliciting contributions from the whole class. It can be used by individual pupils for planning and managing projects, or for representing and developing their understanding of the subject matter. If you provide an initial map for pupils of the formal concept, and then ask pupils to add notes to each component, it helps pupils to manage their learning and increase their independence. It enables ideas to be recorded quickly and then refined and linked; discussion of the links will help develop individual pupils' naïve concepts towards the formally accepted view that is being taught. It helps the teacher to identify pupils' misconceptions and discuss alternative views.

| Task 3.9 | Use mind-mapping software to map your understanding of ICT in teaching and learning. |
|---|---|

## What can you do with virtual learning environments?

A virtual learning environment (VLE) is a web-based system that provides tools for teachers and pupils to help manage learning. It assists teachers to structure the curriculum over a period of time, to communicate objectives, to provide multimedia resources for pupils, and for pupils to access the materials. It helps with setting and scheduling tasks; the tracking, submission and receipt of student work; and the recording and analysis of assessment records. It provides e-mail tools such as bulletin boards and conferences, which support directing, guiding, facilitating and responding to pupils both individually and in groups. These tools also support pupils in working together.

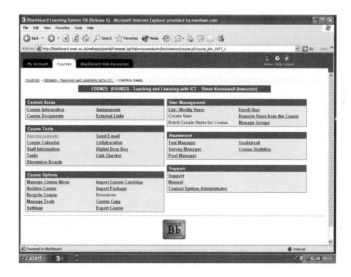

**Figure 3.8**  VLE facilities for course instructors

## What are the concepts involved?

A VLE is a system which deals with the on-line interactions that take place between learners and tutors (Becta, 2003a). It often forms the key component within a larger

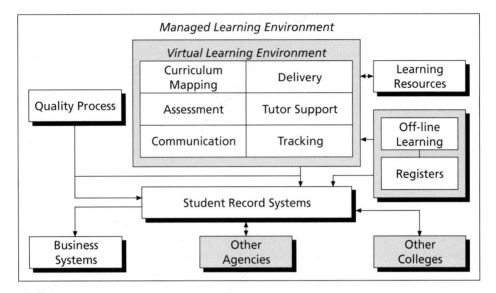

**Figure 3.9**   Diagram of MLE/VLE relationship, from Becta ICT Advice: copyright Becta 2003 http://www.ictadvice.org.uk/index.php?section=te&rid=74

system – a Managed Learning Environment (MLE) – which provides a range of other functions within the school or college that relate directly or indirectly to the management of learning (see Figure 3.9).

## Why are virtual learning environments effective in education?

VLEs have mostly been used in Higher and Further Education at the time of writing. Benefits have accrued to lecturers in more effective management of courses and tracking student activity. Students gain through being able to access materials at the time and place that suits them, and in maintaining contact with tutors and other students whilst working independently without have to arrange meetings. VLEs have been found to increase student participation in discussions (Becta, 2003b). For schools, they offer opportunities to improve support for pupils' work at home and to make minority courses available in a wider range of schools.

---

**Task 3.10**   If you have not already used a virtual learning environment in your courses or training, try to gain access to a course (even if it is just designed for introduction or evaluation).

Consider what is gained and what may be lost from studying with this medium compared with direct teaching by tutors.

## What can you do with direct teaching packages?

This is not a standard type of software; this book uses the term to cover any program which can be used by pupils independently of the teacher to develop knowledge, understanding or skills. Programs may include demonstrations of skills, explanations of ideas (with text, sound, diagrams, animations or video), questioning of the learner, checking of the response, feedback on the quality of the response, remediation material if needed, progression to the next topic. Some of this may be controlled by the teacher by setting the difficulty level or the topic to be presented.

### What are the concepts involved?

These programs are usually in the form of a 'black box': the teacher cannot alter the content itself or the way in which the program sequences material for particular learners. They are usually produced using professional programming languages, although there are a number of tools known as 'authoring packages' that allow teachers to specify content to be presented, questions to be asked, and criteria for success (thus putting the ICT in control of the learner, as opposed to VLEs above which put the learner in control). Some tools available, such as *Hot Potatoes* (see Further reading below) are very simple to use, but limited in their flexibility. Some expensive direct teaching packages, on the other hand, claim to have some 'intelligence' and attempt to build a 'model' of the learner's abilities so that the material presented and the mode of presentation are contingent on earlier responses. These include large-scale packages known as Integrated Learning Systems (ILS) which are commonly used in schools, particularly with small groups of SEN pupils because of their expense. These systems combine a direct teaching element (with tutorial screens, practice exercises and assessment tasks), a pupil record system, and learning management functions. They enable learners to work independently of the teacher, by providing feedback on their work and setting tasks that are at a level of difficulty which is just greater than the level at which learners have been successful previously (see Underwood and Brown, 1997; Trend *et al.*, 1999: scenario N).

### Why are direct teaching packages effective in education?

Putting the computer in control of the learner's activities is attractive in many situations in the classroom, as it is able to give more immediate feedback than the teacher, allows the pupil to work independently of the teacher who can then devote more time to working away from the computer with other pupils, and it can maintain a high level of concentration on difficult subject matter for a longer period of time than other approaches. This is sometimes achieved through an element of competition, either against other pupils, or against a pupil's previous performance. In addition, some programs provide a diagnostic report for the teacher that can identify features of the pupil's abilities that were otherwise hidden. This is not independent learning, however, and can lead to a state of dependency on the computer, and make it more difficult for the pupils to work independently away from the computer. It is thus important for the teacher to review progress with the pupil rather than leaving everything to the computer.

---

**Task 3.11**    Choose a program which is designed to teach a particular topic. How much control over the content presented and the sequence of activities does the learner have? How much does the teacher have?

---

## What can you do with an interactive whiteboard?

Using an interactive whiteboard (IWB) for whole-class teaching purposes involves interaction with standard and specially designed software (including the WWW) on a large display screen using a special stylus or 'boardpen', or even your finger, rather than the mouse. Typically, when running standard software, you are able to add extra handwritten marks electronically using the stylus. These marks can have the aim of focusing (circling or highlighting words) or relating ideas (connecting lines, arrows). You can also write words just as on an ordinary whiteboard, except that you can use handwriting recognition software to convert your writing into standard ICT text. Furthermore, any annotations you make can be stored. The special software provided (usually called either 'notebook' or 'flipchart' software, depending on the analogy chosen by the manufacturers) will provide a variety of extra features in an environment similar to a presentation program. There will be libraries of symbols and shapes which can be displayed, and there will be an on-screen keyboard so that when operating standard software, you can either simulate the usual way of entering data, or you can use handwriting with conversion.

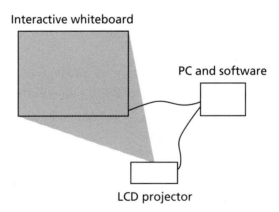

**Figure 3.10**    Interactive whiteboard system

Pupils can easily use the same features in order to represent their ideas to a class or group.

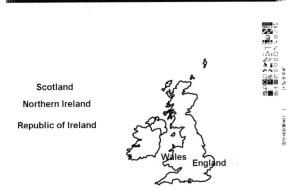

**Figure 3.11**  Interactive whiteboard effects

## What are the concepts involved?

Effective use of the IWB requires some understanding of the technology. The board and a data projector are both connected to a PC; this is running software which serves two functions:

1    to control the display of the screen image on the board through the projector;
2    to receive signals from the board and pen that indicate what the user is doing with it – pointing, writing, or selecting options – and where on the board the stylus is located.

In order to coordinate these two functions and make sure that marks appear where the pen is located on the board, a process of calibration is required whenever the board or projector may have been moved even slightly. This will involve touching the board at a number of standard positions to allow the PC to calculate the relationship between the board location and the projected image.

## Why is an interactive whiteboard effective in education?

The IWB can enhance whole-class teaching when ICT is being used because of the direct interaction with the large image on screen. It can seem as though the whole class is interacting with the same ICT resource when the teacher or pupil works in front of the class, rather than the teacher working with keyboard and mouse away from the board, or all pupils using different PCs. This has benefits when gathering ideas and responses from the whole class and when wanting to emphasise points in the screen display on which pupils are required to focus their attention. However, much of what is done with standard software on the IWB can be achieved with just the PC and data projector. If wireless keyboards and mice, or tablet PCs (see Chapter 12) are passed around the class for entering data, similar effects can be achieved without requiring an IWB.

> **Task 3.12**    Using either a presentation program or special program for your interactive whiteboard, create some material that uses the particular features of the IWB and associated equipment.

## General issues

You also need to be familiar with a number of more general tools and techniques, examples of which are given below.

### Portable computers

This term mainly covers equipment described as laptops, notebooks and 'sub-notebooks'. These all have a full keyboard, although not usually as many extra keys as a desktop PC keyboard. Except for sub-notebooks, they usually have at least a floppy disk drive and CD drive built in, and all have a number of sockets (ports) to connect printers and other peripheral devices. They can also connect to networks using suitable cables or using wireless technology. See Chapter 12 for further discussion of their use in schools.

### Networks

Most of the PCs in secondary schools are connected to a school network. This provides many advantages, although to the non-ICT teacher the disadvantages are often more obvious. The centralised file storage means that you and your pupils can access your work from any PC in the school. If the system is set up in a standard way, then the same software is available and the same operating procedures apply on all machines without users being able to alter things accidentally or intentionally. This feature can be a problem if you need to install software or change settings quickly, however, and it also means that if the network server is out of action, you may not be able to carry out the planned lesson.

### Passwords

In order to keep individuals' work secure on a network, each user is allocated a username (usually based on their own name) and a password which they are responsible for remembering. These codes must be entered when starting to use a network PC ('logging on'), and you need to allow time for this during a lesson – particularly with pupils who are inclined to forget their passwords!

### Intranet

This is a system which provides communications and file access through a browser and e-mail software in the same way as the Internet, except that it only operates within the school or local area.

## File management

It is important to have a system for storing your files on the school network and on a personal PC if you have one, and to separate your files into thematic categories, each with its own folder or directory. A category with a lot of files should be divided into subfolders – you can have as many levels as you like. It is worth giving thought to how you name files, to make it easier to locate them in several months' time. This applies to pupils as well as teachers.

It is important to keep extra copies of your files, known as *back-up* copies, in case the originals are lost or corrupted. You should save your work every few minutes in case your PC fails for any reason, and if you are working on an important document, you should save a version with a new name each time you change it. Make a back-up copy on your network user area, on a floppy disk, on a CD-ROM or USB flash storage.

These operations should be carried out sufficiently frequently that they become routine (see Chapter 6). If you have to think about how to carry out basic file management techniques, they will seem like extra workload and become a barrier to the effective use of ICT.

## Printing

If the use of ICT is to reduce the amount of paper you use, you will need to think carefully about printing documents. With the increasing use of portable computers to work on the move and e-mail to send copies to other people, it should rarely be necessary to print a document until the final version is ready. You can generally preview the printed version from within your software, in order to check that it is displayed correctly on the page.

## Scanning

You will often wish to incorporate some existing printed material or photographs into your work, and a scanner is very valuable. They will usually have Optical Character Recognition (OCR) software with them, so that printed text can be converted into editable files. You should be careful concerning copyright issues, however; unless you have permission from the copyright holder to distribute copied material, you should only scan small amounts for information for academic purposes and acknowledge sources (see Chapter 11).

## Wizards

Many pieces of software offer you a 'wizard' to help you carry out common tasks; this aid will guide you through the steps, offering you a set of standard options at each stage. They can be very useful to achieve a complex task quickly, but they may not give you as much control as you would like. In most cases, it is best to find out how to carry out the process yourself from scratch, and only use the wizard when you know that you want a very standard result.

## Installing

Software is generally supplied on CD-ROM, or downloaded from the Internet, in a form that requires an installation procedure. This usually involves merely responding to prompts from a 'wizard', and for most purposes you can choose the default options. Note that you will not generally be able to install software, or even run it directly from a CD-ROM, on a network PC unless you have special access rights from the network manager.

## Help

Most software has a 'Help' option within it, and this can be very helpful when you know what you want to do but have forgotten what options to choose in order to achieve it. It is not usually the best way to learn from scratch, however, and a tutorial guide (see Further reading below) or a taught course will suit most learners better.

## Virus protection

A virus is a program which can be transferred to your computer without you being aware of it, merely by opening an e-mail or copying a file produced on another computer. They are usually written with the purpose of deleting files or stopping your computer working, and it is wise to make sure that you always have a security program running which checks for viruses and allows you to deal with them safely.

## Further reading

Software course books such as:
> *Access 2000 An Introductory Course for Students*
> *Access 2002 An Advanced Course for Students*
> *Excel 2000 An Introductory Course for Students*
> *Excel 2002 An Advanced Course for Students*
> *Word 2000 An Introductory Course for Students*
> *Word 2000 An Advanced Course for Students*

All published by Learning Matters, Exeter

BBC Learning website (http://www.bbc.co.uk/learning/)

Davis, N. (1997) 'Do electronic communications offer a new learning opportunity in education?', in Somekh, B. and Davis, N. (eds) (1997) *Using information technology effectively in teaching and learning*, London: Routledge, 167–80.

Digital Education Network, free software tutorials and on-line courses (http://www.actden.com/)

Hot Potatoes website, containing software for quizzes, puzzles and text manipulation exercises (http://web.uvic.ca/hrd/halfbaked/)

How Stuff Works, computer section of a very informative website (http://computer.howstuffworks.com/)

Microsoft, free Internet guide and web tutorial (http://www.microsoft.com/insider/guide/intro.asp)

Netskills TONIC, free introductory Internet course (http://www.netskills.ac.uk/TonicNG/cgi/sesame?tng)

The Discovery Channel school website, containing quiz and puzzle software (http://school.discovery.com/quizcenter/quizcenter.html)

# 4 Applications of ICT in the Curriculum

This chapter focuses on the use of ICT in teaching. It is based on case studies of a number of teaching scenarios in which ICT is used, covering all subjects and all ICT tools in various combinations, and explains how the features of capacity, range, speed, automation, provisionality, interactivity, clarity, authenticity and focusability contribute to teaching and learning in ways that can be applied in other subjects. When originally published, the case studies were presented in detail for specialist teachers. In this general book, the ideas have been combined and simplified in order to indicate for the general reader how the teacher exploits the potential role of ICT, and suggestions are given concerning how this affects pupils' learning.

Tasks are set involving reflection on the effects which ICT may have on the learning of each subject. Although the most effective combination of ways in which ICT is used will differ for each subject, there are some issues concerning the role of the teacher that apply to all subjects.

You will probably want to concentrate on your own specialist subject initially, but in due course you should be seeking ideas from other subject areas. ICT helps to provide links between subjects, and, for each case study, there are suggestions for other subjects to which the ideas might be applied. You should be able to find more useful connections and ideas if you read all the sections.

## How can ICT be used in teaching English?

ICT is having a fundamental effect on the nature of text, and consequently is affecting the content of the English curriculum as well as the way it is taught. TTA (1999a) suggests that there a number of ways in which ICT can make a positive contribution to teaching and learning.

'ICT has the potential to make a significant contribution to the teaching of English by:

- enhancing and developing pupils' reading and writing;
- supporting and enhancing the study of literary texts;
- enabling pupils to engage with texts in ways which would not always be possible through a paper-based activity;
- enabling pupils to focus on the content of their writing;
- emphasising the link between the writer and the audience;
- promoting the integration of reading, writing, speaking and listening;
- enabling literacy skills to be extended beyond the reading and writing of chronological and linear text;
- providing a flexible and time-saving resource;
- enabling the teacher to make formative and summative assessments;
- allowing the teacher to focus directly on texts at different levels, using different strategies.'

The following case study shows how some of these factors were exploited in order to produce a more sustained response to a well-designed task, and with a higher quality outcome than with traditional tools.

## Case study: desktop publishing at KS3 (NCET, 1997)

The learning objectives for this unit of work concerned media and non-fiction text study; evaluation of how text is presented; imaginative and intellectual response to reading. The class was of average ability and below, including some pupils whose effort and attainment were normally very poor. In order to help them complete the task, the teacher had developed their abilities in English by requiring them to produce an imaginary first-hand account by someone involved in a disaster, focusing on how it felt personally.

The first task was to summarise, using basic WP functions, a particular newspaper article, selected and provided by the teacher to reflect pupils' interest in the dramatic reporting of disastrous events. Pupils were organised into pairs, with different articles provided for each pair. This basic text was then to be developed in two ways. The first requirement was to produce a newspaper front page using DTP, with the main story concerning an imaginary air crash using a style similar to the one in the article that they had summarised and incorporating a number of imaginary eye-witness accounts. The second part was to script a TV news item, which would be presented on video.

## How did this improve English teaching?

Pupils had opportunities to communicate and process information in order to convey ideas in various forms and to organise, reorganise and analyse ideas and information.

The process of drafting and redrafting of each part of the work was assisted by ICT tools appropriate to the medium of communication, and gave the task a high degree of authenticity. The ICT tools also helped pupils, who often did not work well on their own, to work together and in turn this collaboration aided the development of their ICT skills in order to achieve the task.

The features of this case study are also relevant to RE, MFL, history and citizenship teaching.

## What other applications may improve the learning of English?

There are a number of other ICT tools which English teachers find particularly helpful for themselves and for pupils, and Table 4.1 shows in outline how some of these can be used.

**Table 4.1**   Use of programs in English teaching

| | |
|---|---|
| **Word processing** | If used with a large display or IWB, the teacher can interactively model the writing process and use tools such as 'tracking changes' to help explain the development of effective writing. |
| **E-mail** | This medium enables pupils to explore a new way of generating dialogue (compare also with text messaging) and to collaborate in writing without being together in time or place. |
| **Presentation and web creation** | Presentation and web are new forms of text, and pupils can explore the medium through creating works for a variety of purposes as well as analysing those created professionally. |
| **Information retrieval** | Pupils can access ideas, opinions and images on issues, both for analysis and to adapt for their own writing (TTA, 1999a). |
| **Text completion** | This activity provides teachers with tools for removing words or scrambling texts so that pupils have to use and develop their language skills in order to recreate the original text. |
| **Digital video** | This medium enables pupils to carry out authentic editing on video works, or to film short pieces of activity and experiment with combining them for dramatic effect. |

**Task 4.1a**    Identify how particular items from the TTA list of potential ICT uses in English (see the beginning of this section) contributed to the success of the case study.

What other effects might the use of ICT in this way have on the learning of English compared with traditional approaches?

## How can ICT be used in teaching mathematics?

Mathematics concepts are abstract in their nature and novices do not have the same ability to explore and experiment with mathematical objects such as numbers and variables as they do with physical objects and verbal material. Consequently, teachers have always had difficulty in developing pupils' understanding. ICT is helping both pupils and teachers to provide better visual and dynamic representations of abstract ideas. TTA (1999a) suggests that:

> 'ICT has the potential to make a significant contribution to the teaching of mathematics by:
> - practising and consolidating number skills;
> - developing skills of mathematical modelling through the exploration, interpretation and explanation of data;
> - experimenting with, making hypotheses from, and discussing or explaining relationships and behaviour in shape and space and their links with algebra;
> - developing logical thinking and modifying strategies and assumptions through immediate feedback;
> - making connections within and across areas of mathematics;
> - working with realistic, and large, sets of data;
> - exploring describing and explaining patterns in relationships in sequences and tables of numbers;
> - manipulating graphics images;
> - helping in the preparation of teaching materials;
> - providing flexible and time-saving resources that can be used in different ways and at different times without repetition of the teacher's input;
> - providing a means by which subject and pedagogical knowledge can be improved and kept up-to-date;
> - aiding record keeping and reporting of pupils' progress and attainment'.

The following case study shows the use of spreadsheets to help pupils progress from identifying patterns in sequences and tables of numbers to representing relationships in algebraic form.

## Case study: spreadsheet formulas to represent relationships (SBOLP, 1999)

The learning objectives for the unit of work were to be able to identify a linear relationship between sets of numbers in a table, and to represent that relationship using an algebraic formula (see Figure 4.1). The class was a middle range ability set for mathematics, and was familiar with the idea of a 'function machine' which carried out a fixed set of operations (+, −, ×, /) on any value ($x$) to produce a new value ($y$).

The task involved using the first row of the table to help 'guess' the remaining values in the second ($y$) column. A prepared spreadsheet was provided for pupils, containing ten progressively more difficult 'mystery function' problems of the form shown in Figure 4.2.

| x | y |
|---|---|
| 1 | 5 |
| 2 | 7 |
| 3 | 9 |
| 4 | 11 |
| 5 | 13 |

$$y = 2x + 3$$

**Figure 4.1**   Table and formula for linear relationship

| x | y | |
|---|---|---|
| 1 | 5 | yes |
| 2 | | |
| 3 | | |
| 4 | | |
| 5 | | |

**Figure 4.2**   Spreadsheet 'mystery function' task

As pupils typed possible values into the blank cells in the second column, the spreadsheet responded 'yes' or 'no' by the side. This could be done by trial and error, but pupils were encouraged to think of the function machine idea, and consider what the machine was doing to each value. This particularly helped with the second stage of the task, which was to enter a spreadsheet formula into the second column to achieve the same answers that they had obtained before. This required an algebraic expression to be identified. Although the spreadsheet provided feedback on whether they were correct, pupils were required to write the spreadsheet formula and the corresponding mathematical expression on printed answer sheets, to check that they could use the standard written format. They also had to find what the function did to a large number, in order to appreciate the generality and power of the relationship that they had identified.

## How did this improve mathematics teaching?

The speed and accuracy of calculation and recording enabled the pupils to see patterns and keep potential relationships in their minds whilst trying out possible cases. The instant feedback meant that they could easily discuss results with their partners, and did not have to keep asking the teacher whether they were correct. It helped them develop the abstract idea of a function, since a single formula could work with any number and represent a huge table of values. It also provided a purpose for symbolic representation, as pupils gained the ability to create spreadsheet models.

The use of a spreadsheet to model relationships between variables in this case study is also relevant to science teaching.

## What other applications may improve the learning of mathematics?

There are a number of other ICT tools which mathematics teachers find particularly helpful for themselves and for pupils, and Table 4.2 shows in outline how some of these can be used.

**Table 4.2**  Use of programs in mathematics teaching

| | |
|---|---|
| **Graph plotting** | Especially if used with an IWB, the facility to produce and manipulate large-sized graphs of algebraic relationships immediately and reasonably accurately enables teachers to clarify and extend ideas they introduce to pupils. On individual PCs, pupils can investigate relationships between functions visually. |
| **Presentation** | The dynamic functions of presentation programs, such as rotation and reflection, have potential for mathematics, particularly if used with the IWB. |
| **Spreadsheet** | As well as the use in pre-algebra and mathematical modelling work, spreadsheets can be used to help develop statistical ideas through their instant recalculation and charting facilities. |
| **Dynamic geometry** | These programs are specially designed to make formal geometry dynamic, and the demonstration and exploration of shape and angle properties is transformed, particularly if used with the IWB. |
| **Graphic calculators** | These cheap, individual devices provide much of the functionality of graph plotters, and teachers can project the image using an OHP. |
| **Logo** | This simple programming language enables pupils to develop mathematical concepts through creating short programs themselves which produce shapes or number patterns. |

**Task 4.1b**  Identify how particular items from the TTA list of potential ICT uses in mathematics (see the beginning of this section) contributed to the success of the case study.

What other effects might the use of ICT in this way have on the learning of mathematics compared with traditional approaches?

### How can ICT be used in teaching science?

As with mathematics, ICT is helping to represent abstract ideas in science. It also helps with experimental activities, by enabling new measurement and recording techniques to be used, and experiments to be simulated if they are too time consuming, rapid or expensive to carry out in reality. TTA (1999a) suggests that:

> 'ICT has the potential to make a significant contribution to the teaching of science by:
> - helping pupils understand scientific phenomena;
> - assisting in the recording, presentation and analysis of results;
> - exploring relationships;
> - finding information and researching;
> - communicating ideas;
> - providing flexible and time-saving resources that can be used in different ways and at different times without repetition of the teacher's input;
> - providing a means by which subject and pedagogical knowledge can be improved and kept up-to-date;
> - aiding record keeping and reporting of pupils' progress and attainment'.

The following case study shows how a commercially produced simulation program helps to understand the relationship between populations of creatures involved in a food web.

### Case study: simulation – food web (based on Newton and Rogers, 2001)

The learning objective was to be able to identify relationships between changes in populations of creatures contained within a food web. Rather than using prepared sets of data presented in tables, the software gives the user the opportunity to specify initial values for animal populations and other conditions. It uses a mathematical model (not displayed to the user) to produce population values over several years, with a choice of display options including numbers and graphs.

The pupils were asked to investigate various relationships between the factors involved, such as seasons and reproduction rates and the changes in populations.

### How did this improve science teaching?

The simulation provides a dynamic representation of the relationships, which can be shown in visual form if required. It enables the teacher to explain the theoretical principles behind the model in terms of the effects on real situations. The reduction in the time taken to explore relationships using the model rather than tables of values enables pupils to consider subtle interdependencies.

The features of this case study are also relevant to ICT, mathematics, geography and history teaching.

## What other applications may improve the learning of science?

There are a number of other ICT tools that science teachers find particularly helpful for themselves and for pupils, and Table 4.3 shows in outline how some of these can be used.

Table 4.3 Use of programs in science teaching

| | |
|---|---|
| **WWW** | This enables authentic and educational scientific websites to be accessed in order to obtain images, representations of processes and structures, and data for analysis. |
| **Presentation** | Pupils' own reporting and explaining of events and processes can be improved by the structure and flexibility of a presentation program. |
| **Simulation** | Pupils can carry out the experimental method in simulated situations which would otherwise be too dangerous or expensive to work with practically. They can gather 'data' and form and test hypotheses about relationships between variables. |
| **Graphic organiser** | Mind-maps and concept maps can be used in two ways – for the teacher to help explain links and relationships between ideas, and for pupils to demonstrate their understanding and their misconceptions in such a way that the teacher can help them to restructure their thinking. |
| **Data logging** | This enables practical experiments to be conducted that would otherwise be too fast, slow or inaccurate for pupils to measure variables themselves. The results can immediately be interpreted visually. |
| **Spreadsheet** | The analysis of data from surveys or experiments can be carried out more quickly and accurately, with immediate visual display of various relationships. Hypothesised relationships can be tested and revised quickly. |

**Task 4.1c**   Identify how particular items from the TTA list of potential ICT uses in science (see the beginning of this section) contributed to the success of the case study.

What other effects might the use of ICT in this way have on the learning of science compared with traditional approaches?

## How can ICT be used in teaching design and technology (D&T)?

ICT is intrinsic to the processes of design and manufacture in real life, and this is increasingly reflected in school schemes of work. In addition, ICT can help to provide stimuli for creative solutions to design problems. TTA (1999a) suggests that

> 'ICT has the potential to make a significant contribution to the teaching of D&T by:
> - generating, exploring, modelling, developing and communicating design ideas;
> - making products;
> - controlling electrical or mechanical products;
> - gaining access to a range of information;
> - controlling operations with a computer;
> - designing – computer-aided design;
> - modelling and simulation;
> - communicating;
> - helping with the preparation of teaching materials;
> - aiding record keeping and reporting of pupils' progress and attainment;
> - providing flexible and time-saving resources that can be used in different ways and at different times without repetition of the teacher's input;
> - providing a means by which subject and pedagogical knowledge can be improved and kept up-to-date'.

The following case study is based on a circuit design program which can simulate the function of the circuits designed. It shows how use of the software helps pupils to develop their design skills without the practical problems of faulty components and poor connections that are experienced when using real components.

### Case study: circuit design (TTA, 1999a)

The learning objectives involved designing a circuit to a given brief, using particular components correctly, applying strategies for testing and fault-finding, recognising standard symbols for components, and understanding the constraints of large-scale manufacture.

The task involved three aspects: designing a circuit to achieve a particular effect, making up the circuit using real components, and producing a printed circuit board from their design. The teacher showed the pupils real components and explained the function of each one. He used a large display to show how to select and connect components on the simulation and then test the circuit produced. The circuit design simulation program enabled pupils to try out different components and study their effects in a circuit, thus obtaining feedback on their understanding of the function that the teacher had explained to them.

## How did this improve D&T teaching?

Pupils were able to plan circuits and explore component functions quickly and without the wastage of materials that previously resulted from using real components in faulty designs. The teacher was able to discuss design and fault-finding strategies with the pupils, whereas in the traditional setting, all his time was taken in merely replacing faulty components and fixing connections. Pupils were still able to develop their practical skills of making real circuits, but in the knowledge that their tested circuit would achieve the desired effects. They were also able to experience the authentic manufacturing process by transferring their designs to printed circuit board software.

## What other applications may improve the learning of D&T?

There are a number of other ICT tools which D&T teachers find particularly helpful for themselves and for pupils, and Table 4.4 shows in outline how some of these can be used.

**Table 4.4**  Use of programs in D&T teaching (Kennewell *et al.*, 2003)

| | |
|---|---|
| **WWW** | In order to be effective as designers, pupils need to have active imaginations that are engaged by external stimuli such as the work of professional designers, videos, photographs of existing products. |
| **CAD/CAM** | These design packages are capable of communicating work to a printer, a plotter, a computer-driven milling machine, a sign writing machine or sewing and embroidery machines. |
| **Process control** | Pupils can create programs to control models they have designed and built. |
| **DTP or graphics** | These are excellent aids for pupils to produce high quality work. |

> **Task 4.1d**  Identify how particular items from the TTA list of potential ICT uses in D&T (see the beginning of this section) contributed to the success of the case study.
>
> What other effects might the use of ICT in this way have on the learning of D&T compared with traditional approaches?

## How can ICT be used in teaching modern foreign languages (MFL)?

The teaching of MFL is based on communication, and again ICT is a natural medium for most communications between nations and language groups in real life. ICT can also help to provide opportunities for practice in communication in the absence of a fluent target language speaker. TTA (1999a) suggests that:

> 'ICT has the potential to make a significant contribution to the teaching of MFL by:
> - developing and improving all four language skills;
> - enhancing pupils' language learning skills;
> - helping to develop independent learning skills;
> - providing different levels of support to match different pupils' language learning skills;
> - communicating with people in the target language;
> - accessing a range of resources in the target language and identifying with the people of target language communities and countries;
> - providing a flexible and time-saving resource;
> - allowing teachers to respond to different stages in a pupil's writing'.

The following case study shows how ICT can help to generate authentic communications with target language speakers in their own country for the real purpose of exchanging information about their everyday lives.

## Case study: e-mail contacts with Spanish pupils (TTA, 1999a)

The learning objectives were for pupils to develop their knowledge of vocabulary concerning household work, to be able to select and apply appropriate language to communicate survey findings and elicit information from Spanish peers, and to understand similarities and differences between their own lives and those of people in Spain.

The context was a unit of work concerning families and homes, and pupils had carried out a survey within their own class, using Spanish, to find out pupils' experiences concerning household chores. They analysed the data using a spreadsheet and presented their findings in terms of graphs. The teacher set up e-mail contacts with a similar school in Spain, and arranged links between individual pupils so that they could send the results of their survey (as attachments) and ask questions about Spanish children's experiences. This gave them practice in using vocabulary, framing questions and interpreting responses. The exchange of e-mails was scheduled carefully to ensure that a rapid response was obtained.

The pupils were then required to use their own survey, together with responses from Spain, to design a presentation for the class in Spanish, so that they could produce and refine their material to a high standard using a presentation program and also practice their oral communication skills in Spanish.

## How did this improve MFL teaching?

The e-mail environment enables learners to pursue interesting, authentic tasks and sustain contact with native speakers over a period of time. Pupils were inclined to be more adventurous in their use of the target language because of the support of an on-line dictionary and the facility to make changes to a draft after consulting the teacher. The quick responses provided rapid feedback on the effectiveness of the communication.

The features of this case study are also relevant to English, RE, geography and citizenship teaching.

## What other applications may improve the learning of MFL?

There are a number of other ICT tools which MFL teachers find particularly helpful for themselves and for pupils, and Table 4.5 shows in outline how some of these can be used.

**Table 4.5**   Use of programs in MFL teaching

| | |
|---|---|
| **WWW** | This gives access to large amounts of authentic and educational material in target languages. |
| **Presentation** | This enables pupils to easily produce quite authentic class presentations in the target language at an appropriate level, such that the visual images support their language use (TTA, 1999a). |
| **Text adaptation** | Word processing can be used to edit a prepared text for an alternative purpose, gender or time. |
| **Text completion** | This type of software provides teachers with tools for removing words or scrambling texts so that pupils have to use and develop their language skills in order to reconstruct the original text. |
| **Database** | Using or creating databases enables pupils to practise the use of vocabulary in the context of authentic tasks. |

**Task 4.1e**   Identify how particular items from the TTA list of potential ICT uses in MFL (see the beginning of this section) contributed to the success of the case study.

What other effects might the use of ICT in this way have on the learning of MFL compared with traditional approaches?

## How can ICT be used in teaching geography?

The processing of data and analysis of relationships concerning human activity and the natural environment have been transformed by ICT, not least in the area of mapping the distribution of variables. Furthermore, access to information concerning distant locations is significantly easier. TTA (1999a) suggests that

'ICT has the potential to make a significant contribution to the teaching of geography by:

- enhancing geographical enquiry skills;
- extending skills of graphical, statistical and spatial analysis;
- extending the range of primary and secondary sources;
- developing understanding of geographical patterns, processes and relationships;
- simulating or modelling abstract or complex geographical systems or processes;
- communicating and exchanging information with people in contrasting localities;
- helping the teacher keep up-to-date in geographic subject knowledge and pedagogy;
- saving time by providing varied and flexible resources;
- providing a source of resources for pupils'.

The following case study shows how ICT can be used in the field as well as in the classroom to help collect and analyse data and present results.

## Case study: river study (based on Hassell and Warner, 1995)

The learning objectives involved understanding the relationships between factors involved in river cross-section and flow and the ability to measure, analyse and interpret data concerning these factors and relationships.

The teacher took the class to a local river bank, positioning groups in different places in order to carry out specific measurements of the depth and velocity of the stream and the size of the bed load. The data was entered on the spot into a pre-prepared spreadsheet on a laptop computer. The velocity was measured both manually and with an automatic flowmeter. In addition, pupils took photographs of the area where measurements were taken using a digital camera.

On return to the school, the class worked in pairs, using the PCs in an ICT room, together with printed guides on using the spreadsheet for this activity, to analyse the data graphically concerning the cross-section of the river, the average velocity and the bed load. They produced word-processed reports which described the investigation that they had carried out, showed the tables and graphs produced, set them in context using the photographs taken, and compared the results with text book descriptions of rivers. The results at different places in the river were then compared and reasons for the differences discussed with the class.

## How did this improve geography teaching?

The use of ICT enabled more data to be collected and analysed, with more accuracy and in a much shorter time than when manual calculations and graphs were required. This enabled pupils to focus on the analysis and comparison of relationships between variables, and improved both the amount and presentation of work, particularly for the lower ability pupils. They gained a better understanding of the process of geographical investigation and developed their ability to organise, refine and present different forms of information for specific purposes.

The features of this case study are also relevant to science and mathematics teaching.

## What other applications may improve the learning of geography?

There are a number of other ICT tools that geography teachers find particularly helpful for themselves and for pupils, and Table 4.6 shows in outline how some of these can be used.

**Table 4.6**   Use of programs in geography teaching

| WWW | The Internet provides access to up-to-date data, images and reports from all parts of the world. |
|---|---|
| **Presentation** | Pupils' own reporting and explaining of events and processes can be improved by the structure and flexibility of a presentation program. |
| **Simulation** | Processes that are too slow or inaccessible can be investigated through simulations that allow the pupil to form and test hypotheses about relationships between factors. |
| **Database/GIS** | Databases that specify a location for each record can be used or created, and the location of particular features plotted and distribution of different factors shown by colours on an outline map. |
| **Graphic organiser** | Mind-maps and concept maps can be used in two ways – for the teacher to help explain links and relationships between ideas, and for pupils to demonstrate their understanding. |

**Task 4.1f**    Identify how particular items from the TTA list of potential ICT uses in geography (see the beginning of this section) contributed to the success of the case study.

What other effects might the use of ICT in this way have on the learning of geography compared with traditional approaches?

## How can ICT be used in teaching history?

The work of historians, too, has changed with the availability of source data and images of artefacts through ICT. The retrieval and analysis of information is quicker and easier, with more sources being accessible from any location. The use of the Internet brings questions of validity into sharper focus, however, and the greater range of opinions and interpretations that are now publicly available makes the skills of evaluation and criticism even more important. TTA (1999a) suggests that:

> 'ICT has the potential to make a significant contribution to the teaching of history by:
> - asking historical questions;
> - investigating change, cause and consequence;
> - assessing, evaluating and using a wide variety of sources critically;
> - organising information and ideas to communicate effectively;
> - understanding, analysing and constructing data;
> - locating sources and interpretations that can be adapted by teachers for use in the classroom;
> - saving time by providing varied and flexible resources;
> - enabling teachers to respond to different stages in a pupil's writing;
> - enabling teachers to focus directly on the different characteristics of sources'.

The following case study shows how a large pre-prepared database of data concerning castles can be used to investigate aspects of work on medieval realms.

## Case study: castles 1066–1500 (Martin and Walsh, 1998)

The learning objectives involved pupils further developing their understanding of the medieval period by investigating aspects of change over five centuries, using their basic knowledge of the topic to form and test hypotheses, developing their own constructions of the past, which are supported by evidence, and recognising that the simple interpretations that they meet in school books and other media may not correspond fully to source data.

The pupils had been introduced to aspects of castles and wider issues of the medieval period through a range of activities, and the current task is focused on the key question 'Were all medieval castles the same?' In the history teaching room, they were introduced to the structure of the database and the nature of the 450 records it contained, using a large display at the front of the class, so that the teacher could explain the field names and discuss the reliability of the data, which was still somewhat incomplete and based on historical judgements where primary evidence was missing. The pupils were then taken to the ICT room and set an initial task to help develop their familiarity with the data, the sort of hypotheses they might create and test, and with the way in which enquiries had to be expressed in order that the database could carry out the search or sort that they required (see Figure 4.3).

The teacher then carried out a review with the whole class in order to compare what different groups of pupils had found, reflect on what they had learnt, and focus their thinking on the overall question. The teacher also demonstrated the graphing facility to help them answer questions concerning patterns and trends over the full time period. Pupils then continued with the database task, using the questions shown in Figure 4.4. The more able pupils were encouraged to devise and answer their own

## TASK SHEET 1

### Key question: **Were all medieval castles the same?**

A **Getting started**

To get used to the way the database works, answer questions 1 and 2.

1. When was the first castle with a portcullis built?

2. Is it correct to say that castle builders did not use brick before the 15<sup>th</sup> century?

**Hint**: Sort the records by **Start of building** – this lists the castles in the order in which they were built.
Then narrow down the list by searching the field **Details** for 'portcullis'.
When the castles with portcullises come up on screen, the first one will be the earliest!

**Hint**: Make sure that you have all records selected. Search the **Materials** first for 'brick'.
Sort or graph the records found by 'century'.

B **True or false?**

Here is a list of statements about castles. Using the database, say whether you believe the statements to be true or false. You need to be able to explain why!

| Statement | True or false? |
|---|---|
| More castles were built in the 12<sup>th</sup> century than in any other century. | |
| No wooden castles were built after 1070. | |
| Concentric castles were not introduced until the 13<sup>th</sup> century. | |
| Shell keeps were no longer used by the 12<sup>th</sup> century. | |
| More Welsh castles were built in the 13<sup>th</sup> century than any other century. | |
| Very few castles were built in England in the 13<sup>th</sup> century. | |
| The only shell keeps built in England were built between 1100 and 1240. | |

C **Testing ideas**

The statements below are ideas or 'hypotheses'. Historians put forward hypotheses as possible explanations of events. Use the database and your own knowledge of the period to decide whether you support this historian's hypotheses about castle building. You will need to have evidence!

| Hypothesis to test | Do you support it? |
|---|---|
| Square keeps were developed during the reign of Henry II. | |
| Edward I built more castles in Wales than in England. | |
| All the castles built in England in the 16<sup>th</sup> century were on the coast. | |
| All the castles built in the 14<sup>th</sup> century were built by barons. | |

**Figure 4.3** Task sheet 1 from Martin, D. and Walsh, B. (1998) *History using IT: searching for patterns in the past using spreadsheets and databases*, Coventry: NCET and the Historical Association, p. 34

questions, whilst all pupils completed the basic task. Finally, pupils were asked to produce a poster, setting out their response to the questions, together with evidence to support it. The qualities of these posters were then discussed with the whole class in order to help develop a clear understanding of the changes over the five centuries and the importance of basing this knowledge on evidence, and what constituted evidence in this case.

## TASK SHEET 2

---

### D Enquiry: Were all castles the same?

**Information**

You have probably looked at many castles in the course of your history studies, but could you say for sure whether all castles were the same or not?

To be confident about this, we need to know the answers to questions like these:
• Were they all built using the same design?
• Were they all built using the same materials?
• Did they all have keeps?
• Were all keeps the same?

**Task**

Now use the database to answer these questions for:
1. all the castles built in the 11th and 12th centuries
2. all the castles built by Edward I in Wales
3. all the castles built in the 15th century
4. all the castles built by Henry VIII.

**Extension work**

Add more questions to the list in the Information section and then try them out on the castles listed in the Task.

---

**Figure 4.4** Task sheet 2 from Martin, D. and Walsh, B. (1998) *History using IT: searching for patterns in the past using spreadsheets and databases*, Coventry: NCET and the Historical Association p. 35

How did this improve history teaching?

The use of ICT enabled a far greater quantity of data to be used in the investigation and made the process of collating responses to questions about it much quicker and more accurate. This enabled the pupils to focus on the higher order skills of historical enquiry, particularly concerning the seeking of evidence to support conjectures. They were able to develop and understand relatively complex interpretations of relationships and events compared with traditional classroom materials.

The features of this case study are also relevant to geography, D&T, science, mathematics and citizenship teaching.

## What other applications may improve the learning of history?

There are a number of other ICT tools that history teachers find particularly helpful for themselves and for pupils, and Table 4.7 shows in outline how some of these can be used.

**Table 4.7**  Use of programs in history teaching

| | |
|---|---|
| **WWW** | Historical source documents, data, images, oral reports and films are available for study and analysis without visiting the particular site, museum or library where they are held. |
| **Presentation** | Pupils' own reporting and explaining of events and relationships can be improved by the structure and flexibility of a presentation program. |
| **Simulation** | The decision-making situations faced during key events in the past can be simulated to some extent, although a model that allows alternative outcomes to the actual one will always be a matter of conjecture. Background information is presented in multimedia form for pupils to evaluate, draw conclusions and gain feedback on their own decisions in relation to subsequent events. |
| **Database** | Databases can be prepared (by publishers, teachers or pupils) from historical sources such as census data, parish records and commercial registers so that pupils can pursue enquiries using clearly legible data; rapid, accurate searching, and flexible display of results. |
| **Graphic organiser** | Mind-maps and concept maps can be used in two ways – for the teacher to help explain links and relationships between ideas, and for pupils to demonstrate their understanding. |

**Task 4.1g**   Identify how particular items from the TTA list of potential ICT uses in history (see the beginning of this section) contributed to the success of the case study.

What other effects might the use of ICT in this way have on the learning of history compared with traditional approaches?

## How can ICT be used in teaching physical education (PE)?

The use of digital video is now fundamental to analysing and developing performance in sports and other physical activity. Automatic measurements of the way the body is functioning during physical performance and the way players and equipment are moving during games also enables performances to be analysed more quickly, more accurately and with more information available. TTA (1999a) suggests that:

> 'ICT has the potential to make a significant contribution to the teaching of PE by:
> - developing pupils' knowledge, understanding and skills;
> - helping pupils review, evaluate and improve their performance;
> - compressing or expanding time;
> - developing pupils' understanding of the human body, physiology and health education;
> - supporting teachers in their administrative role'.

The following case study shows how digital video can be used by the teacher to demonstrate good performance without being an expert in the activity, and by pupils to record and review each others' performance.

### Case study: basketball shots (TTA, 1999a)

The learning objectives included knowledge and understanding of the lay-up shot in basketball, skill in creating shooting opportunities in the game, and improvement in shooting skills.

The teacher used a recording of a good basketball player demonstrating a shot to show pupils the elements of good technique. He was able to replay this, each time focusing pupils' attention on different aspects of the player's movements. He could play sections of the video to break the shot down, and play it slowly, even frame by frame, in order to examine closely the footwork and body position at particular points.

Pupils were then able to record their performances, and replay the video on a large screen for the whole group to discuss with the teacher how each pupil had performed in comparison with the demonstration.

### How did this improve PE teaching?

The digital video technology supports a focused analysis of performance which would be impossible otherwise.

The features of this case study are also relevant to science, mathematics, geography and D&T teaching.

What other applications may improve the learning of PE?

There are a number of other ICT tools which PE teachers find particularly helpful for themselves and for pupils, and Table 4.8 shows in outline how some of these can be used.

**Table 4.8**  Use of programs in PE teaching

| | |
|---|---|
| **WWW** | Information about sports, results and players, can be obtained easily from all over the world for comparison and analysis. |
| **Presentation** | Teachers can represent points using a mixture of images, video, diagrams and words using a single prepared source, and pupils' reports can be structured effectively in multimedia format. |
| **Graphics and video** | Detailed analysis of still and moving images can be carried out by manipulating images and video material appropriately. |
| **Data logging** | Measurements and recording of physical processes can be carried out even during fast movement, with very rapid or very slow rate of reading if needed. |
| **Spreadsheet** | Analysis of physical data can be carried out using calculations and graphs, either comparing several people or a single person over a period of time. |

**Task 4.1h**  Identify how particular items from the TTA list of potential ICT uses in PE (see the beginning of this section) contributed to the success of the case study.

What other effects might the use of ICT in this way have on the learning of PE compared with traditional approaches?

## How can ICT be used in teaching religious education (RE)?

TTA (1999a) suggests that:

'ICT has the potential to make a significant contribution to the teaching of RE by:
- analysing information to pose and answer questions;
- exploring the consequences of decisions on religious, social or moral issues;
- assessing and evaluating a wide variety of sources critically;
- understanding, analysing and constructing differing interpretations;
- organising information and ideas to communicate effectively;
- communicating with faith communities, organisations and experts;

- providing a flexible and time-saving resource;
- enabling teachers to respond to different stages in a pupil's writing;
- allowing the teacher to focus on the different characteristics of sources;
- helping teachers to locate sources and interpretations that can be adapted for use in the classroom;
- aiding record keeping and reporting of pupils' progress and attainment'.

The following case study shows how ICT can enable pupils to explore themes in religion through rapid access to key texts and a range of ideas that would not otherwise be accessible.

## Case study: exploring the theme of suffering (TTA, 1999a)

The learning objectives concerned knowledge of how the concept of suffering is approached in different religious traditions, understanding how suffering is treated in particular religions, understand approaches to suffering in particular situations, and considering why apparently 'good' people suffer.

The teacher evaluated the CD-ROM in advance, in order to identify content at an appropriate level for different pupils. He also searched the WWW to find and bookmark particularly useful sites for the topic and an RE site which acted as a 'portal': it provided links to a selection of other sites, which had been checked for appropriate educational content. After a brief whole-class discussion of the ideas in the RE classroom, pupils worked in groups of three in the school's resource centre to explore a range of resources including CD-ROM and websites as well as books in order to explore what others have thought and written on suffering and identify the different approaches and perceptions. Each group used a word processor to produce a report on their findings.

## How did this improve RE teaching?

Pupils were able to gain perspectives of other faiths from direct sources, as well as interpretations in books. They were able to access text and images on screen from all around the world, and particularly recent writings and the rare and sacred texts that would be otherwise inaccessible. The speed of access allowed pupils to engage in deeper thinking.

The features of this case study are also relevant to English, history, MFL and citizenship teaching.

## What other applications may improve the learning of RE?

There are a number of other ICT tools that RE teachers find particularly helpful for themselves and for pupils, and Table 4.9 shows in outline how some of these can be used.

**Table 4.9**  Use of programs in RE teaching

| Presentation | Teachers can represent points using a mixture of images, video, diagrams and words using a single prepared source, and pupils' reports can be structured effectively in multimedia format. |
|---|---|
| Graphic organiser | Mind-maps and concept maps can be used in two ways – for the teacher to help explain links and relationships between ideas, and for pupils to demonstrate their understanding. |
| Database | The structuring, collecting and analysis of data helps pupils to understand the factors involved and to make informed comparisons between faiths. |

**Task 4.1i**   Identify how particular items from the TTA list of potential ICT uses in RE (see the beginning of this section) contributed to the success of the case study.

What other effects might the use of ICT in this way have on the learning of RE compared with traditional approaches?

## How can ICT be used in teaching art?

ICT has influenced art in two main ways. Digital media provide new art forms, and also provide new ways of exploring more traditional ideas. Novice artists no longer require traditional skills with media such as pencil, paint or clay; they can produce images using the electronic equivalents of these tools, together with a whole array of new tools and effects. They can experiment, evaluate and quickly change their work if they do not like the effect. Furthermore, they can manipulate images by selection of particular parts, replication, and transformation in size, shape, form, texture or colour. TTA (1999a) suggests that:

'ICT has the potential to make a significant contribution to the teaching of art by:
- researching and developing ideas;
- aiding in the creative process;
- creating a finished piece of work;
- contributing to an extension activity;
- providing a medium that can be used to explore visual phenomena and experiment with a visual language;
- extending the range of tools and techniques used in art;
- enabling teachers and pupils to develop their ideas and maintain a visual record of the process and final outcome of their work;

- extending pupils' knowledge experience and critical skills; enabling pupils to share their own and other pupils' artwork;
- helping to locate resources and interpretations of contemporary art practice, which can be adapted for use in the classroom'.

The following case study shows how ICT can be used in accessing and capturing images, focusing and manipulating them in response to a particular theme and a variety of stimuli and in preparation for producing a 3-D outcome.

## Case study: Travellers' Tales (Virtual Teachers' Centre, 2003)

The learning objectives in a vocational course for 16–17 year-olds included:

- developing research skills;
- understanding the value of ICT in the production of art and in the communications media;
- understanding of contemporary art issues;
- awareness of culturally diverse artists.

More precisely, students were to investigate and experiment with a variety of ideas and techniques for making photographic imagery, become familiar with relevant vocabulary, collaborate on investigations and learning, manipulate photographic images, document their progress and critically evaluate the process and product of the work.

The teacher wanted the students to investigate, experiment with and document their responses to the theme of travellers' tales. The students were given trigger questions for an initial brainstorm and used a graphic organiser to represent their ideas and the links between them. A professional photographer from Brazil, who came to show and talk about his work, left his e-mail address for the students to ask questions and to continue discussions. The students chose their favourite theme from the ideas generated, and were given particular websites and other stimulus materials concerning life and art in different cultures to explore, including books, maps and a wall covered with inspirational images. They discussed how various images could be transformed, and were shown how to download images from the Internet, operate a digital camera and a scanner. They were then shown how to use graphics software to resize, crop, cut-and-paste, filter and otherwise manipulate the appearance of images.

They were required to devise a non-traditional way of displaying their photographic work in a 3-D structure, and they used the WWW to research alternative ways of displaying photographic images as well as investigating the work of other artists in the field. They produced a range of outcomes, involving traditional photos, photocopies and inkjet prints.

## How did this improve art teaching?

The teacher was able to point students towards stimulus material that would not have been available otherwise. Students were able to explore ideas quickly, without requiring traditional craft skills and without having to produce time-consuming 2- and 3-D studies.

## What other applications may improve the learning of art?

There are a number of other ICT tools that art teachers find particularly helpful for themselves and for pupils, and Table 4.10 shows in outline how some of these can be used.

**Table 4.10**   Use of programs in art teaching

| | |
|---|---|
| **WWW** | Images are available for stimulus and analysis without visiting the particular gallery or library where they are held. |
| **Presentation** | The development of visual ideas during an investigation or preparatory study can be structured effectively and shown easily to a class or group to discuss. |
| **Graphics** | An image can be captured easily and then all or selected parts of it manipulated in terms of colour, size, and form. Images can be easily juxtaposed, overlaid or combined in other ways to create new effects. |

**Task 4.1j**   Identify how particular items from the TTA list of potential ICT uses in art (see the beginning of this section) contributed to the success of the case study.

What other effects might the use of ICT in this way have on the learning of art compared with traditional approaches?

## How can ICT be used in teaching music?

The influence of ICT on music has perhaps been the most revolutionary of all subjects, with digital sound production now pervading most popular music and digital methods being dominant in recording, editing, reproduction and transmission. Even novice musicians can explore original combinations of sounds and manipulate recorded pieces in ways that would have been impossible when performance skills with an instrument were required for composition and presentation of musical ideas. TTA (1999a) suggests that:

> 'ICT has the potential to make a significant contribution to the teaching of music by helping:
> - pupils to respond and review their own and other pupils' work;
> - pupils to develop musical skills by applying knowledge and understanding of musical elements, devices, tonalities and structures;

- pupils to develop knowledge and understanding of specific procedures and conventions used in certain musical genres, styles and traditions;
- pupils to develop knowledge and understanding of the impact of ICT on the way music is created, performed and heard;
- teachers to locate materials for personal information and classroom use;
- to maintain an easily accessible library of recordings;
- to provide a flexible and time-saving resource;
- to save and archive pupils' work;
- to offer flexible stylistic recorded accompaniments;
- to maintain a database of information'.

The following case study shows how work on major and minor sounds can be enhanced by using prepared sequencer files for demonstration and music programs on the PC for pupils to explore, experiment, evaluate and perform without requiring skills in playing an instrument.

## Case study: major and minor sounds (TTA, 1999a)

The learning objectives involve developing knowledge and understanding of major and minor scales, improving aural recognition of major and minor keys, the ability to distinguish between changes in key and changes in other features, and the appreciation of contrast between major and minor keys when composing.

The teacher reviewed previous work on major and minor using instruments, and then used prepared MIDI files on a sequencer to demonstrate particular points concerning major and minor sounds. Pupils were then asked to use a music program to compose (in pairs) a short piece of melody, and then transform it from major to minor or minor to major. They were able to play both versions in quick succession for comparison. The more able pupils used the program to change each note themselves, whilst the less able used a program which enabled them merely to drag the melody to a different position in order to change key automatically. Some pupils' work was played to the whole class at the end of the lesson, so that pupils could practice identifying whether an unknown piece was major or minor.

## How did this improve music teaching?

ICT enabled the teacher to prepare polished pieces for demonstration and make rapid transition between pieces in order to focus pupils' thinking on comparison, without having to read sheet music or think about the performance whilst in front of the class. It enabled pupils to make changes to work very quickly and easily in a way that they would not have been capable of if they had to manipulate acoustic instruments or keyboards.

## What other applications may improve the learning of music?

There are a number of other ICT tools which music teachers find particularly helpful for themselves and for pupils, and Table 4.11 shows in outline how some of these can be used.

**Table 4.11**  Use of programs in music teaching

| | |
|---|---|
| **WWW** | Musical sources from all over the world can be sought and explored easily. |
| **Presentation** | Multimedia presentations allow pupils to combine their own compositions and/or performances, or selected pieces from other sources, together with visual images. |
| **Composition and sequencing** | Music can be composed in draft form and edited easily in order to explore different effects, without having to manually record notes or use an instrument effectively. Separate parts can be combined in flexible ways. |

**Task 4.1k**    Identify how particular items from the TTA list of potential ICT uses in music (see the beginning of this section) contribute to the success of the case study.

What other effects might the use of ICT in this way have on the learning of music compared with traditional approaches?

## How can ICT be used in teaching ICT?

This may seem like a strange question, but it is important to consider how ICT may be used to help pupils understand ICT concepts, not just to practise techniques. TTA (1999a) suggests that:

'ICT has the potential to make a significant contribution to the teaching of ICT by:

● allowing different options to be demonstrated, explored and discussed;
● helping to prepare teaching materials;
● providing flexible and time-saving resources;
● providing a means by which subject and pedagogical knowledge can be improved and kept up-to-date;
● aiding record keeping and reporting of pupils' progress and attainment'.

The following case study shows how pupils' understanding of the social, ethical, economic and environmental effects of ICT can be developed through the use of ICT itself. It also helps contribute to pupils' understanding of global citizenship and sustainable development, at the same time as developing pupils' skills in information retrieval and developing web pages.

## Case study: effects of ICT

The teacher wanted to set a project task for a GCSE group within the theme of global citizenship and sustainable development. He decided to ask the pupils to create a website for other GCSE students concerning ICT's effects on the environment and on the gap between rich and poor countries. He grouped them into teams, each group having a separate question to research and then construct web pages in order to publish their findings. The questions included the following.

- What happens to old computers and phones when they are no longer wanted? Are they recycled?
- In the UK, most homes have at least one PC. How much energy does this use? What if every home in the world had a PC?
- Does the use of ICT reduce the amount of paper used?
- How many homes have PCs in other countries around the world? How many are connected to the Internet?
- How many people work in the ICT industry in different countries? What do they earn?
- Which companies are the biggest computer manufacturers worldwide? In the UK? Where do they have their factories? Where are their components made?

All pupils were reminded about search strategies and sifting results from web search engines, and the harder questions were given to groups containing the most able pupils. They were provided with a web page template within which each group chose how to set out their findings. Each group's pages were then linked into an index page prepared by the teacher. The whole site was then reviewed by the class, with each group explaining how they found and selected information for their pages and how they set the site out. The teacher and other pupils suggested improvements, and questioned them about the points made on their pages to check that they were correct. The pupils then had a short time to make any changes before the teacher published the pages on the school's website. Finally, the teacher asked them to suggest projects in other subjects where they could use the same approach.

## How did this improve ICT teaching?

The learning objectives involved the ability to use effective search strategies to identify helpful websites for a particular brief, the development of a simple website for a particular audience, and the understanding of differences in access to ICT in rich and poor countries and of potential uses for redundant ICT equipment. Whilst dealing with wider issues, the task had a worthwhile purpose within the subject itself: pupils were clearly learning about ICT's effects as well as developing their web-searching and web-creation skills. The task enabled pupils to structure their reports of plans/ discussions in a non-linear fashion and to make the results available beyond the school. Pupils were learning to learn autonomously, and to work as a team. The teacher provided support for transfer of skills to other subjects by asking pupils to identify opportunities to use the ICT skills that they had developed.

## What other applications may improve the learning of ICT?

There are a number of other ICT tools which ICT teachers find particularly helpful for themselves and for pupils, and Table 4.12 shows in outline how some of these can be used.

**Table 4.12** Use of programs in ICT teaching

| | |
|---|---|
| **Presentation and web creation** | Pupils' own reporting and explaining of events and processes can be improved by the structure and flexibility of a presentation program; quizzes can be created by teacher and pupils. |
| **Database and spreadsheet** | Pupils' knowledge of database principles, construction and use can be applied to ICT factors such as speed, size, capacity, cost when investigating and designing systems |
| **E-mail or text messaging** | Debates, role play and hot-seating (see Kennewell et al., 2003) can be continued beyond the constraints of the classroom and lesson time. |
| **Graphic organiser** | Mind-maps and concept maps can be used in two ways – for the teacher to help explain links and relationships between ideas, and for pupils to demonstrate their understanding. |

**Task 4.11** Identify how particular items from the TTA list of potential ICT uses in ICT (see the beginning of this section) contributed to the success of the case study.

What other effects might the use of ICT in this way have on the learning of ICT compared with traditional approaches?

## How can you analyse the role of the teacher in these scenarios?

ICT in the classroom does not automatically help with teaching and learning. The case studies illustrate some of the planning and careful management that goes into the use of ICT, and this is why the teacher's role is so important.

First, the teacher has planned the teaching in order to enable the pupils to achieve certain learning objectives. Assuming that the pupils have not already attained these, then there will be a gap between what the pupils already know and what the teacher plans for them to know as a result of the teaching. This book will refer to it as the *learning gap*. In order to bridge this gap, pupils will need to engage in some activity that enables them to gain the required knowledge, skills and understanding – this may involve passively listening to the teacher, or it may involve actively creating a product. Most pupils will need some help and support in completing the activity. The teacher will plan to provide much of the necessary support, and pupils may be able to help each other. The teacher will also prepare resources to supplement their own ability to provide support for pupils, and this is where ICT fits into the process. The assistance needed will depend on pupils' existing abilities in relation to the activity. The teacher will assess pupils' needs and increase or decrease the support that they provide themselves and the support the resources provide. This idea of 'orchestrating' (Kennewell, 2001) the resources in order to provide just enough support for pupils' learning activity is at the heart of using ICT in teaching and learning, and subsequent chapters will develop it further.

| Task 4.2 | How is ICT used in your placement school department? Identify particular features of the setting which provide potential and structure for ICT activity. |
|---|---|

## Further reading

Cox, M. J. and Abbott, C. (eds) (2004) *ICT and attainment: a literature review*, Coventry: British Educational Communications Agency and Technology London: DfES

Leask, M. and Pachler, N. (eds) (1999) *Learning to teach using ICT in the secondary school*, London: Routledge

Poole, P. (1998) *Talking about ICT in subject teaching*, Canterbury: Canterbury Christchurch University College

Trend, R., Davis, N. and Loveless, A. (1999) *Information and communications technology*, London: Letts Educational

Underwood, J. (1994) *Computer based learning: potential into practice*, London: David Fulton

One book has been selected for each subject as a starting point. For most subjects, there are other books dealing with the use of ICT in the subject, and institutional libraries should be able to help you to locate them. The journals of subject associations also frequently contain articles concerning the use of ICT in teaching and learning.

Dugard, C. and Hewer, S. (2003) *Impact on learning: what ICT can bring to MFL in KS3*, London: CILT

Hall, A. and Leigh, J. (2001) *ICT in physical education*, Cambridge: Pearson Publishing

Hassell, D. and Warner, H. (1995) *Using ICT to enhance geography: case studies at KS3 and KS4*, Coventry: NCET and the Geographical Association

Hickman, R. (2002) *ICT in art and design*, Cambridge: Pearson Publishing

Hughes, S. (2001) *ICT in religious education*, Cambridge: Pearson Publishing

Martin, D. and Walsh, B. (1998) *History using IT: searching for patterns in the past using spreadsheets and databases*, Coventry: NCET and the Historical Association

Mill, D. (2001) *ICT in music*, Cambridge: Pearson Publishing

Newton, L. and Rogers, L. (2001) *Teaching Science with ICT*, London: Continuum Press

Oldknow, A. and Taylor, R. (2000) *Teaching mathematics with ICT*, London: Continuum Press

Shreeve, A. (ed.) (1997) *IT in English: case studies and materials*, Coventry: NCET

In addition, a series of booklets *Using ICT to meet teaching objectives in secondary* . . . (produced by TTA) provides case studies in each subject. For example, TTA (1999) *Using ICT to meet teaching objectives in secondary geography*, London: Teacher Training Agency.

Becta's ICT Advice website www.ictadvice.org.uk also provides advice concerning the use of ICT in each secondary subject.

# 5   How Pupils Learn with ICT

This chapter explains and exemplifies key elements of learning theories that underpin the way ICT supports learning. It analyses further the Chapter 4 case studies from the perspective of pupils' learning and explores the role of different learning styles and of reflection in learning with ICT. It explores the relationship between ICT and other key skills when learning in subject lessons, using examples from different subjects.

## What types of knowledge are there?

For the purposes of this chapter, knowledge can be categorised under three headings:

- Knowing that
- Knowing how
- Knowing why.

The first of these involves purely factual knowledge, or knowledge of terminology, such as 'the capital of Italy is Rome', 'Shakespeare wrote Romeo and Juliet', or '6 times 9 is 54'. It may not involve any understanding of the relationships involved.

The second concerns what are usually referred to as 'skills'. This term covers a wide variety of types of skill, from low order skills such as writing letters of the alphabet, through techniques such as long multiplication, more complex processes such as translating a work of French literature into English, to higher order skills such as evaluating a solution to a design problem.

The third type of knowledge concerns the vital element of understanding, for example the role of a capital city, the plot of Romeo and Juliet, the purpose of multiplying numbers, the structure of sentences, the associative law of arithmetic, the role of idiomatic expressions in conveying an author's meaning, and the nature of the human needs for which a technological solution was designed.

All these types of knowledge are essential, and all school curricula are based on them. The learning of each type may be assisted with the use of ICT, but there are likely to be different ways in which ICT can help in each case.

| Task 5.1 | Identify a situation in which you have used ICT in learning, or where you have observed others using ICT. Which type of knowledge did ICT assist with? How was ICT used? |
| --- | --- |

## What learning theories can help us to understand the role of ICT?

It is important to review briefly some of the key theoretical ideas concerning learning that may be used to help understand what is happening during the use of ICT processes. By focusing on points relevant to ICT, the analysis will be brief and selective to the point of oversimplifying some of the issues involved, and you should refer to the recommended further reading in order to develop your understanding of learning theories.

### Behaviourism

During much of the twentieth century, the ideas of behaviourism were most influential on teaching approaches. The work of B. F. Skinner was based on the idea that humans learned from experience through the mechanisms of stimulus–response and operant conditioning. The key elements of the learning process involved the frequency of the activity to be learned and the reinforcement of it in terms of positive feedback. This implied a very limited role for the teacher, involving the repeated presentation of highly structured material to the learner, recognition of correct responses from the pupil, and dispensing rewards accordingly. Once a particular point was mastered, the next point was presented in the same way. Skinner applied his theories in the practical form of teaching machines, which presented material, asked the learner an assessment question, and either presented new material or remedial material depending on the response. He argued that machines would perform this role better than teachers (Skinner, 1968), as they could represent and replicate the most expert knowledge of content, presentation and sequencing.

Although highly developed empirically and theoretically, this view denies any role to conscious thought, or cognition, on the part of the learner. It corresponds closely to naïve, intuitive ideas about teaching and learning. Its influence on practice in schools is less than it was 50 years ago, but it may still be seen in tasks where learners practise a skill repetitively and unthinkingly, and in the principles of behaviour modification to develop children's social skills. To this extent it does have a role to play, as conditioning and habituation are important in making skills automatic, that is they can be carried out without conscious thought. This is a valuable feature of some skills, for example basic operation of machinery (such as a car or a mouse) which needs to be used without distracting the user from concentrating on higher order matters (such as the road conditions and route, or the design of the presentation being produced), and this point will be considered further in relation to developing ICT skills in Chapter 6. As far as learning with ICT is concerned, it has been particularly influential since the first examples of computer-aided learning (CAL) which were based heavily on Skinnerian teaching machines. Programs that present material and then repetitively test knowledge and skills ('drill') are still common, particularly in primary schools in developing basic skills of literacy and numeracy, and the same principles are used to a certain extent in integrated learning systems (Underwood and Brown, 1997).

## Constructivism

At the same time as behaviourism was influential, Jean Piaget was developing his theories of cognitive development. He also emphasised the role of experience in learning, but his key theoretical idea was the development of schematic structures in the mind which constituted understanding. These structures developed through a natural process of generalisation through reflection on experience, and enabled humans to apply knowledge in unfamiliar situations. They evolve in individuals through gradual extension of schemata in the mind in order to assimilate new information and through major reconstruction (or accommodation) in response to conflict between concepts and experience. This conceptual change is the most powerful form of learning and is difficult to bring about (see, for example, Adey and Shayer, 1994).

For Piaget and many educationists since, knowledge is constructed by the learner from experiences in interacting with their environment. This has led to the term *constructivism* for this type of learning theory. This implies that mere exposition of ideas by teachers will not be enough for pupils to learn anything worthwhile, and explains many of the difficulties teachers have traditionally faced in 'transmitting' their expert knowledge to novices. It suggests the most important goal for teachers is to stimulate conceptual change, which implies a very different role for ICT than for repetitive practice of basic skills. The constructivist role involves providing learners with experiences that may conflict with naïve ideas, allowing the teacher to intervene to help resolve the 'cognitive conflict' through conceptual change. This is particularly valuable in science, mathematics and other subjects where models and simulations of situations, which are difficult to experience practically, can be implemented with ICT (see Chapter 4).

Reflection has a vital role to play in constructivist theories, for without a reflective stage it is unlikely that experiences will have any effect on mental structures. Indeed, for Abbot (1994, cited in Watkins *et al.* (2000)), learning is precisely 'that reflective activity which enables the learner to draw on previous experience to understand and evaluate the present, so as to shape future action and formulate new knowledge'. However, reflection does not have to be carried out consciously, subsequent to the experience concerned. Schön (1987) highlights the role of *reflection-in-action* rather than *reflection-on-action* for improving performance in professional activity, and this involves the continual planning and monitoring of actions carried out during tasks. This type of metacognitive activity – thinking about one's thinking – is of great importance and the whole field is considered below. For pupils, such processes need to be learned and both the teacher and ICT can play an important role in stimulating reflective activity and supporting metacognition. The idea of concept mapping (see Chapter 3) is one way of generating reflection, and the graphic organiser enables ICT to support this activity.

## Social constructivism

The constructivist approach primarily focuses on the development of the individual mind, and at the same time as Piaget was developing his ideas in the first half of the twentieth century, Vygotsky was pursuing a similar analysis of cognitive development based on social interactions rather than individual experience as the source of learning. The ideas developed from Vygotsky's seminal works (for example, Vygotsky, 1978) have been characterised as socio-constructivist or socio-cultural, highlighting the need to consider not just interactions between individuals, but the cultural setting in which they take place. These theories have much more to say directly about teaching as well as learning. Indeed, Vygotsky's fundamental law was that knowledge is created in the interaction between people before it becomes internalised by the individual learner, and so we would expect the role of the teacher to be paramount. It also suggests that collaborative activity has an important role to play in learning.

Vygotsky proposed a specific feature of the process of learning called the zone of proximal development (ZPD). For a particular learner, there will be tasks that they can already perform confidently, and others that they cannot begin to engage in because of the unfamiliarity of the subject matter. The range of activity in between may be carried out by the learner with support, and this is the ZPD. Activity of this sort is the most likely to result in learning. The support may be from a teacher, a fellow learner, or from tools and resources. Vygotsky attached great significance to the role of cultural tools, particularly that of language, which he saw as essential to higher forms of cognition. Although he did not live to see the rise of the mass communications media, his ideas can suggest much about the value of these, and the role of ICT in particular. The value of collaborative learning has been explored in many contexts, and the role of ICT tools has been highlighted in many of these. Crook (1994) has analysed learning from collaborative interactions:

- with computers;
- in relation to computers;
- at computers;
- around and through computers.

The idea of teaching being characterised as support within the ZPD was refined further by Wood and Bruner (see Wood, 1988). They used the term 'scaffolding' for the assistance given by a teacher, tutor, colleague, parent or other more knowledgeable person which is contingent on the learner's response to a task. It is only provided while the learner is constructing knowledge, and should be withheld once the learner can work independently. This process is commonly seen in individual tutoring, but quite rare in busy classrooms where the teacher cannot spend enough time with individuals to provide contingent support (Bliss *et al.*, 1996). This idea has been the basis of many approaches to using ICT in the classroom, with some designers trying to represent all the thinking that the teacher does in the computer program (such as an ILS), and others recognising that the learner can make useful judgements about the support they need in a resource-rich environment.

## Situativity

The constructivist theories suggest that conceptual knowledge will transfer to unfamiliar situations, but there is much evidence that this rarely happens in the way that would be expected (Lave and Wenger, 1991). As proponents of 'situated cognition', Lave and Wenger claim that it is wrong to consider knowledge as something that we acquire individually and carry around with us. Instead, learning is just a part of our participation in activity in different social settings, the knowledge gained is situated in that setting and we would expect a change in setting to require new learning. We can make use of experiences gained elsewhere to the extent that features of the new setting are similar to those in the original. The implications for teaching of these ideas are that teaching should be based in real-life settings rather than the school as a purely 'educational' setting, or at least that authentic tasks should be used in the classroom. To implement these ideas fully would require a fundamentally different curriculum, but there may be value in using them in combination with reflective activity, which considers the concepts underlying the authentic tasks. It is appropriate, therefore, to look for ways in which ICT can improve the authenticity of classroom activity.

## 'Brain-based' ideas

Most recently, much has been made of a loose amalgam of ideas that have emerged from research on cognition in terms of the function of the brain (Smith, 1997). These include the idea of preferred learning style. This idea is based on the claim that, although we all use visual, auditory and kinaesthetic (physical movement and touch) activity in learning, we each have a preference for which suits us best. Variations in fundamental cognitive style have also been characterised (Riding and Rayner, 1998), particularly along two independent dimensions: the *verbaliser–visualiser* scale and the *wholist–analyst* scale. The 'verbaliser' has a preference for using words, whereas the 'visualiser' has a preference for using images as aids to thought; the 'wholist' likes to grasp the 'big picture' first, whereas the 'analyst' prefers to focus on details in order to understand matters. These thinking styles also influence learning, and are likely to be related to the preferred learning style. Furthermore, Gardner (1993) has characterised 'multiple intelligences', claiming that one's natural ability in learning and performance is not based on a single quality of intelligence, but varies over a whole range of factors including:

- linguistic;
- logical-mathematical;
- musical;

- bodily-kinaesthetic;
- spatial;
- interpersonal;
- intrapersonal.

Unfortunately, although there seems to be much value for teachers in recognising the individual differences between learners which these ideas imply, there is not yet a single theoretical framework that accounts for these differences. Each team of psychologists that investigate behaviour and learning in these terms has produced a new characterisation of differences (Adey *et al.*, 1999). However, there is general agreement that the most successful people are those who can employ a variety of styles and strategies, recognise their weaknesses and work to improve them. There are two main issues for teachers to consider.

- How to 'accelerate' learning by exploiting the full range of individual learners' strengths.
- How to help learners to improve their abilities in strategies that are naturally weak.

One potential role of ICT in accelerating learning is clear, in that multimedia presentation that incorporates images, animation and sound is likely to be more effective than only oral/verbal exposition. In addition, the interaction with ICT through mouse and keyboard seems to offer the kinaesthetic element which is often difficult to incorporate in classroom learning activities.

## Metacognition

Metacognition is a difficult term to define, and it is often described as 'thinking about your own thinking'. It involves both knowing about your cognitive abilities and being able to control them strategically. The classic definition is that of Flavell:

> Metacognition refers to one's knowledge concerning one's own cognitive processes and products or anything relating to them, e.g. the learning-relevant properties of information or data . . . Metacognition refers, amongst other things, to the active monitoring and consequent regulation and orchestration of these processes in relation to the cognitive objects on which they bear, usually in the service of some concrete goal or objective.
>
> (Flavell, 1976: 232)

Metacognitive knowledge, or *knowing what you know*, is important because knowing how well they are likely to perform in a situation will affect the way pupils approach a task and how successful they are likely to be. Knowing that they can do something – a feeling of self-efficacy – will make them more likely to choose to do it and to take the risk of being wrong. It is also important whether they think that success is due to effort rather than factors outside their control.

On the other hand, metacognitive skill concerns 'when, why and how' pupils explore, plan, monitor, regulate and evaluate their progress. Muijs and Reynolds (2001) suggest that for pupils to learn more effectively, self-regulation needs to become a conscious process. This skill can be developed by guiding the pupil's progress through a task by asking questions that focus their attention at critical points, and requiring them to verbalise or otherwise articulate their thinking as a first step towards internalising the processes for themselves. In order to stimulate pupils' metacognition, then, teaching approaches would include:

- significant pupil autonomy in the selection of tools and resources;
- active participation by pupils in the process of planning and evaluating the use of tools and resources in problem situations;
- that pupils be given opportunities and encouragement to reflect formally on their ICT learning.

(Kennewell *et al.*, 2000)

## Affective aspects

One further theoretical aspect deserves consideration here, in addition to the range of ideas concerning the cognitive aspect of learning. The influence of the 'affective' aspect is also well established. Learning is influenced by the degree to which pupils are motivated by the activity they are engaged in and by longer term aims related to the subject matter and teaching strategy (Cox, 1999). Although the most effective learning may involve a struggle, this does not need to be an unpleasant experience; Papert (1996) refers to 'hard fun' as characterising many of the leisure activities such as games which children engage in with ICT. The self-esteem of pupils is also significant: they are more likely to learn if they feel good about themselves in relation to the setting for activity. There is evidence that these factors are improved for many pupils in an ICT environment, although it may not be true for all pupils. In particular, fewer girls than boys are motivated merely by the use of ICT, and they also tend to underestimate their abilities with ICT (Kennewell *et al.*, 2000). This suggests that the purpose and outcome of any task should be considered carefully, rather than using ICT for its own sake.

Disaffected pupils may find more incentive to use ICT, first because it can provide the potential and structure for action that they need on a continual basis but cannot get from the teacher, and second because they do not realise that they are 'investing effort in learning' (Black and Wiliam, 1998: 9), rather they think they are 'doing ICT'. If disaffected pupils can gain success when ICT is used, an immediate positive assessment of their subject learning (not just their ICT capability) combined with appropriate praise may give them encouragement to continue their effort. However, this will only spread to other tasks if they are assisted to reflect on what they have learned; otherwise, their enthusiasm will remain limited to 'doing ICT'.

| Task 5.2 | Analyse some teaching that you have carried out or observed in relation to these theories. |

## A practical synthesis

The list of ideas catalogued above does not form a coherent whole; indeed, there are conflicting elements in the different points of view. A useful synthesis of principles which may help to guide your practice can be found in the *Do-Review-Learn-Apply* cycle (Imison and Taylor, 2001) (see Figure 5.1).

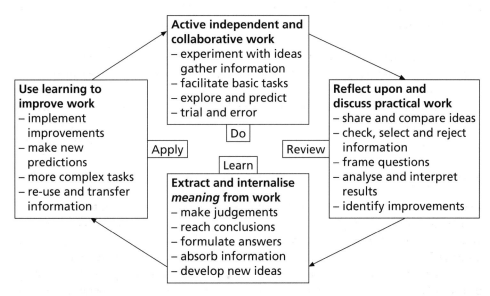

**Figure 5.1** *Do-Review-Learn-Apply* cycle, based on Imison, T. and Taylor, P. (2001) *Managing ICT in the secondary school* Oxford: Heinemann p. 54, Figure 2

Although all the aspects of this cycle apply to learning in general, the approach is particularly recommended for ICT-based activities.

## How do they explain the ways in which ICT can aid learning?

Unfortunately, as might be expected from some of the ideas presented above, knowledge of the theories in isolation does not provide much help to novice teachers. Teachers' pedagogical knowledge is developed primarily through copying others, trying out one's own ideas, and reflecting on practice. Formal learning theories may help to explain events in the classroom, but do not readily predict them. Instead, teachers develop their own informal, practical 'craft knowledge' to guide their everyday activity. They tend to think in terms of cases and images drawn from experience rather than theories (Brown and McIntyre, 1993). However, when introducing and developing a new feature, such as ICT, it is valuable to consider what the underlying principles of learning suggest about its role in teaching.

So far, this chapter has indicated some of the implications for the use of ICT associated with each of the principles introduced, and this next section will bring these points together and characterise them according to the type of activity in order to explain the potential role of ICT in improving it. (Based on findings presented by NCET (1994).)

## Strategies aided by ICT

### Whole-class teaching

The whole class approach is particularly valuable for the reflective phase of a lesson, and ICT facilitates the drawing together of points that have arisen during the lesson. When the teacher is communicating with the whole class, the key challenge is to involve all pupils. This management issue will be explored further in Chapter 7.

### Challenging activities

ICT can bring difficult tasks within the ZPD of more pupils through screen cues that provide scaffolding not available from the teacher. Tasks can be more motivating and enjoyable because of the interactivity. Conjecture and risk taking are encouraged by the provisionality so that pupils can learn constructively from their mistakes. This fosters perseverance which enables pupils to meet the high expectations placed on them and appreciate the role of personal effort in achieving success.

### Experimentation and hypothesising

This type of activity fosters concept development and analytical and divergent thinking, also through encouraging conjecture, risk taking and learning from mistakes during interactive tasks.

### Representing concepts

This is not common in traditional classrooms, as it involves a focus on metacognition and reflection; ICT can help by making abstract ideas more visible and even 'concrete'.

### Independent learning

The key challenge in enabling pupils to work independently is to give them the metacognitive skills required to manage their work on the task and the motivation to stay on task and persevere to a satisfactory conclusion. ICT helps to supplement pupils' metacognition, and it helps them to achieve high expectations and focus on the role of personal effort in achieving success.

### Authentic tasks

Pupils are motivated by work that seems to have a real purpose, and they enjoy achieving professional results; ICT helps make this realistic in the classroom by scaffolding complex tasks, providing the same tools that professionals use and enabling contact with the world of work.

### Group work

This type of activity enables different features of ICT to come into play; the easy and quick exchange of ideas and information with others and the visibility of work on screen aids cooperation with peers, and the range of resources that can be employed facilitates the involvement of all members of a group and highlights the role of personal effort in achieving success.

*Skills practice with reward*

This also creates motivation and enjoyment, because of the automation of the response, the immediate positive feedback on performance, and the reward for progress. This helps pupils to achieve the 'over-learning' required for automaticity of basic skills, although often without any worthwhile context.

In any of these types of activity, and others which are not listed, learners are carrying out a task with a particular goal, whether their task is listening to the teacher so that they can answer questions if required, or whether they are producing an artistic work with the aim of pleasing those who view it. Their progress towards the task goal depends on the support for appropriate action provided by the features of the setting, together with their abilities. This support comprises *potential* (when the features make them more likely to choose a particular course of action) and *structure* (when the features constrain them to particular courses of action). Their abilities relate to the subject they are learning, to other key skills such as literacy, numeracy, and working with others, and ICT if relevant. For example, in the biology classroom, the task of describing the heart may be supported in various ways. The potential for successful action may be increased by displaying a large diagram of a heart on the wall, or by the showing of a film. The structure may be increased by giving pupils a writing frame or a version of the task in which they merely have to fill in missing keywords on a printed version of the required description.

Activity takes place within a particular *setting*; the classroom setting includes the pupils, the teacher, other adults available to help, the ICT resources, other resources such as printed materials and wall displays, and the general culture in the classroom. The *features* of the setting which may support the task thus include the abilities of other people (teacher, classmates, classroom assistants); ICT tools; images, text (printed and electronic) and sounds; instructions, prompts and advice from the teacher and others; the culture of the classroom through which pupils know what sort of work and behaviour is expected without needing explicit instructions.

Figure 5.2 shows the Tasks-Abilities-Features (TAF) model, and in order to illustrate its use in practice, some of the examples from Chapters 1 and 4 will be analysed.

## How does the TAF model help analyse teaching and learning?

In Example 1.1 in Chapter 1 (see p. 7), the Internet was selected by an English teacher to help pupils prepare for a debate on the topic of capital punishment. It enabled pupils to work in small groups, using books and bookmarked websites on the WWW through networked PCs in the Resource Centre, to find information and opinions from a wide range of sources, both from the UK and from countries which have the death penalty. It also enabled each group to send a summary of their arguments by e-mail to other pupils who were acting as speech editors in preparation for the formal debate.

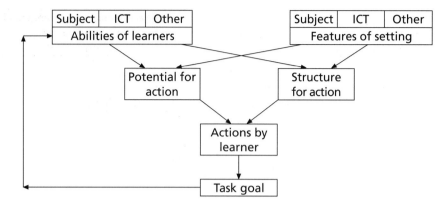

**Figure 5.2**   Model for learner activity, based on Figure 1 in Kennewell (2001)

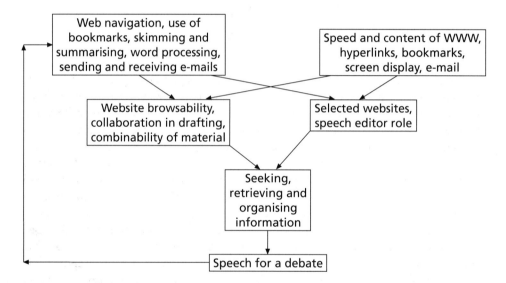

**Figure 5.3**   TAF analysis of Internet activity

The TAF analysis of this activity is shown in Figure 5.3.

In Example 1.4 in Chapter 1 (see p. 8), a dynamic geometry program was selected by a maths teacher to help pupils develop their understanding of the angle properties of parallel lines and triangles. The teacher was able to demonstrate certain effects and techniques using the software with an interactive whiteboard, and as the image was manipulated, the teacher asked pupils questions to focus their attention on what was changing and what was not. The pupils were then able to use the software in pairs in the ICT room to investigate the relationships between angles made by a line crossing two parallel lines, to make conjectures and test them out with instant feedback.

The TAF analysis of this activity is shown in Figure 5.4.

In Example 1.5 in Chapter 1 (see pp. 8–9), a geography teacher presented video clips, each of which illustrated a particular point that she wanted pupils to note. She played

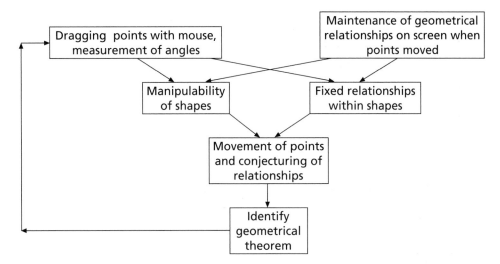

**Figure 5.4** TAF analysis of dynamic geometry activity

the clips, first without sound in order to focus their attention on what they could see, and then with sound. She asked pupils questions and, depending on their answers, showed appropriate clips in order to help pupils to develop their understanding. She encouraged pupils to formulate their own questions and replayed particular clips to help with responses. She used a word processing program, with a large, clear typeface, to record key points as they arose. She switched the display between the video and the document frequently, and developed a long list of ideas that was stored and retrieved for later discussion. The pupils were then required to make summary notes for themselves about what they had learned. This was followed up with a task where pupils worked in pairs on networked PCs, using mapping software to plot the distribution of different social and economic factors across Italy. They were able to draw conclusions about differences between North and South by visually examining the map shading for general patterns concerning population, employment, car ownership, etc. Printouts of each pair's map were displayed on the wall and the conclusions discussed. Pupils then extended their own notes about their learning.

The TAF analysis of the mapping activity is shown in Figure 5.5.

In the history case study from Chapter 4 (see p. 72), the pupils had been introduced to aspects of castles and wider issues of the medieval period through a range of activities, and the current task is focused on the key question 'Were all medieval castles the same?' In the history teaching room, they were introduced to the structure of the database and the nature of the 450 records it contained using a large display at the front of the class, so that the teacher could explain the field names and discuss the reliability of the data, which was still somewhat incomplete and based on historical judgements where primary evidence was missing. The pupils were then taken to the ICT room and set an initial task to help develop their familiarity with the data, the sort of hypotheses they might create and test, and with the way in which enquiries had to be expressed in order that the database could carry out the search or sort that they required (see Figure 4.3).

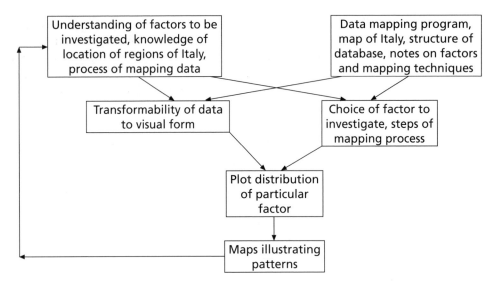

**Figure 5.5**    TAF analysis of mapping activity

The teacher then carried out a review with the whole class in order to compare what different groups of pupils had found, reflect on what they had learnt, and focus their thinking on the overall question. The teacher also demonstrated the graphing facility to help them answer questions concerning patterns and trends over the full time period. Pupils then continued with the database task, using the questions shown in Figure 4.4. The more able pupils were encouraged to devise and answer their own

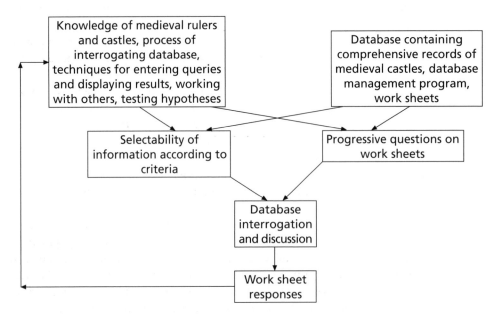

**Figure 5.6**    TAF analysis of database activity

questions, whilst all pupils completed the basic task. Finally, pupils were asked to produce posters, setting out their response to the questions together with evidence to support it. The qualities of these posters were then discussed with the whole class in order to help develop a clear understanding of the changes over the five centuries and the importance of basing this knowledge on evidence, and what constituted evidence in this case.

The TAF analysis of this activity is shown in Figure 5.6.

Chapters 8 and 9 will develop this model for planning further.

---

**Task 5.3**   Consider a task that you have carried out with ICT in your course. Analyse the task goal, and the potential and structure for action provided by the features of ICT resources and by your abilities.

What did you learn from the task?

---

## How can you match types of ICT resource to the intended learning?

As noted in Chapter 4, the role of the teacher is crucial. The teacher makes a number of decisions in relation to the learning objectives, including the following.

1   What approach to take to learning activity in each phase of teaching. The main approaches can be characterised as teacher-centred activity (where the teacher controls activity directly, usually from the front of the class) and learner-centred activity (where the pupils work on tasks, more or less at their own pace).

2   What tasks to set in order to enable pupils to bridge the learning gap between their current abilities and the objectives. Again, different approaches are available (see Chapter 2):
   * *instructive:* in which the learner reacts to content provided, particularly during whole-class teaching and skills practice;
   * *constructive-directed:* in which the learner produces the content which the teacher expects, particularly during the representation of concepts, and challenging tasks;
   * *constructive-creative:* in which the learner designs original content, particularly during group work, authentic tasks, experimenting and hypothesising.

3   What resources to employ, including the teacher's exposition, questioning, and review; books and other traditional media; ICT and other equipment in order to support the pupils' activity. This choice, including whether and how to use ICT, is related to decisions 1 and 2: indeed, the availability and potential of ICT may mean that the best approach for the topic changes from a traditional teacher-centred exposition to learner-centred investigation; this was the case in the history case study in Chapter 4. The change may be the

other way round, too; for example, if the features of an interactive whiteboard may make it possible to have a whole-class discussion on something that previously had to be carried out in groups. The choice of resources will almost certainly make a difference to what task is the most appropriate.

4    How the teacher will orchestrate the use of resources (see the last section of Chapter 4). The teacher may do this indirectly, in that the resources may be designed to adjust the support available to pupils automatically (for instance, using an ILS), or directly, in which case the teacher may plan in advance to be pro-active, or plan to respond to pupils' actions (reactive): see Figure 5.7.

5    What actions by learners are to be allowed, which actions are to be supported if required, and which actions are to be actively stimulated by the teacher; and where ICT is to be used, what actions are allowed by ICT, which are supported, and which are actually stimulated by ICT.

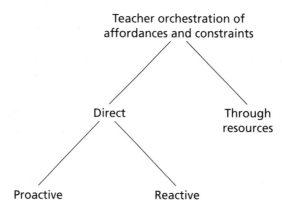

**Figure 5.7**   Modes of teacher orchestration of resources, based on Figure 3 in Kennewell, S. (2001) Using affordances and constraints to evaluate the use of ICT in teaching and learning, *Journal of IT and Teacher Education*, **10**, 101–16

Chapter 8 will examine the design of tasks and orchestration of resources in more depth.

---

**Task 5.4**    Identify a learning outcome in your subject and outline a task for a particular group of pupils that will help to achieve that outcome. Identify the expected learning gap and consider how ICT may help learners. Explain what ICT resource might be appropriate.

---

## How does ICT relate to other key skills?

Key Skills are fundamental aspects of learning that underpin the learning of a wide range of subjects across the curriculum. The Key Skills within the National Curriculum for England are listed as being:

- application of number;
- communication;
- improving own learning and performance;
- information technology;
- problem solving;
- working with others.

(DfES, 2001a)

Three of the Key Skills are very closely associated with particular subjects within the National Curriculum. For example: 'application of number' will obviously draw on knowledge, skills and understanding developed in mathematics. However, this does not mean that the skills will be learned solely in their associated curriculum subject. Although Key Skills are of great significance for effective teaching and learning within schools, they are most often learned on the way to learning something else rather than by direct instruction (Tanner, 2003).

Not only will ICT be learned whilst using ICT in other subjects, but so will literacy and numeracy (Poole, 1998). Indeed, there will be many occasions where a certain level of ability in literacy or numeracy will be required in order to use ICT effectively, and other occasions where a certain level of ICT ability is needed to demonstrate adequate literacy or numeracy. In Example 1.1 in Chapter 1 (see p. 7), the quality of pupils' debating speeches will depend on an effective interplay of their ability to read and summarise text, to cut/paste and edit text using ICT, to combine different files, and to adapt text for oral presentation. In Example 1.2 in Chapter 1 (see p. 7), numeracy comes into play, with pupils' response depending on their appreciation of relative sizes of large numbers and their selection and interpretation of graphs, as well as their ability to implement the techniques using ICT. The teacher recognised the need to support pupils with these aspects; he provided much of the structure needed for solving the problem by suggesting that pupils produce a graph, and provided hints concerning the relationship for pupils whose numeracy was insufficient. Pupils also used their literacy to abstract relevant information from the printed material provided, and to organise this into their reports.

Example 1.3 in Chapter 1 (see p. 8) illustrates the role of working with others in order to achieve success. ICT is often used for pupils working in pairs or small groups; sometimes this is because there are limited resources, but often the task is designed to be achieved through cooperative effort, and ICT can support the activity indirectly by making it easier for pupils to work together. A desktop screen is easily seen by a number of pupils, and pupils can be trained to share the keyboard and mouse or given particular roles to play in the activity.

The sort of challenge given to pupils in Example 1.5 in Chapter 1 (see pp. 8–9) or the history case study in Chapter 4 (p. 72) shows the role of ICT in supporting problem-solving; this key skill involves higher order and metacognitive activity, and the role of ICT can be one of helping to plan and organise the strategy, or it can be one of rapidly and accurately carrying out low order tasks so that learners can give more attention to higher order aspects.

There are also important relationships between the use of ICT and the improvement of pupils' own learning. When pupils are practised at the sort of concept-mapping activity suggested in many subject areas for identifying current knowledge and reflecting on learning, they have a powerful tool for metacognitive activity. This can underpin improvements in learning across the curriculum.

| Task 5.5 | For the task you devised in Task 5.4, identify what key skills pupils will need and how these can be developed further. |

## Further reading

Davis, N. *et al.* (1997) 'Can quality in learning be enhanced through the use of IT?', in Somekh, B. and Davis, N. (eds) (1997) *Using information technology effectively in teaching and learning*, London: Routledge

Glover, D. and Law, S. (2002) *Improving learning: professional practice in secondary schools*, Buckingham: Open University Press

Turner, T. (2001) Active learning, in Capel, S., Leask, M. and Turner, T. (eds) *Learning to teach in the secondary school: a companion to school experience*, (3rd edition) London: RoutledgeFalmer

Underwood, J. (1990) *Computers and learning: helping children acquire thinking skills*, Oxford: Blackwell

# 6 ICT Capability and its Development

Chapter 1 introduced the idea of ICT capability. In order to exploit ICT effectively in your subject, you will need to develop your own ICT capability, and you will need to be aware of what level of ICT capability to expect of different groups of pupils. You also need to know how you can help your pupils to improve their ICT skills further when appropriate in your lessons, in order to help them learn with ICT in your subject and as a contribution to a whole-school key skills policy.

This chapter explains and exemplifies what is involved in developing ICT capability, including techniques, processes, concepts and higher-order skills. It builds on the understanding you will have gained through work during Chapter 3, and then develops and explains the relationship between learners' ICT capability and their use of ICT in the curriculum, using further realistic examples from the classroom.

## What is ICT capability?

This idea was introduced with the National Curriculum for ICT in England and Wales in 1990, and you saw in Chapter 1 that it is represented slightly differently in each nation of the UK. In England, the National Curriculum for ICT sets out the requirements for 11–14 year olds as shown in Appendix B.

As with all NC subject orders, eight levels of attainment are specified in the attainment target, and most pupils are expected to have reached level 4 on entry to secondary school:

> Pupils understand the need for care in framing questions when collecting, finding and interrogating information. They interpret their findings, question plausibility and recognise that poor quality information leads to unreliable results. They add to, amend and combine different forms

of information from a variety of sources. They use ICT to present information in different forms and show they are aware of the intended audience and the need for quality in their presentations. They exchange information and ideas with others in a variety of ways, including using e-mail. They use ICT systems to control events in a predetermined manner and to sense physical data. They use ICT-based models and simulations to explore patterns and relationships, and make predictions about the consequences of their decisions. They compare their use of ICT with other methods and with its use outside school.

(DfEE/QCA, 1999: 41)

This may be illustrated by the following example:

Pupils were asked to investigate the Elgin marbles. They used various information sources, including the Internet, to gather information about the marbles. The teacher asked the class to create a presentation incorporating two contrasting points of view about the future of the marbles. Pupils cut and pasted information from the WWW and created a scrapbook of information. They synthesised this information to create bullet points to use in a presentation. They combined pictures and text within the presentation. They presented their work to other classes in the year group. Later, pupils conducted a survey to establish which point of view was most common within the school.

(http://www.ncaction.org.uk/subjects/ict/progress.htm)

Progression in ICT has been characterised by increasingly independent and depersonalised activity, from initial exploration through to applying knowledge in designing systems for others:

- exploration of tools;
- purpose in the use of ICT;
- development of ideas and improvement of work;
- interpretation of results gained from using ICT;
- qualitative and quantitative information processing;
- range and complexity of application;
- selection of tools and design of solutions to problems;
- design of systems for others to use.

(Imison and Taylor, 2001)

There are no standardised assessment tasks or central collection of data on attainment levels in ICT at the time of writing, and so it is unclear to what extent this expectation is being met. However, despite encouragement for primary schools to use a standard scheme of work for ICT (QCA, 2003b), Ofsted (2004) report a wide variation in ICT provision between primary schools and this is inevitably reflected in the varying levels of experience of pupils on entry to secondary education. The government's concerns about children experiencing repetition and lack of challenge in secondary school has led to a specific strategy for 11–14 year-old pupils in England which involves a one-hour ICT lesson each week, a standard scheme of work, ready-made lesson plans and materials, and a large investment in training for teachers of ICT. The key messages of this strategy for teachers are:

- high expectations and clear objectives conveyed to pupils in simple language: 'What I am looking for is pupils who can . . .';
- both medium- and short-term planning that clearly identifies the progression for pupils;
- structured lessons, with an engaging starter, new skills and ideas introduced in well-planned stages in the main part of the lesson, and a summary of the lesson in a concluding plenary;
- challenging and engaging activities and tasks to interest both girls and boys;
- manageable differentiation based on work common to all pupils in a class, with targeted support to help those with less experience, and genuine challenge for the more able;
- interactive teaching of whole classes, small groups and individuals, using a combination of exposition, demonstration, modelling, instruction and dialogue;
- effective questioning, giving pupils time to think, air views and hear the views of others, and to explain and justify their reasoning and decisions;
- time for pupils to reflect on their learning and progress, and evaluate their own and other pupils' work.

(DfES, 2002a: 1)

There are also messages for pupils:

Through Key Stage 3 pupils will become increasingly independent, discerning users of ICT. They will:
- develop an ability to judge when and how to use ICT;
- be able to make judgements about the quality and reliability of the products they have developed;
- engage in increasingly complex tasks with a clear focus, efficiency and rigour.

(DfES, 2002a: 1)

The National Curriculum in Wales has largely preserved the previous structure for IT (note that the name of the subject is different from the term used for resources):

- *communicating and handling information* – for example producing documents, presentations and drawings, exchanging e-mails; searching for information in a database or on the WWW, producing graphs to compare sets of figures, structuring information so that it can be retrieved;
- *modelling* – for example, using a spreadsheet to explore or specify relationships between variables.

TTA (1998) used the NC themes (see p. 12) for ICT capability as a basis for what teachers should be able to do, in relation to the subject they teach.

Subjects such as English, Welsh and MFL will naturally require most emphasis on 'exchanging and sharing information', whereas science, mathematics, geography and history will require most emphasis on 'finding things out' and 'developing ideas and making things happen'. In broad terms, the main contributions to learning in other subjects can be characterised as follows:

- communicating information involves refining learners' ideas through interaction with others and through evaluation of presentation;
- handling information involves identifying facts and relationships which were not previously known;
- modelling involves representing, testing and refining hypothesised relationships between variables.

(Imison and Taylor, 2001)

An analysis of the different types of skill that make up ICT capability suggests a number of components (Kennewell *et al.*, 2000):

- basic skills or routines;
- techniques;
- underpinning concepts;
- processes;
- higher order skills and knowledge.

## Basic skills or routines

These are operations that are carried out without significant conscious thought. This means that you can think about other aspects of the task, or other matters completely, whilst doing these operations, without affecting performance. Routines include motor operations such as *mouse movement, click to select an object, drag-and-drop to move an object*, and *double click to start a program*. More complex operations, such as *cut-and-paste* or *using an 'undo' option* to restore the previous text, may become routines as a result of practice (mental automaticity) or of developments in hardware/software (technological automation).

Routines tend to be associated with the use of specific software and hardware systems, thus creating a potential problem and a need to 'unlearn' familiar techniques when using different resources.

| Task 6.1 | Consider the operations listed as possible routines above. Do you carry these out 'without significant conscious thought'? |
|---|---|

What other operations come into this category for you?

## Techniques

These are operations that still require a degree of conscious thought or prompting. They are context-specific methods that are known to achieve specified effects, for example: *editing a text* by deleting a phrase and typing a different one; *saving successive versions* of an important document with different names; *copying an element of a graphic design to make a regular pattern* or *selecting margins from the format menu* in a word processor in order to adjust the margins of a document to make a piece of text fit on a page. When first experienced, techniques are likely to be highly context- and situation-specific, with limited potential for transfer. Initially, they are also likely to make the task more difficult using ICT, since a part of the conscious mind must be allocated to controlling the technique.

One aspect of the learning of techniques is practice in order to achieve automaticity. The development of automaticity frees the mind to concentrate on the problem situation rather than the cognitive overhead or ICT interference factor (see p. 117). When automated in this way such techniques have become routines. However, there is a danger that techniques learned in this manner are likely to be applied in reaction to superficial features of problems met, and thus have limited potential for transfer to new situations.

It is difficult to generalise from a single context, but if techniques are met in a variety of situations and contexts, the potential for reflection and concept development grows. The learning of techniques is supported by the progressive understanding of key concepts (see below) and general ICT principles, which enable ICT capable learners to explore confidently when solving problems. Reflection on the use of techniques across contexts and situations is more likely to generate principles, ideas and strategies that are abstracted from their initial situation.

The techniques selected in a particular problem situation are a function of the context, the resources available and the strategic knowledge of the user. They are underpinned by concepts, but their application also depends on the features and structure offered by the technology and the user's knowledge of its opportunities and constraints.

> Identify ten techniques that you have used with a word processing or desktop publishing program. Which of these could you transfer immediately to a different word processing program? Which transfer to a spreadsheet program?

## Key concepts

The main concepts that underpin knowledge of techniques and processes are relatively few, and these are the most important at present (each concept has the main specialist terminology relevant to it highlighted in bold):

- **item of data**: a set of symbols that can be processed electronically as a unit, and can also be interpreted to provide meaningful information;

- **file**: a collection of related data that can be accessed and transferred as a unit (associated terminology: **directory**, **icon**, **file size**, **file type**);
- **window**: an area of the screen that can be operated independently of other areas (associated terminology: **dialogue box**, **help**);
- **menu**: a list of options that can be displayed and selected (associated terminology: **button**);
- **text**: as a continuous string of characters, including codes that are not displayed (associated terminology: **format**);
- **object**: a unit of data within a file that can be selected, formatted, moved, resized, copied, deleted and transferred to other locations; types of object include text, image, movie, sound (associated terminology: **handle**, **link/embed**);
- **publication** or **drawing**: a collection of objects of various types and their positions (associated terminology: **frame**);
- **presentation**: a sequence of objects and associated animation effects/timings (associated terminology: **multimedia**, **slide**);
- **database**: an information structure that can be searched in a meaningful way, and selected information displayed (associated terminology: **flat-file**, **relational**, **table**, **record**, **field**, **field name**, **query**, **filter**, **report**);
- **model**: an information structure that represents relationships amongst variables; (associated terminology: **formula**, **auto-update**, **dynamic**);
- **spreadsheet**: a grid in which each location can contain a value or a formula in order to implement a model (associated terminology: **cell**);
- **hypertext**: an information structure containing links that allow quick access to chosen options; (associated terminology: **CD-ROM**, **hyperlink**);
- **procedure**: a sequence of instructions that achieve a specified result (associated terminology: **control**, **program**, **procedure**, **macro**, **condition**, **loop**);
- **measurement/monitoring**: process that records data from outside the ICT device (associated terminology: **sensor**, **data logging**);
- **message**: text together with a destination and return address (associated terminology: **e-mail**, **address**, **list**, **conference**, **chat**, **synchronous/asynchronous**);
- **website**: a hypertext structure that can be accessed remotely from any location (associated terminology: **World Wide Web**, **web server**, **web page**, **home page**).

When first meeting a particular concept in any subject, learners tend to apply their more informal knowledge of the idea or to assume that the idea is similar to something with which they are already familiar. These situations are often referred to as *misconceptions* (see, for example, Adey and Shayer, 1994). Pupils' errors and inefficient processes will often indicate that their concepts are naïve. For instance, when using a word processor, children will commonly use the backspace key to delete a whole section of text, just to change one word at the beginning of it. When developing a presentation, some pupils will save each slide as a separate file – particularly if they have only ever created single page documents when using a word processor or DTP program. Others will use a spreadsheet program whenever they need a table layout for a document. And when introduced to a database, pupils will assume that it works in the same way as a spreadsheet because of the grid structure that appears on the screen. For this reason, it is important for you to be clear yourself about the concepts, and to explain them to pupils where appropriate. It is quite reasonable to use a spreadsheet program to carry out database functions, such as searching for cases that meet particular conditions, as long as you make it clear to pupils that this is what they are doing.

| **Task 6.3** | Think back to when you started to use a particular program or device. Can you recall any misconceptions? How did you overcome them? |
| --- | --- |

The specialist terminology associated with techniques and concepts is important. It should not be written off as mere jargon, as it is necessary to have specific terms for the key concepts and common techniques in order to be able to communicate with others about one's work with ICT.

It is much easier in the long run for learners if you can say 'click on the "print" button and check the option you need in the dialogue box' rather than 'use the mouse to move the pointer to the little picture that means what you want to do, press the left button, find the option you need in the extra box that appears on top of your work, move the pointer to the circle by the side of it and press the left button on the mouse'.

## Processes

Processes such as developing a presentation or finding information from a database, are sequences of techniques designed to achieve an overall goal. The sequences will vary according to the circumstances, but will always include certain operations characteristic of the process. Such combinations of techniques will gradually be learned by following explanations, trying examples, working with more capable peers and attempting to solve real problems.

Sometimes the user's choice of technique will not produce the desired effect, and a different technique will be tried. Reflection on this 'mistake' will lead to learning, which improves the user's ability to make an appropriate choice in the future.

## How do the components combine in practice?

Consider the task of producing a work sheet for pupils, which will contain an eye-catching heading, images to illustrate the key points, and some empty boxes for pupils to fill in answers to questions.

### Step 1 – planning the task (higher order skill)

You will first consider what the outcome is intended to achieve, and then break it down into smaller steps (processes) which you can carry out in turn. Although you are always told to plan carefully before starting a task, in practice planning will continue throughout the task as you think of things that you need to take into account. Which program are you going to use to do the task? This will depend on what programs you have available, your confidence with different programs, whether you have time to learn new skills, and your understanding of the concepts involved in each one. You could use a word processor or DTP program for this task; there is no 'right' answer, but it will be assumed that you use a word processor.

## Step 2 – process of producing the heading

The techniques will depend on whether you use simple text or 'Wordart'. If using simple text, you may enter the text in default style and then select the heading text and change the size, the emphasis (to bold, for example), the font, and the justification (to centred, for example). If pupils are to complete the work sheet using ICT, you may decide to change its colour. If you are a regular user of the program these techniques will probably be routine.

## Step 3 – process of entering the text

This will certainly be routine, but you may use your higher order skills to consider the needs of pupils as you go along and interrupt your automatic activity in order to add *emphasis* to the text or perhaps a hyperlink to further material on the WWW if pupils are using the work sheet on-line.

## Step 4 – process of adding images

This process involves a sequence of techniques that may be less familiar, and will depend on whether you are using a clipart library or pictures specially photographed or scanned. Your higher order skills will intervene to consider copyright, of course, and your concept of copyright (see Chapter 11) will guide you concerning whether you need to seek permission to use images from other sources. You may also need to develop your concept of objects and their relation to text in your document, and learn the technique for controlling text flow around an image in order to create a good layout.

## Step 5 – monitoring the progress of the task (higher order skill)

As you go along, you will be thinking continuously about how effectively you are carrying out the task and whether you are on course for achieving a good enough result in the time available. You may decide to use a simple, familiar set of techniques for carrying out a process rather than taking the time and trouble to learn a new, better method. For the empty boxes, for instance, you may think of creating some blank lines and using the drawing tools to produce an empty rectangle; or you may consider putting a border round the blank lines; or you may think of inserting a text box. The one you choose will depend on:

- your knowledge of techniques;
- which techniques have become routine;
- which method will produce the best work sheet – it does not make much difference if you are just printing and copying it, but the rectangle will be useless if pupils are to complete the work sheet using ICT; the text box will be confusing for pupils who are not familiar with this technique themselves, so the border is probably the best compromise.

## Step 6 – process of producing the pupil response boxes

Three techniques are probably required here: for instance, the creation of blank lines using the 'enter' key, the selection of these lines by dragging over them, and then the selection of the border tool. This process is underpinned by understanding the various ways white space is achieved in a document (note that it is very different if you are using DTP).

## Step 7 – Evaluating the outcome in relation to its purpose (higher order skill)

You should take time to think through what your pupils will make of it, particularly in terms of the amount of writing, language level, size/style of text, and clarity of instructions. Consider revisions to improve it at this stage; for instance, you may decide to put all the text into text boxes so that you can position different sections of text more flexibly in relation to the images. You may also decide to produce different versions for different pupils. After the lesson, consider it again; you will no doubt identify further improvements in the light of pupils' reactions in the classroom, and you may well see more possibilities when you collect in pupils' work for marking.

| Task 6.4 | Consider the task of producing a presentation to introduce a topic. Analyse the task in the same way as the example above. |
|---|---|

## How and when does ICT capability develop?

Two ways of classifying the aspects that make up ICT capability have been considered: the range of purposes (strands) and the component skills. Neither the components nor the strands are hierarchical, however, and these classifications do not tell us how ICT capability develops. We do not necessarily learn to communicate information before handling it, nor do we learn techniques in isolation from processes and concepts, although sometimes ICT is taught this way, unfortunately.

Instead, it is necessary to look at two other dimensions to explore how learners make progress (Birnbaum, 1989). The first concerns experience of a wider *range* of contexts; concepts can be developed and skills can be consolidated by applying them to new situations where information needs to be acquired, processed, presented, communicated or relationships can be modelled. In school, this situation arises when knowledge gained in one subject is applied to another; this is notoriously difficult to bring about in some cases, but seems to be easier when ICT is involved (Kennewell *et al.*, 2000). Pupils may learn to use a spreadsheet to produce graphs and explore relationships between variables in an ICT lesson or in a mathematics lesson, and then apply their skills in science. It is important to provide pupils with sufficient practice of skills in order to for them to retain them in the long term, and in a sufficient variety of contexts to avoid loss of interest in learning. It is also important to allow time for pupils to reflect on what they have done and how they have done it using ICT.

The second dimension is in terms of greater *depth* of thinking employed in using ICT; this is seen both as learners meet more complex or unfamiliar settings in the curriculum, or are able to implement increasingly sophisticated solutions to the tasks set. It is important to provide progressively more difficult challenges, and for these to drive the learning of new concepts, processes and techniques.

Furthermore, although most pupils are keen to learn specific ICT skills and often learn a lot just by trying things out for themselves and seeing what others are doing, they do not easily develop their general higher order skills independently. These are largely independent of ICT and continued support for their planning, monitoring and evaluating will also be needed in all subjects. This support should be steadily reduced as pupils gain the skills for themselves.

Learners should be encouraged to seek opportunities for challenge, exploration, practice and application of ICT. But it is not possible ever to be fully ICT capable – personal ability can always be improved and in any case ICT is not a fixed body of knowledge.

---

**Task 6.5** For your own subject:
1  identify a piece of software specific to your subject that you might introduce pupils to, thus increasing the range of ICT resources that they can use;
2  identify a task in your subject that can be carried out using a generic ICT tool but requires a greater depth of knowledge than is taught to pupils in ICT lessons.

In each case, consider how you would manage the ICT learning that is required.

---

## How is ICT capability used in learning another subject, and what skills do pupils need?

Consider Example 1.3 in Chapter 1 (see p. 8). The teacher required pupils to engage in four processes:

- retrieving information from websites;
- retrieving information from CD-ROM;

- taking photographs with a digital camera;
- producing a presentation.

The pupils had used presentation software previously in their ICT lessons to produce a presentation about a chosen leisure interest, and so the RE teacher did not demonstrate techniques to the whole class. Instead, she focused pupils' thinking on higher order skills of planning, monitoring and evaluating in relation to the purpose of the presentation. She was aware that pupils had not been systematically taught strategies for information retrieval, but they had all used the WWW either at home or in other lessons. She therefore discussed with the whole class various ways of retrieving information from the web and CD-ROM using specific web addresses, on-screen menus and search engines. She expected that some pupils would not have the combination of ICT capability and literacy levels required to use a search engine effectively and make sense of the information that appeared, so she prepared a set of bookmarks and showed relevant pupils how to use them. For the photography, she showed one pupil in each group how to use the digital camera and upload the pictures to a PC (she found that many already had experience of this) and asked them to make sure that all the rest of the group learned how to do this. In all the processes, she ensured that most pupils did not have to devote too much of their efforts to thinking how to use ICT and were able to concentrate on the subject matter. ICT was therefore a means of helping pupils to achieve success in a challenging task without doing too much for them. This made it effective in bringing about learning in RE (based on TTA, 1999a).

The history case study in Chapter 4 (see p. 72) illustrates the use of different aspects of ICT capability. In order to develop hypotheses about relationships between factors concerning medieval castles, pupils had to be able to explore the nature of the data in the database. They also needed to be able to carry out searches using specified criteria before they could formulate questions which would provide evidence to test their hypotheses and translate these questions into formal search criteria. They also had to be aware of the way in which the software allowed them to produce graphs, in order to decide how they would use ICT to help provide evidence for trends over a period of time. Finally, they needed graphics and DTP skills in order to represent their conclusions effectively on a poster.

| Task 6.6 | Analyse the ICT capability requirements of the activity you chose for Task 2.6. |
|----------|----------------------------------------------------------------------------------|

## How does the subject teacher help to develop pupils' ICT capability?

Earlier in the chapter, it was suggested that progression in ICT capability depends on both increasing the range of contexts in which knowledge and skills are applied, and tackling more complex and unfamiliar situations with ICT. Pupils gain ICT experience from a variety of sources:

- ICT lessons;
- extra-curricular activities;
- home;
- subject lessons.

(Kennewell *et al.*, 2000)

The role of experience in subject lessons will be particularly important in achieving both range and depth of contexts. The examples analysed in the previous section indicate how the subject teachers recognised when pupils' ICT capabilities would need to be developed before they could apply them to the subject task, and planned opportunities to familiarise pupils with new resources and skills. In the case of the database activity in history, quite a large amount of time was spent in developing pupils' skills to a level where they could make sense of the activity and gain benefits from the speed, automation, capacity and provisionality of ICT.

It is important to be able to build on skills developed elsewhere, too, and you may be able to take advantage of pupils' access to ICT outside school hours by setting homework that involves the use of ICT. You may need to provide some extra help for those who do not get opportunities for learning ICT at home, and your school may cover this in its ICT policy.

---

**Task 6.7**    Find out about:

- your pupils' access to ICT at home;
- opportunities for pupils to use school ICT facilities outside lessons (in Homework Clubs, for instance);
- your school's policy on homework involving ICT.

---

Whilst engaged in tasks designed for learning your subject, there will be occasions when pupils need to develop their ICT capability in order to complete the task set. There will also be occasions when you plan to develop their ICT capability as part of the departmental scheme of work, because your subject provides a good context for understanding and applying an aspect of the ICT curriculum.

For instance, NCET (1998) describes a case study in Internet use in English teaching that was ideal for developing pupils' skills in searching the WWW. The levels of ICT capability, expressed in general terms in the NC orders, were adapted to set out specific criteria for levels of capability that could be used for assessment and targets in the lesson. For example, level 4 (see above) was represented as:

> Formulates a simple search with care. Formulates more than one search routine. Produces a range of materials from a variety of sources. Evaluates

adverts (for example in terms of visual impact). Compares the use of the
Internet with other advertising media.

(NCET, 1998: 39)

Progression to level 5 requires that a pupil:

> Refines and improves the search routine in the light of results obtained
> (for example, use different combinations of keywords). Organises a range
> of materials into a simple report. Evaluates adverts, and compares results
> from different sources. Assesses own effectiveness.

(NCET, 1998: 39)

The most appropriate component to focus on is the process, rather than individual
techniques, although you should consider which techniques may be unfamiliar to
pupils and plan to introduce or revise these carefully. If you do not do this, you may
experience the 'ICT interference factor' (Birnbaum, 1990): pupils may fail to learn
what you intend about your topic because of the difficulties in using ICT. You should
discourage pupils from spending excessive time on improving the appearance of their
work rather than the content.

You also need to give careful attention to the management of the ICT classroom,
too, in order to ensure a good learning atmosphere and pace to the lesson. Chapter 7
will consider this further.

It is important to help develop pupils' higher order skills. Teaching approaches
should therefore emphasise:

- significant pupil autonomy in the selection of tools and resources;
- active participation by pupils in the process of planning and evaluating the use of ICT in problem situations;
- teacher intervention in the form of focusing questions to assist pupils in the formation of generalisations;
- discussion about the features offered by the ICT resources and processes that they have experienced;
- the development of pupils' enthusiasm and confidence about ICT;
- opportunities and encouragement for pupils to reflect formally on their ICT learning.

(Kennewell et al., 2000)

| Task 6.8 | For the teaching you have carried out using ICT, identify the ways in which pupils' ICT capability developed through the work carried out, and what contribution you made to this development. |
|---|---|

As your teaching develops, it is important to collaborate with specialist ICT teachers
and discuss with them when and how they introduce particular techniques and concepts.

However, your main role as a subject teacher is in providing a context for ICT, practice in application, support for choosing appropriate techniques, reminders of how to carry out processes and techniques, and reflection on how and why ICT is used.

## Further reading

Imison, T. and Taylor, P. (2001) *Managing ICT in the secondary school*, Oxford: Heinemann

Kennewell, S., Parkinson, J. and Tanner, H. (2000) *Developing the ICT capable school*, London: RoutledgeFalmer

# 7  Managing Learning in the ICT Classroom

This chapter explains how computers can be used effectively in different ways for a variety of teaching purposes:

- a single computer for whole-class interaction with important ideas;
- a small number of computers for group work on projects;
- an ICT room for individual and pair work on differentiated tasks.

The chapter provides strategies for organising pupils to use computer rooms and small numbers of computers in subject rooms. It discusses school policies and computer room rules; health and safety issues; monitoring behaviour; giving demonstrations and instructions; managing transitions; monitoring engagement in tasks; intervening and supporting learners' progress.

## How can you use a single computer in a classroom?

Most secondary schools now have at least one networked PC in each classroom. There is a variety of practice in how these are configured and used, however, and you may find any of a number of different approaches being used in the classrooms in which you are working. The choice may depend on school policy, departmental policy or individual teacher preference. It will not usually be advisable to change the way the PC has been configured, because this will affect the school network management, but there may be some flexibility in how it is used.

### Whole-class teaching

In this model, the PC is essentially a teacher's aid. It is used by the teacher at the front of the class, with a large display so that all the class can see. With the right equipment, such as a wireless keyboard and mouse, a tablet PC or electronic 'slate' attached to an interactive whiteboard, the teacher can move around the class whilst still controlling the display that the pupils are watching. It does not have to be used exclusively by the teacher, however; pupils can be asked to use the PC to show their ideas to the whole class. If the school has a wireless network, this idea can be extended to passing a laptop or tablet PC around the class and an IWB may not be needed. Chapter 12 will discuss these new developments further. Most teachers find ICT effective in helping to involve pupils in this way, because pupils find it easier to respond and their efforts have a better appearance than with manual blackboards and whiteboards. This is particularly so in the case of an interactive whiteboard, where pupils can often respond merely by clicking or dragging an object directly on the board, or their writing can be converted to a clear typeface.

## Research

In this model, pupils can reserve the PC for short periods of time in order to carry out research for a project. They will need to make written notes or print out the information that they find, to work with manually back at their desks.

## Project

A small number of pupils are allocated time on the PC to carry out a more substantial part of a project, which they complete on the PC.

## Rota

The whole class uses the computer in turn to carry out a particular task and pupils are allocated a particular period of time. When their turn comes, they will leave whatever they are doing back at their desks and return to it later, with the obvious disadvantages of discontinuity. There will inevitably be a long delay between initial briefing and the task itself for some pupils, so that a printed or on-screen guide may be useful.

## Carousel

A number of short activities, each with a specific purpose, are carried out in turn by groups in the class. Most will be manual activities, but one will be PC-based. In this way, all pupils carry out the ICT activity over a relatively short period of time without interrupting their concentration on something else. You need to ensure that each activity can be completed in a similar amount of time in order to maintain the pace of the lesson for all pupils.

Rota and carousel activities have to be complete activities in themselves, and are often based on a particular piece of direct teaching or game software, on a simple simulation, on an Internet search, web quest or a text completion exercise (see Chapter 3 for details of these uses of ICT). In order to consolidate pupils' learning and relate it to their understanding of the topic as a whole, it is important to:

- brief pupils about the purpose of these activities;
- ensure that they keep a record of what they have achieved in the activity;
- plan a review of activities when all pupils have completed them.

You could ask them to send you the outcome of the task in an e-mail, so that you can give individual feedback where appropriate and gain an overview of pupils' progress before you review the work with the class.

All these approaches can be organised individually or in groups. Collaboration during pair and small group work can be supported by ICT because of the easy visibility of the screen for all pupils (although this is less convenient with portable devices). However, you need to consider the balance of abilities between the group members; as well as their ability in your subject, their ICT capability may vary considerably. The advantage of this is that it may increase the contribution of a pupil with low ability in the subject; the disadvantage is that the most ICT-capable pupil may end up doing all the work and reducing the others' opportunities for learning.

Different models will suit different subjects and teaching styles; the carousel is probably used most in MFL and the rota in mathematics, whereas the project model is used most in practical subjects.

| Task 7.1 | Plan a short ICT activity that could be used in rota or carousel mode. |

There is another category which can still be observed in some classrooms: the PC is not used at all in teaching and learning. You will need to suggest tactfully to the teacher that you switch it on and see what it will do, explaining that it is part of your course to explore the use of ICT. The next stage is to suggest using it in one of your lessons! Most teachers will be very pleased to have your help in using ICT, and will learn from what you do, as long as you seek their advice on lesson content and classroom management and take account of it in your planning.

## Why is ICT effective in whole-class teaching?

There are a number of benefits of whole-class teaching:

> Students have also been found to be more likely to be on task during whole-class sessions than during individualised instruction. This is mainly because it is easier for the teacher to monitor the whole class while teaching than to monitor individual students. Whole class teaching also allows the teacher to easily change and vary activities and to react quickly to signs that students are switching off, either through lack of understanding of the content or through boredom. It also allows mistakes and misconceptions made by students to be illustrated to the whole class.
>
> (Muijs and Reynolds, 2001: 5)

This section will consider first how ICT might promote these benefits, and then discuss whether it can ameliorate some of the disadvantages.

The teacher uses whole-class teaching to communicate the objectives and purpose of the lesson, and to model the sort of thinking expected in the subject. ICT facilitates this by virtue of making ideas more visually explicit (through concept mapping, for instance). Pupils need to be given opportunities to share their experiences, and this can be made easier using the IWB, whereby pupils' board writing skills do not need to be good, and by passing around an interactive 'slate' device or wireless laptop computer for pupils to contribute from their seats. This can be followed up with probing questions from the teacher and by hearing and responding to other pupils' views. Teachers need to create a clear structure to the lesson, and manage the class so that they have the opportunity for contact with individuals. ICT can help improve these aspects in three main ways:

- allowing a variety of material to be quickly and smoothly accessed;
- clarity of presentation – prepared and ad hoc – using a variety of media;
- retrieval of material for review.

(Kennewell and Beauchamp, 2003)

In Example 1.2 in Chapter 1, the teacher introduced the ideas by showing animated images from a CD-ROM to the whole class and asking questions about the experience that the class had shared to focus pupils' attention on the relative position and movement of planets.

---

**Task 7.2**    Explain why you think the teachers used whole-class teaching with ICT in Examples 1.4 and 1.5 in Chapter 1.

Why do you think the teachers did not use whole-class teaching in Examples 1.1 and 1.6?

---

There are some disadvantages to whole-class teaching, such as the fixed structure to presentation of material, a reduction of pace in order to accommodate the slowest pupil, unconfident pupils' reluctance to respond. Using ICT, pupils who need to work slowly can review the material for themselves afterwards, and pupils who wish to structure the ideas differently can work through it again in a different way. As noted in Chapter 5, the key challenge in a whole-class teaching approach is to involve all pupils, not just those at the front/middle of the room or those most interested, most able or most extrovert. If ICT is used with a large display, this involvement is aided by:

- incorporating multimedia (and preferably an interactive whiteboard) to cater for a variety of learning styles;
- providing different forms of scaffolding appropriate for different pupils;
- allowing contributions from all pupils, even if incorrect, because of the provisionality of the display;

- enabling the teacher to focus on particular items on the screen for emphasis; rapid change of display in order to maintain interest and concentration;
- promoting a positive atmosphere by providing visible success and immediate reward for progress.

## What do you need to consider in managing whole-class teaching with ICT?

You obviously need a large enough display for the group of pupils you are teaching, but you also need to consider the following:

- How will you place the pupils? Can each pupil see the screen?
- What will your position be in relation to the class? Can you see every pupil?
- Can you still face the class while using the keyboard?

You can overcome some logistical difficulties by having a capable pupil demonstrating under your instruction, although difficulties can arise because of differences in interpretation of the instructions.

During questioning, the usual rules apply to the management of oral interaction during whole-class teaching using ICT, with one person speaking at a time, nominated by the teacher. There may be additional ways of achieving a response to a question from all pupils using an interactive whiteboard.

---

**Task 7.3**    Observe an experienced teacher using a single computer with a whole class. Focus on:

- where the teacher is positioned;
- how all pupils are enabled to see;
- who controls the computer and how;
- how the teacher involves pupils in the activity;
- what rules of behaviour are operating.

Are there any differences compared with when the teacher is not using a computer?

---

## When is an ICT room needed?

There will be some occasions when it is important that all pupils in the class gain a particular experience at the same time. This usually provides benefits for teaching when you need to introduce a new ICT process or technique, if you want to set a difficult challenge which will need class discussion concerning strategy and progress, and also if you want pupils to present and discuss their experiences immediately as a whole class to help stimulate conceptual change. Having all pupils using ICT at the same time gives you an extra opportunity for reflective activity. Pupils, too, may prefer carrying out a task as a whole class, and peer support is easier to manage than in the normal classroom.

The ICT room also has some advantages when pupils are working independently. This is most obvious when you want all pupils to work individually or when time is short for completing a project or unit of work involving ICT, and the classroom or departmental equipment is insufficient to allow all pupils to complete using a rota. However, the fact that there is one PC per pupil does not mean that you have to allocate PCs individually. In many situations it will benefit pupils to work in pairs or even groups of three if space allows.

The continuous availability of a PC also aids autonomous learning, as the resources will be there on demand. Pupils can also use a word processor in a separate window to type out their own notes on what they are learning. This can be stored and retrieved at any time and even e-mailed to a fellow pupil should the need arise.

The disadvantages of the ICT room concern setting and time. In a subject classroom, there are other resources, wall displays and an association in pupils' minds with the subject culture. In the ICT room, the culture is of 'doing ICT' and whilst the ICT processes may be easier for pupils, it can be more difficult for them to develop subject concepts in this setting. If you want pupils to carry out a non-ICT task, the ICT room may have insufficient working space, and in any case the computers can be a distraction to learners. This problem can be overcome with careful planning and movement of resources, but time limitations are almost unavoidable. Particularly if there is a significant amount of ICT subject teaching in the school, bookings for general ICT rooms may be rationed, often have to be made for precise dates a term in advance, and are difficult to change. A resource room or cluster of PCs in each department can be scheduled much more flexibly, although it may not offer as many PCs (see What other ways are there of organising the classroom to use ICT? below).

| Task 7.4 | For the activity that you designed in Task 7.1, identify the advantages and disadvantages of using an ICT room. |

## What do you need to consider in managing the computer room?

### Rules and routines

There are some special points to consider when pupils are using ICT, particularly if they are in a computer room. You should check school policies, however, and use those if they differ from this advice. The head of ICT may have particular procedures to be followed in computer rooms, and may even specify particular ways in which ICT tasks are to be carried out. You should seek advice on:

- dealing with log-on problems and Internet access;
- movement – should pupils move around the class? How does the teacher circulate the room?
- saving – do pupils have their own user area and/or specific folders for each subject?
- printing – who decides when to print and when printout is collected?

**Task 7.5**    The rules and routines applied at the start of the lesson are crucial to the success of the lesson as a whole. Observe a variety of experienced teachers at the start of the lesson and analyse the following.
- What routines do the pupils and the teacher follow?
- What rules apply concerning pupil behaviour on entry to the class and up to the start of the lesson content?
- How does the teacher ensure that these rules are applied?

## Clear briefing

As with any practical activity, it is important to give a clear briefing to pupils. The nature of the briefing will depend on the type of pupils as well as the type of task. With a group of good learners, you may provide a minimal briefing which indicates the required outcomes of the task and the intended learning. With a younger or less able group, you may need to give very detailed instructions, and then question pupils to check that they remember and understand them before they start the activity. If you do not do this, the ensuing fuss and confusion may spoil a potentially good activity. Be careful not to give too many instructions initially, however; pupils will need reminding later on and it may be better to plan to stop them when some pupils have complete the first stage of the task and give them the next part of the briefing then.

In order to maximise your use of the time available in the ICT room, you may give the main briefing in the subject classroom in the previous lesson, and just provide a brief reminder through questioning in the ICT room.

## Start of the lesson

For safety and security reasons, pupils will not normally be allowed into the classroom before a teacher arrives. It is important to arrive before the pupils if possible, so that they are not waiting in the corridor – this makes a poor start to the lesson. Supervise pupils carefully as they enter the room and set a welcoming atmosphere, whilst emphasising the computer room rules where necessary.

The start of the lesson should set the scene for the work to be carried out; it also sets the tone of the lesson and it is important that you manage it efficiently and reinforce your expectations of work and behaviour. In most cases the lesson should start away from the computers, although this is not always possible because of class layout. If you have to talk to the class when they are seated at computers, ensure that they are turned to face you, with hands away from the keyboard and mouse. It may be a good idea to tell pupils to switch their screens off while you talk to them – this is routine in many schools.

Pupils could also be allowed to sit at computers immediately if they are continuing with a familiar task or have already been briefed in another room. You should allocate pupils to appropriate places in the room initially, in order to lay down the ground rules and establish control. Having fixed positions initially also helps with learning names. This is particularly difficult when you often just see the backs of pupils' heads, but it is vital in establishing your authority and developing a constructive relationship.

You can relax the constraints later, once a sound relationship has been established and you can rely on pupils to sit down, log on and give you their full attention when you are ready (Hughes and Kennewell, 2003).

If you plan to introduce new ideas or revise important techniques, you need to consider carefully how you will do this. The best approach will depend on a variety of factors: pupils' abilities, the resources available, and the support you will have from other adults in the classroom such as the class teacher, another student teacher, or a technician. Note that you will need to discuss in advance with colleagues what their role is to be in managing the pupils' learning, the pupils' behaviour, and the ICT resources.

Hughes and Kennewell (2003) suggest a number of possible approaches, detailed below.

### Demonstration

The issues here are essentially the same as for whole-class teaching.

### Step-by-step handouts

These are useful as *aides mémoires* or revision guides but most pupils find it difficult to follow detailed instructions and will tend to ask you or their friends rather than reading the handout. They can work well with limited content or with the most able pupils, but pupils will still tend to seek reassurance that they are 'doing it right' and screen illustrations should be included at key points. Pupils following detailed instructions may not learn the key elements of the exercise but just blindly follow the instructions on the sheet, without comprehension.

### Whole-class talk through

This involves the teacher explaining each step of the process to the whole class while they work on the PC. It requires every pupil to complete each step successfully before the whole class moves on. This is useful to quickly get a class or group to a particular starting point, for example, loading a template, but it is a risky strategy for longer processes. Be prepared for pupils not keeping up or computer problems that will cause the pupil to disrupt your flow by calling out. Very capable pupils will tend to experiment for themselves or try to move ahead. It is better to ask them to help slower pupils.

### Trial and error

With a capable class and intuitive software, you may only need to give a brief demonstration of the facilities or potential of a package. You can then set pupils the challenge of producing a particular outcome, or suggest that they 'play with it' and see what they can do with loose guidance as to the required outcomes. As long as all pupils succeed, this approach has the benefit of increasing confidence, quicker learning, transfer of skill, and developing autonomous learning. You will need to plan carefully a plenary session in order to discuss the terminology for the techniques and concepts, and how to combine techniques in order to carry out complete processes.

### Cascade

This involves showing the next phase or a more advanced technique to a small group, and then each member of the group can show the pupils around them. Alternatively, show the technique to every fifth pupil around the class, and then these 'peer teachers' can show the other pupils near to them. The use of peer teaching is a valuable strategy, and it can benefit the pupils who do the teaching because of the need to reflect on their knowledge in order to communicate with their peers. However, you need to ensure that the peer teachers do not miss out on more advanced learning because they are always helping others with basic skills, and that they are briefed to *explain* what to do and not just take over the task from their less capable classmates.

*Combinations of the above*

The approaches detailed above are not mutually exclusive. You may take the class to a suitable point via whole-class talk through, then bring the class together for a demonstration and support the pupils on their return to the computer with a handout or notes on the board. This has the advantage in that there is a fall-back situation if one strategy fails.

---

**Task 7.6**   Discuss with experienced teachers the approaches that they use for introducing new techniques. Do these approaches vary with different topics? Do they vary with different classes? Why might teachers use different approaches in different circumstances?

---

## Handling of transitions between activities

After your introduction to the main points of the lesson, the transition to the next phase of the lesson will require careful thinking and planning. There needs to be a clear demarcation point between the two phases and, before any movement occurs, you need to make clear exactly what you want the pupils to do when you give the signal. You may need to specify how they are to move – for instance who goes first – if space is limited or the pupils are poor at organising themselves. It may be helpful to ensure that they have a written note of the procedures and/or expectations to be carried out when they move to the PCs. One of the most important factors in maintaining a working atmosphere and preventing misbehaviour is *momentum*. You need to ensure a smooth flow of activity, avoiding delays when pupils are uncertain of what to do and vacillation between one activity and another (Muijs and Reynolds, 2001).

While the class are working, bear in mind that casual comments have little or no effect, and rather than 'talking over the class', it is best to save up points to tell the class in a single intervention rather than saying them when they come to mind. When pupils reach a planned point at which further briefing or explanation is needed, or when several in the class have the same problem, call the whole class together and ensure you have everyone's attention. You could do this with a subset of the class if you are confident that the others can make progress.

If you do need to stop them, then the point you want to make should be important; re-directing, focusing, highlighting are all valid purposes. Ensure that you give a clear signal to stop, and ensure that you have their full attention before making your point. They should face you, turning chairs if necessary, with hands clear of equipment. This procedure will also enable you to make an effective transition from individual or group work to a plenary session.

## Managing the class

Your ability to control pupils can be largely influenced by the layout of the room. If you are in the centre, there are always going to be pupils who are behind you and you are going to have to move around continually so that there are only a few seconds when any pupil is out of sight. Consider where in the room you can see all the pupils, and they can see you. If, for example, there are two pupils behind an island, consider moving them for the purpose of a demonstration, whole-class questioning or board work. When you turn to the board or to help a pupil with a problem on their computer do you lose contact with the class? If you have to turn your back, try to make it on the side with the least number of pupils. Try different stances when dealing with a problem on a computer or writing on the board. Preparing work in advance for projection will mean that you can face the class continuously. Make sure that you do not have to bend down or turn to operate the projector, mouse or keyboard. If you are working with a particular pupil, however, you will find it easier to keep an eye on the whole class if you stoop down next to the pupil. This stance will also be less threatening to the pupil you are helping. Make a point of commenting to pupils who are in the distance or behind you frequently.

There are other matters of organisation that can affect the success of the lesson.

- Bags, coats and books all need to go somewhere, particularly on a wet day during the winter.
- Pupils need surface space if they are going to write in their books or folders.
- If you intend to separate pupils who can be disruptive when together, you need to decide where they can be placed so that they cannot try to communicate across the class.

It will be important to give these points attention when you are responsible for organising classes, especially those containing 'difficult' pupils (Hughes and Kennewell, 2003).

---

**Task 7.7**   Look at various teaching and ICT rooms. In each, place yourself at various points in the room and try to identify the following.
- Where is the focal point of the room?
- Are there any blind spots or seats where pupils will have their back to you?
- Where will bags and coats go?
- Are you able to move around the room?
- If you give support to a pupil, will you lose sight of the rest of the class?

---

Establish a routine in your class and try to keep rigidly to it, for example pupils should not call out or talk beyond their immediate neighbours. It is important to show quiet confidence and efficiency, which will lead to a relaxed atmosphere (Hughes and Kennewell, 2003). This comes from careful and detailed preparation: when you are inexperienced in a teaching situation you need to know exactly how you intend the activity to proceed and explain this clearly to the pupils.

It is important to check that your resources and instructions work on the actual equipment to be used, as machine specifications and configurations will vary between home or college and school, and from room to room within the school. Make sure that you check the actual set up in the room you intend to use, as versions may differ. Log on as though you are a pupil if possible, to check that they have access to the resources that you expect.

Events may still deviate from your intentions for reasons beyond your control, however. In this case, you may not know how to solve the problem yourself. There will often be pupils in the class who know more than you do, and you can listen to their suggestions or even ask for their advice. If the problem concerns the network, however, you will probably need help from a technician, so find out in advance how you can contact them. If all fails, you will need to switch the class quickly to another activity, and it is important to have contingency plans for non-ICT work in the case of complete resource failure.

Pupils may be used to a more informal atmosphere in the ICT room, and this can be difficult to manage when you are inexperienced. You should make your routine and guidelines for the class clear; for instance, if you decide on a policy of 'no movement around the class', you need to enforce it rigidly. Think through the implications in advance, however, so that you are not caught out during the lesson: printout will need to be distributed by you rather than collected by pupils. Pupils learn a great deal through talk in the ICT room, whether they are working collaboratively on a task or asking their neighbours about a technique. Tell pupils that conversation should be kept to relevant matters, should only be with the person next to them and should be quieter than normal. As soon as the noise level approaches that where you can hear individual voices then there is too much. There is a different sound from 'working noise' compared with general chatter, and you should learn to detect the difference so that you can intervene early when you perceive pupils stopping work on their task.

Maintain vigilance and circulate systematically around the class, watching for fast/ slow progress and off-task behaviour as well as responding to questions and difficulties. Note that off-task behaviour using ICT can be obscured easily by pupils, and you should check the bar at the bottom of the screen that shows all the programs/files they have open. Pupils who are surreptitiously playing games, sending social messages or accessing prohibited websites should be reprimanded and disciplined according to school policy. There is potential for other antisocial misdemeanours, from merely touching someone else's keyboard through to hacking into their user area. There will be different perceptions concerning what constitutes misbehaviour, however, and you should seek advice on how particular actions are viewed by the class teacher and in school policy. The value of a consistent policy concerning misbehaviour in empowering teachers is considerable (Macrae and Quintrell, 2001), and you should make every effort to know, understand and apply your school's policy concerning procedures for the use of ICT resources from the very start of your teaching.

## Supporting pupils in using ICT

A variety of techniques are available to assist pupils who need help with the ICT aspect of the activity:

- demonstration with descriptive or explanatory commentary (mainly used in introducing the ideas to a group or the whole class);
- monitored instruction (the teacher gives instructions step-by-step and checks that the pupil is following);
- monitored repetition (the pupil tries to repeat the technique with the teacher filling in what the pupils cannot do);
- guided discovery (the pupil tries to work out the steps with the teacher providing questions/prompts to help them recognise relevant cues, concepts and familiar techniques);
- guided repetition (pupil tries to repeat the technique with the teacher providing questions/prompts to help the pupil recognise relevant cues and concepts);
- quick fix (the teacher solves a problem without explanation to enable the pupil to focus on their intended objectives).

Try to give prompts and ask questions rather than giving instructions or demonstrations. You will usually be able to look with them at their work on screen, and you can take the opportunity to point out (literally) particular matters that need attention. This provides a model of the sort of self-regulation that you want them to adopt. Never snatch a mouse or keyboard; this is likely to leave the pupil with a sense of helplessness. If you need to demonstrate something, ask if you can 'borrow' the mouse or keyboard for a moment.

> **Task 7.8**    Observe an experienced teacher working with pupils who are using ICT. Focus on:
> - how the teacher monitors pupils' ICT work;
> - when the teacher intervenes to support pupils in their work;
> - what sort of support is provided;
> - how the teacher monitors pupils' behaviour;
> - how the teacher controls misbehaviour.

## Review and ending

As much of ICT work is ephemeral and a final printout does not record learning, an evaluation of work, review of learning and recap of key points is essential. For safety and security reasons again, dismiss pupils as carefully as you brought them in.

> **Task 7.9**    You have already planned the lesson structure and organisation in outline, and the tasks for pupils in detail. Now use the prompts in this chapter to produce a more detailed plan concerning the organisation of pupils and activities during the lesson so as to make the most of the use of ICT in learning.

## What other ways are there of organising the classroom to use ICT?

There are a number of alternative ways of organising a classroom for ICT:

- a cluster of four or five PCs in a subject teaching room: these can each be used by one pupil to carry out independent activities, using a rota to ensure that the whole class has a turn; or one can be allocated to each group of five/six pupils for a collaborative activity;
- a number of pupils can be sent to work independently in a resource base where PCs are supervised by a librarian or technician;
- a set of portables may be booked for use with the class, often on a one-per-pair basis.

Each of these methods has different management implications. For the cluster, you will need to ensure that not only the pupils using the PC are purposefully occupied and making progress, but that the rest of the class, or the rest of the group if several pupils are working together, are also making progress. If you send pupils to a resource base, you will need to check and follow procedures for pupils leaving the class, and make sure that they are well briefed and prepared to work effectively without your direct supervision. It will help to discuss this with the librarian or technician beforehand. With the portables, you will need to consider the procedures used for allocating PCs to pupils, whether pupils are familiar with using the equipment (for instance, if there is a trackpad rather than a mouse), how long the PCs will work before recharging is necessary, whether pupils can take the machines home, how files can be transferred to the school network and how printing can be carried out. The extra management time needed during a lesson for all this means that it is unwise to plan to use portables for short lessons (Bowell *et al.*, 1994).

## Further reading

Bowell, B., France, S. and Redfern, S. (1994) *Portable computers in action*, Coventry: NCET

Cox, M. (1999) Motivating pupils, in Leask, M. and Pachler, N. (eds) (1999) *Learning to teach using ICT in the secondary school*, London: Routledge

Davison, J. (2001) Managing classroom behaviour, in Capel, S., Leask, M. and Turner, T. (eds) (2001) *Learning to teach in the secondary school: a companion to school experience* (3rd edition), London: RoutledgeFalmer

Muijs, D. and Reynolds, D. (2001) *Effective teaching: evidence and practice*, London: Paul Chapman

# 8  Developing Pedagogy with ICT

This chapter introduces a framework for planning and analysing teaching based on the Task-Abilities-Features (TAF) model for learning activity introduced in Chapter 5. The chapter explains and exemplifies how the framework can be used to design and evaluate lessons in which ICT is used in subject teaching, focusing on the contribution of introduction, task and plenary. The examples referred to are all introduced in Chapter 1.

## What is the role of the teacher when ICT is used in teaching?

Many ways of using ICT that may aid learning have been introduced, including:

1   aiding exposition by teacher (see Example 1.2, p. 7);
2   providing exposition independently of teacher (see Example 1.6, pp. 9–10);
3   assessment/diagnosis (see Example 1.6, pp. 9–10);
4   enabling learners to express ideas (see Example 1.3, p. 8);
5   access to information by learners (see Example 1.1, p. 7);
6   processing of data by learners (see Example 1.5, pp. 8–9);
7   structuring of learners' problem solving (see Example 1.4, p. 8).

Some programs may be designed specifically for one or more of these approaches, but a generic package or the Internet may be used in various ways according to the teacher's intentions or even the learners' choice.

The thinking carried out by expert teachers in making decisions about the design of activities and materials, the selection of resources (including ICT), and the management of learning in the classroom is usually tacit and difficult for them to explain to novices. The Task-Abilities-Features (TAF) model of learning through activity, which

> **Task 8.1**   For one particular item of software or ICT activity specifically designed for your subject, identify which of the methods 1–7 above are appropriate.
>
> Can you identify any other ways in which ICT may aid learning?

you met in Chapter 5, can be used to make explicit and analyse the way in which the teacher brings together dynamically the features of the resources in relation to the tasks set and the learners' abilities. Figure 8.1 incorporates the main elements of the learning framework represented by Figure 5.1 – the features of the setting, the

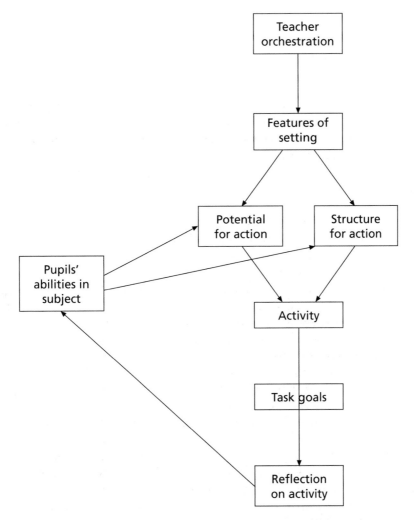

**Figure 8.1**   Teacher orchestration of features to support learning through activity. Based on Figure 2 in Kennewell, S. (2001) Using affordances and constraints to evaluate the use of ICT in teaching and learning, *Journal of IT and Teacher Education*, **10**, 101–16

potential and structure for action that they offer, the abilities of the learners, the task goal, the activity carried out and the important loop back from the activity to the improved abilities which represents learning.

The framework contains two important extra elements that characterise effective teaching. The teacher provides the overall structure of the lesson and can decide to increase or reduce the features of the setting that provide potential and structure for action. The teacher responds to the needs of the learners in order to maintain an appropriate learning gap – not so small as to make the task trivial, and not so large as to make the task goal unattainable and the activity frustrating. This tailoring of the resources may be judged in relation to the abilities of the class in general, or to the needs of individuals. The teacher will be a particularly important resource within the setting, because of the feature of contingency: the ability to respond to the actions of the learner, so as to provide sufficient instructions and guidance for the learner to complete the task. This process is often described as 'scaffolding' (see Chapter 5, p. 91).

In addition, the teacher ensures that the activity involves a reflective phase, perhaps at stages during a complex task when the learners look back on their progress, evaluate their strategies and plan the next stage (with appropriate scaffolding for this process as needed). Certainly, reflection is required on completion of the task, when their attention needs to be switched from the task outcome to the learning that has resulted from the activity. This learning needs to be explicitly linked to what else they know and where else they might apply the knowledge.

This framework enables us to see how the teacher can set a challenging task, and provide differentiated support according to learners' needs. ICT is not explicitly shown in Figure 8.1; it can be considered merely as one of the features of the setting. But it is necessary to consider its relation to the abilities of the learners as well, and it is helpful to show specifically the need to consider the ICT capability of pupils as well as subject abilities if they are going to carry out a task involving ICT (see Figure 8.2). You may be able to help pupils develop their ICT capability, and put an extra arrow looping back from the activity to pupils' abilities in ICT!

You may find it helpful, too, to consider other key skills in the same way as ICT capability, particularly literacy and numeracy, but also problem solving, working with others and improving own learning. You may need to take account of pupils' existing abilities in these skills as well as ICT, and to help them develop them further.

You can use this framework for analysis when pupils are not interacting directly with ICT themselves. If the teacher is using ICT with the class, there is still activity leading to a task goal and the TAF model (see Chapter 5) can still be applied to pupils' learning as long as they are involved in the activity through questioning. Pupils' ICT capability will be of less importance, however, unless the teacher involves them in ICT decisions as well.

The framework can help you to plan specific developments in the teaching of topics using ICT and to evaluate the effects of these changes by focused observation of how the features of ICT provide potential and structure for both action and reflection.

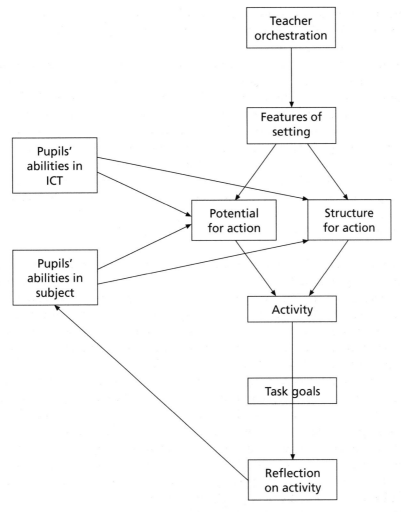

**Figure 8.2** Adding ICT to the features and abilities. Based on Figure 2 in Kennewell, S. (2001) Using affordances and constraints to evaluate the use of ICT in teaching and learning, *Journal of IT and Teacher Education*, **10**, 101–16

## Deciding whether to use ICT

It will not always be appropriate to use ICT. The main issue is whether the features of ICT provide potential and structure for action, and whether this is helpful in manipulating the learning gap and thus supporting pupils' learning. Your decision on whether to use ICT will depend on many factors, however: the topic, the class, the resources available, and your own ICT capability. However, as a trainee teacher you are required to gain experience of using ICT in the classroom, and you should discuss with your school-based tutor or mentor as soon as possible in your placement which particular classes and topics will give the best opportunity for practising the use of ICT in teaching and learning.

> **Task 8.2**  Identify a particular class and topic where there is likely to be some benefit for pupils' learning from the use of ICT.

## Aims and objectives

You need to be clear about what learning you intend to achieve in the lesson or unit that includes ICT work, so that the ICT is not seen as an end in itself, or just as a means of improving presentation.

You need next to consider pupils' prior knowledge:

- of your subject: will the intended work make a high or low demand on pupils?
- of ICT: again, will the intended work make a high or low demand on pupils?

It is important to identify the nature of the learning gap for pupils concerning the subject matter, and make sure that it is:

1   not too large for pupils to bridge even with the combined support of your teaching and ICT resources;
2   not so small that pupils will find the work trivial or boring.

If the ICT skills required are unfamiliar to pupils, you need to consider whether the ICT may interfere with the subject learning, rather than enhancing it (see Chapter 6). It may still be worth using ICT in this case, as most pupils pick up what to do with ICT quite quickly, but it would be a good idea to start with an easy activity to familiarise them with the skills needed.

> **Task 8.3**  For the topic/class you chose in Task 8.2, identify the aims for the topic and a number of particular learning objectives. Which particular objectives will ICT help to achieve?

## Selecting ICT resources

The next stage is to consider what resources are available that may provide the required features – these may be subject specific, such as a simulation program or CD-ROM database, or they may be generic, such as a DTP or spreadsheet program. You will also need to check that they are:

- accessible at the right time, place, and on a sufficient number of computers;
- relevant to the topic, age and ability of the pupils;
- effective in exploiting the features of ICT that enable pupils to do things which would otherwise be difficult or time consuming.

You will also need to consider what further resources you may need to provide in addition to the ICT and other published material if you are using a pack. Such resources could include:

- help sheets for pupils;
- posters to provide reminders or stimuli;
- versions of material adapted for different pupils, including those with special needs;
- extension activities to challenge the most able.

Chapter 9 will consider these aspects in more detail.

You are most likely to learn yourself from using ICT in the classroom if the activity you choose is successful in promoting pupils' learning. You should therefore seek advice from your mentor, tutor and published literature in order to find out whether the resources have been used successfully in the past. At the current stage of development, however, you may well be in a pioneering position. Since you must gain experience of using ICT in the classroom, you will sometimes need to take some risks and try out ideas which are new to everyone involved.

| Task 8.4 | Decide on the resources you are going to use for the work with your chosen topic/class, and identify what role they will take. |
|---|---|

## Developing your own knowledge of the resources

It is important that you are thoroughly familiar with the resources, particularly if you expect pupils to use them, so that you can plan effectively what you expect the pupils to do in order to achieve the learning objectives, and so that you can anticipate most difficulties and overcome problems as they arise. Even if you are only using a program yourself, if you are in front of the whole class you want to be prepared for anything that might arise.

There are two main aspects to this knowledge; one is the structure and purpose of the program you are using, and how it relates to subject knowledge. If it is a subject-specific program, or a website with subject-specific content, you need to know the scope of its content, how the author is representing the subject concepts, and whether there are any errors or differences in approach which could cause confusion. If it is a generic tool such as a web editor or spreadsheet, you need to consider how its functions represent subject-specific processes. A spreadsheet, for instance, uses different structure and notation for formulas than conventional mathematics, and a web has a different structure from traditional text.

## How can the framework be used?

### Structuring lessons and planning the work of learners

You may be expected or recommended to use a standard lesson structure, for example a three- or four-phase pattern (see, for instance, Hughes and Vass, 2001):

1    overview/recap/orientation
2    main input
3    process activity
4    review.

The role played by ICT will be different in each phase. During the initial phase, the capacity of ICT storage may be used to retrieve material used in the previous lesson or created during the previous lesson, such as notes made on an interactive whiteboard. Alternatively, the automation may be used to carry out a class brainstorm in mind-map format using graphic organiser software.

The main input may again use the capacity feature, in that a large amount of material can be prepared beforehand. It can also use the range feature in that material can be drawn from a wide variety of sources, and presented in different ways – through words (written and oral), images and sounds in order to cater for different learning styles (see Chapter 5). It will use the feature of speed in that it can be made available quickly in the classroom. It may use the feature of interactivity, with slides in a presentation hyperlinked so that the teacher can easily branch to different options depending on pupils' answers to questions. This feature also makes it easy to involve pupils at the board, since they will only need to touch the screen rather than writing or drawing on the board. Prepared material also takes advantage of provisionality, in that it can be changed for future use following evaluation and it can be tailored to different classes.

ICT will have a different role in the process phase of the lesson, where the focus is on pupils' activity. The features will provide support for action in ways that depend on whether pupils are using ICT instructively or constructively, however (see Chapters 2 and 5). In the case of instructive use, the computer is managing the task as a surrogate teacher, and pupils are responding to what appears on the screen or through the speakers/headphones. You need to consider whether in that case the ICT resource is able to orchestrate support features adequately itself, or whether you need to plan to monitor and intervene when appropriate to ensure that the support from the ICT is neither so great that the task is trivial nor so little that the task is too difficult and pupils become frustrated. If the use is constructive or creative, the learner is more involved in managing the resources employed in the task, but they may need some assistance from the teacher to ensure that they gain help at the right time – not so soon that they do not get a chance to think for themselves, and not so late that they have become bored and frustrated.

In the final phase, the range feature can be valuable again in enabling the teacher to collate different pupils' work for display and discussion with the whole class.

It is important to identify possible learning problems that might arise and either plan to avoid them, or plan to deal with them when they arise. Problems may occur in the following areas.

*Subject learning*

ICT may well help with pupils' learning, but it will not do everything, and you need the same sort of awareness of pupils' potential difficulties with subject skills and concepts as with any other activity. This will be gained through experience and advice, although the particular issues concerned with a topic in relation to ICT may not be familiar to many teachers.

*ICT capability*

For most of the time, your main teaching focus in each phase will be the relevant subject topic, but there may be some lessons or phases of a lesson in which ICT is the main focus because you need to develop pupils' ICT capability before they can carry out a particular process that is required for subject learning. It is wise in this situation to make the subject information they are going to handle as simple as possible whilst the focus is on ICT, so that the overall learning gap is not made too large.

*Other key skills*

Most, if not all, ICT tasks will require a contribution from other key skills, and you should check whether pupils' skills, particularly in literacy and numeracy, are going to be adequate, and, if not, how you are going to help to develop these skills during the task. The same applies to working with others and problem solving in tasks where these skills apply. It is easy to assume that pupils can handle cooperation in group tasks when they lack the social skills to do so, and that they can cope with being 'stuck' or in a state of uncertainty when in the past they have always had specific instructions on how to proceed.

| Task 8.5 | Produce an outline plan for the structure of the lesson and organisation of pupils for your class/topic, and discuss with your mentor. |
|---|---|

- Identify the learning objectives.
- Consider the present abilities of pupils in the subject topic.
- Design a task that requires the learning gap to be bridged.
- Identify possible resources to be provided initially, possibly including ICT.
- Plan the sequence of activity in the classroom so that pupils are engaged with the learning objectives, are motivated by the task, and start on the task.
- Plan changes in the features, contingent upon pupil performance, in order to complete the task.
- Design reflective activity in order to consolidate and evaluate the pupils' learning.

You should also consider the role of homework. Increasingly it is becoming realistic to set homework requiring the use of general ICT tools such as the Internet or word processing because of the availability of ICT in the home (Tanner, 2003). There are different features involved in the use of ICT in the home setting, particularly the human support for exploratory and constructive tasks (Kennewell, 2002). You can take account of this and set different types of challenge from the traditionally common tasks of repetitive practice or finishing off. To help with this, pupils may have access to the school network from home in order to work with files provided by the teacher or stored in their own user areas. If this is not the case, teachers may provide material for download through the school website and pupils can e-mail their work to themselves at home.

## Why is the framework effective?

The TAF model helps us to recognise where and how ICT can contribute to motivating pupils to engage with subject learning, to supporting the achievement of learner tasks and to structuring learning activities that take place in and beyond the classroom. The framework for teaching incorporates key ideas from learning theories, including the role of activity in learning, scaffolding within the ZPD, and reflection in order to develop conceptual understanding. It involves planning to integrate ICT into lessons and interacting with pupils in the classroom, rather than 'bolting on' ICT or 'handing over' the teaching to ICT.

Furthermore, relating the resource organisation to pupils' abilities (in the subject, in ICT and in other factors including learning styles and key skills) means that other important features of teaching strategy such as lesson phases and differentiation can be incorporated into the framework rather than having to consider each one separately.

## How can the use of ICT in a lesson be evaluated?

There are two main issues to consider:

- is ICT better than other approaches?
- is ICT used in the best way in the circumstances?

The answers to these questions depend on a variety of factors, including the particular tasks set and resources used. Chapters 9 and 10 will consider the evaluation of tasks and resources in more depth. Other factors will not be under your control, such as the school's policies and equipment. This leaves the evaluation of the overall design of the lesson and the role of ICT within it. There are some general issues related to the evaluation of lesson structure and teaching approaches, including the following:

- Was your choice of teaching strategy successful in stimulating pupil learning?
- Was the lesson structure effective? Did you maintain a good pace and finish on time?
- Did pupils understand what was expected of them?

- Did pupils succeed in the task as expected? Did all achieve your baseline?
- Were all pupils motivated and interested? Did they persevere with the task?
- Did you interact with every pupil? Did you provide feedback and targets?
- Was the classroom management effective in maintaining a good working environment?
- Did most pupils achieve your learning objectives for the lesson?

(Kennewell et al., 2003; Ellis, 2002)

Each of these factors will be influenced by ICT, and you should consider whether or not ICT is helping you to achieve your teaching aims. If it is not, then try to identify how you can change your lesson structure, teaching approach, tasks or resources in order to exploit the features of ICT more effectively – or use a non-ICT approach next time!

According to the TAF framework, the most important issue in evaluation is the relationship between activity and learning. ICT should support the activity in such a way as to facilitate learning, and this will happen when it enables pupils to achieve challenging tasks which would have been too difficult or time-consuming for them otherwise. It should not make them too easy, however, or they will not need to think deeply about the matters you want them to learn. And, of course, ICT must not create difficulties that get in the way of the pupils' focus on the subject matter concerned.

## Further reading

Cox, M. J. and Webb, M. (eds) (2004) *ICT and pedagogy: a literature review*, Coventry: British Educational Communications Agency and Technology London: DfES

Ellis, V. (2002) *Learning and teaching in secondary schools*, Exeter: Learning Matters

Leask, M. (2001) Improving your teaching, in Capel, S., Leask, M. and Turner, T. (eds) (2001) *Learning to teach in the secondary school: a companion to school experience* (3rd edition), London: RoutledgeFalmer

Muijs, D. and Reynolds, D. (2001) *Effective teaching: evidence and practice*, London: Paul Chapman

Scrimshaw, P. (1997) Computers and the teacher's role, in Somekh, B. and Davis, N. (eds) (1997) *Using information technology effectively in teaching and learning*, London: Routledge, 100–13

# 9 Preparation and Evaluation of ICT Resources

This chapter explains and exemplifies the principles and practice of producing teaching and learning materials for whole-class teaching, group and individual work. It examines the problems of providing an appropriate level of challenge, structure and information according to the abilities of the learners, and suggests solutions for a variety of teaching situations by designing differentiated tasks for pupils, including those with SEN. It provides and explains criteria for selecting from existing school and commercial materials, evaluating their suitability for learners and designing activities that exploit their features.

## Designing tasks for learning with ICT

The process phase of the lesson is a vital component of the learning experience. The design of tasks for pupils to carry out, and of the resources you will provide to support pupils' work, are both very important if you are to be successful in teaching. When you are preparing activities for the pupils to work on in the classroom, you should consider various factors. For each of these, the role of ICT will have an influence on your decision making.

### Is the task appropriate for the learning objectives?

You should first focus on the learning objectives for the lesson or unit of work, and then consider the pupils' existing abilities in ICT, in the subject matter you are teaching, and in other key skills. Ensure that the learning gap that you identify is a reasonable one for the pupils to bridge with the help of your teaching and the support of ICT, and then plan a task that will provide potential and structure for the intended learning.

## Is it a worthwhile task for pupils?

There is no fixed definition of 'worthwhile'. In general, tasks should not be too trivial, but the subject matter should at least be comprehensible to pupils, the task goal should be something the pupils want to achieve, the learning objectives should be seen as relevant to their aspirations, and the task should clearly help them to achieve the learning objectives. The role of ICT should also be worthwhile, rather than merely 'doing ICT' for the sake of it.

Consequently, you need to consider some more detailed questions when planning a task for pupils.

- What is the purpose of the task in terms of learning outcomes?
- What will the product be, and hence the goal for pupils?
- How does the task help them with their subject learning?
- How does ICT help them with the task, in terms of potential and structure for action?
- How does ICT affect their subject learning, in terms of managing the learning gap?

## What is the learner's intended role in relation to ICT?

Chapters 2 and 5 classified tasks in terms of the learner's intended relationship to the ICT resources as either instructive activity (in which the learner reacts to the content), constructive-directed activity (in which the learner develops content, with the emphasis on a specific product) or constructive-creative activity (in which the learner develops content, with the emphasis on imaginative design). You need to be clear about the learner's role in any task where ICT is involved. The first reason for this is in order to check that it is likely to be effective in bridging the learning gap for the pupils. The second reason is to identify what sort of briefing and review of prior learning the pupils will need; a constructive task is likely to need preparatory work in order for pupils to gain optimum benefit from it.

## How will you make your expectations clear to the pupils?

Your activity will not be successful unless pupils are clear about your expectations of them, in terms of the task outcome, the process you expect them to engage in, and what you intend them to learn from the process – they need to be aware of 'the big picture'. This is particularly important with a constructive learning task. To this end, pupils need to know what is to be assessed and how (more about this in the next chapter). Even if you specifically decide that you want them to explore a situation without a particular goal, you need to explain this to them, and tell them the ultimate purpose, or else they will think you are merely disorganised. You particularly need to consider how you will explain:

- what skills and resources you expect them to use;
- what specific outcomes you require, and when;
- whether it is intended to be a straightforward task or a challenge;
- how long you expect it to take;
- what you expect them to learn from doing it;
- how the work will be assessed.

## Can all pupils get started?

The early stages of the task are crucial. However well you give instructions, it is likely that some pupils will not have been listening or will have misunderstood. If the class is in an ICT room, you should move around the class, checking that each pupil is engaged with the first steps of the work before you deal with any more complex enquiries. If using a single PC, check each pupil or group as they start their turn on the PC in order to ensure that no time is wasted. In planning this stage, consider the following questions:

- Are they familiar with the context?
- Is the first stage clearly explained?
- Do they know the techniques required?

## What outcomes are expected from the task?

It is likely that the pupils' main concern will be the nature of the product that they are required to produce. Some pupils may treat the process as a race, and you will need to be clear about the criteria for a *good* piece of work, as well as the minimum requirements for task completion. It is helpful to show pupils an example of good work, and to discuss how the results were achieved. It can also be helpful to consider poor quality work, and to discuss how to avoid it, but it is advisable to keep the example anonymous in such cases.

You may often ask pupils to finish a task at home, and you need to check whether this is feasible when ICT is required. Pupils who do not have adequate PCs at home will need to know when they can gain access to school or other public facilities outside school hours.

Much ICT work is ephemeral, that is it appears on the screen just long enough for the purposes of the task, and there is no permanent record. It is important that pupils have some way of recording what they have achieved – it gives greater status to the task, allows you to give written feedback and parents to find out what pupils have done (see Chapter 10). In planning, then, consider whether you require:

- a printed work sheet to be completed;
- an electronic work sheet to be completed;
- an oral report;
- a handwritten or word processed report;
- homework.

## Are pupils clear about the role of resources available to help them complete the task?

You should make clear what resources are provided and how they should be used to help with the work. It is particularly important to explain how to extract key points and illustrative examples from sources of information, rather than just reproduce them. Most pupils are adept at cutting and pasting any material that has superficial relevance to the topic, but will learn little from doing so. Similarly, when they are 'stuck' they should not expect the teacher or another pupil to do things for them; they should try something for themselves and ask for advice and guidance that is related to their own ideas. In planning, consider the role of:

- printed material – work sheets, information sheets, books, etc.;
- ICT – programs to be used, files such as templates or prepared data, websites, specialist devices;
- artefacts such as physical models;
- human assistance – teacher, other adults, peers.

## Can they develop, evaluate and improve their work?

It is important that pupils develop the ability to monitor their activity and regularly evaluate their progress on the task. In some cases, there will be right answers and it will be clear to pupils when they have attained these. Usually, however, there is a value judgement involved in assessment, and you should aim to share with pupils the qualities and criteria that represent your high expectations for their work. In planning, then, consider the following.

- Is the work self-checking?
- Are they aware of assessment criteria?
- Are there stages to the task?
- Are there choices for the pupils?
- Can they tell when it is finished?
- Can they judge how good it is?
- How will you give them feedback during their work and at the end?

## What is the minimum requirement for completion, and is there extension work for the more capable?

The issue of task completion may well be quite complicated if you have differentiated the task in some way, but most situations will be covered by planning what is the minimum you will accept in order to achieve your objectives (this may vary from pupil to pupil within the class), and what extra will be expected from the most able. It is important to maintain a sustained effort from those inclined to be satisfied by the minimum (or less), and it is often helpful to set individuals or groups of pupils specific short-term targets, such as 'You've just got five minutes to finish section 3'. At the other end of the scale, enthusiastic and able pupils will often be able to devise their own extension work; indeed, it is quite normal for them to set themselves greater challenges than you have! In planning, consider the following.

- What is the minimum requirement?
- For extension work, should pupils produce more material or improve their existing work to meet more demanding criteria?
- Can pupils identify further needs/opportunities?

## How are you going to monitor the work?

For any classroom activity, teachers use two main criteria for observing and monitoring what pupils are doing. They aim first to maintain the 'normal desirable state' of pupils' activity, and second to ensure that progress is made with the task (Brown and McIntyre, 1993). Therefore you need to consider at all times what you expect pupils to be doing, whether it is sitting silently, listening to you; talking quietly in groups, or typing data individually at a keyboard. You also need to develop an expectation of how quickly each pupil should complete any task. You should develop a continual awareness of class activity, supplemented by systematic rotation around the class, checking on each pupil's efforts in detail. This enables you to intervene if the normal desirable state is broken or progress slows too much. In planning, then, consider the following.

- What do you expect pupils to be doing at each stage?
- How can you judge whether they are progressing as expected?
- How will you recognise when pupils need prompting or explanation?

## When will you intervene?

With a complex task or with a low-ability class, it is often wise to split up the task into stages, and only explain the next stage when a number of pupils have completed the current one. You will therefore plan particular points in the lesson when you will stop the class to review what they have done and explain the next stage. There may also be occasions when your monitoring indicates that an unforeseen difficulty has arisen, or that the general pace of progress is slow, and that an intervention is required (see Chapter 7). In planning, then, consider:

- planned points, in order to explain/demonstrate something which was not appropriate at the start, or to question pupils about what they are doing;
- unplanned points, when a number of pupils have the same problem: try to predict these difficulties;
- how to drive the pace forward, perhaps setting more specific targets.

## How will you conclude the work?

The end is as important as the beginning if the task is to be successful in achieving learning. Timing of conclusions is one of the greatest challenges for the novice teacher, and you should take careful account of advice from those who are more experienced. In planning, consider whether to end:

- when all pupils have achieved a product: this must not take too long, and you might set pupils a number of short-term targets during the activity;
- after a fixed time: pupils will want something to show for their efforts, and will need to know how long they have to do the work;
- evaluation with the whole class of the quality of products and the learning which has been achieved: this is usually valuable, and may be essential if the task outcomes are ephemeral (see Chapter 10).

---

**Task 9.1**  For your topic/class, think now about the tasks you want pupils to work on, using the prompts listed above. Again, discuss these with your mentor.

---

## What potential and structure do features of different ICT tools provide?

The framework for teaching based on the TAF model developed in Chapters 5 and 8 will be used to frame the discussion of how to select and produce effective tasks and resources. Whilst this book will focus on the role of ICT, the same principles can be applied to non-ICT aspects of preparation for teaching.

An effective learning task will involve bridging the gap between what learners can already handle confidently on their own and what you would like them to be able to do. This should require some cognitive effort on their part, but will also involve utilising the features of the setting to help them achieve the desired goal. These features, in combination with their own abilities provide both potential for action and structure for action. The teacher can manipulate the features of the setting in order to increase or decrease either the potential, the structure or both in order to ensure that the learners achieve the task goal. Sufficient gap must be left in order for learning to take place, and learning should be consolidated and conceptualised through reflection on the activity and the features involved in carrying it out.

For example, the task of writing a report on a science experiment or a historical event re-enacted on video may be aided by providing a portable PC or word processor for each pair of pupils; the provisionality of this medium increases the potential for action. For some pupils, the structure may be increased by providing a writing frame in a word processing or DTP format (see Chapter 3), whereas other pupils will be able to structure the task for themselves. The potential could be increased further by including images, such as photos or diagrams, in the prepared template for the report in order to prompt pupils to respond appropriately in each section. Using a multimedia program, sounds or even video clips could be included. It is important that the extra features are not provided indefinitely, however, or else ICT can become 'a crutch to avoid learning' rather than 'scaffolding to assist learning' (Tanner and Jones, 2000: 168). Pupils will come to rely on them rather than thinking for themselves, and cognitive effort will be insufficient to stimulate learning.

The next stage would be to provide the page structure and allow pupils to insert the images or other objects to illustrate their report, before removing the page structure once pupils have learned the process of reporting and can use their own abilities to provide sufficient potential and structure for the task.

Other ICT resources provide potential and structure in different ways, and Table 9.1 shows how a number of features listed in Chapter 3 can help with learning tasks.

**Table 9.1**  The potential and structure for action provided by different features of ICT

| Feature | Potential for action | Structure for action |
|---|---|---|
| Tabulation in WP or DTP | Identification of categories and qualitative relationships between them | Listing – optional provision of headings |
| Bulleted lists in presentation | Identifying factors | Listing – optional provision of headings |
| Formulas in spreadsheet | Identification of quantitative relationships between variables | Specification of relationships using standard notation and syntax |
| Queries in database program | Identifying items that meet particular criteria | Specification of conditions using standard notation and syntax |
| Reply option in e-mail program | Responding to communication | Addressee and subject already inserted |
| Bookmarks in web browser | Reaccessing useful information | Record of where to find useful information addressed by topic |
| Hypertext in web or presentation | Rapid access to information | Linking of related ideas |
| Notes in graphic organiser | Recording of more detailed thoughts about an idea | Notes kept with heading |
| Symbol libraries with interactive whiteboard | Rapid display of visual cues | Sets of images stored hierarchically by subject |

## How can features be adapted to suit the needs of learners?

In Example 1.3 in Chapter 1 (see p. 8), the teacher provided two different ways of accessing information from the WWW: through search engines and by providing

> **Task 9.2**    For the task you designed for the lesson in Task 8.5, identify how the
> ICT tools used provide potential and structure for pupils to act. If
> pupils are having difficulty, explain how you can either:
> 1 increase the potential, perhaps by providing additional help or resources;
> 2 increase the structure, perhaps by providing additional instructions or chang-
>   ing program settings in order to keep pupils on the right track.

bookmarks for specific websites that the teacher knew contained relevant information. This is a simple example of *differentiation*, defined as a process that involves:

- recognising the variety of individual needs within a class;
- planning to meet those needs;
- providing appropriate delivery;
- evaluating the effectiveness of the activities in order to maximise the achievements of individual pupils.

(Becta, 2003c)

This example could be refined further, with a range of different approaches tailored to particular pupils; for example:

- full search engine;
- child-friendly search engine, with prompts for search options and clear display of results indicating which are most relevant;
- CD-ROM search tool only, so that results are selected from material designed for the target level of ability;
- bookmarks for a range of known sites with some difficult content;
- bookmarks for a limited number of known sites with simple content.

This strategy for differentiation involves providing different resources as appropriate to pupils' abilities. In the next section, we will look at this strategy further, and suggest a number of others.

## Providing for a range of levels of ability in the same class

Ability is not a single attribute: prior knowledge and experience of subject matter, ICT, literacy, numeracy, other key skills, learning styles, learning strategies (see Chapter 6) all contribute to pupils' abilities to learn in a particular context. A general cognitive ability, traditionally known as 'intelligence', also seems to have considerable influence. Measurements such as cognitive ability test (CAT) scores have been found to give a general prediction of how effectively pupils are likely to learn, but this can be misleading in particular cases. You should try to build up a profile of each pupil's abilities and not base your expectations of what individuals can achieve either on the perceived ability of the class as a whole, or on a single measure of an individual's ability or attainment (more information about this will be provided in Chapter 10).

In order to cater for differing abilities, there are a number of well-established strategies that can be used. The suitability of each strategy will depend on the subject matter and the activities planned.

*Task*

Different tasks, or different versions of the same task, are set for different pupils in the class. The tasks can cover the same topic, but the less able may have more limited learning objectives or they may be expected to address them in a simpler way. This can be implemented with group work, too, using homogeneous ability groups.

*Response*

The same task is set for all pupils, but it can be completed successfully in many different ways. The most able pupils are encouraged to produce responses that are deeper, more complex, more detailed or wider-ranging than less able pupils.

*Support*

The same task is set and the same sort of response is expected from all pupils, but the most able are expected to manage their own learning to a large extent so that the teacher's time can be spent providing scaffolding for the less able. This strategy can also be implemented by using mixed ability groups, so that much of the support for the less able can be given by the more able – as long as the most able pupils do not do all the work.

*Resource*

A variation on differentiation by support, in which pupils' work on the task is less dependent on scaffolding from the teacher, and depends largely on whether they can work independently with the resources.

## The role of ICT in providing differentiation

These approaches can all take advantage of ICT, which has features that make it particularly valuable in tailoring support and resources to pupils' needs.

*Differentiation by task*

With the sort of project-based activity that ICT supports, it is normal for different pupils to be working on different aspects of the topic in their projects, and this feature can be used to set project briefs suitable for particular pupils or groups. In Example 1.1 in Chapter 1 (see p. 7), for instance, groups researched different aspects of the issue and the most able pupils were given editing roles in order to involve the whole class whilst ensuring that the key points were made clearly in the debate.

*Differentiation by response*

During an investigation, the interactivity of ICT allows able pupils to go beyond the basic learning objectives for the class, making and testing their own conjectures. In Example 1.4 in Chapter 1 (see p. 8), some pupils discovered and justified the properties required very quickly, and the teacher encouraged them to see what else they were able to find out about angle relationships. These pupils were thus able to carry out more authentic mathematical activity.

*Differentiation by support*
In Example 1.5 in Chapter 1 (see pp. 8–9), pupils were supported in their understanding of the differences between regions in Italy by the teacher asking probing questions in relation to video clips, and using the speed of ICT to switch instantly to alternative clips to emphasise and clarify pupils' responses when they showed a lack of understanding.

*Differentiation by resource*
ICT can aid the teacher in preparation of a range of related resources in the same time that a single resource could be produced using manual methods. In Example 1.2 in Chapter 1 (see p. 7), the printed information provided for pupils was available in different formats. The teacher had used the same basic information to create a range of publications that varied in the level of language used and the amount of text in relation to images. You can utilise the readability level analysis feature in some word processors (or use a separate program for this purpose) to check whether your language is at the appropriate level for your pupils.

   These forms of differentiation are not mutually exclusive, and experienced teachers will use a combination of approaches according to their judgement of pupils' needs.

---

**Task 9.3**   Identify what forms of differentiation might be appropriate for Example 1.3 in Chapter 1 (see p. 8).

Suggested answers are given in Appendix C.

---

## Special Educational Needs and inclusion

A child is defined as having special educational needs if he or she has a learning difficulty which needs special teaching. A learning difficulty means that the child has significantly greater difficulty in learning than most children of the same age. Or, it means a child has a disability which needs different educational facilities from those that schools generally provide for children of the same age in the area.

The children who need special educational provision are not only those with obvious learning difficulties, such as those who are physically disabled, deaf or blind. They include those whose learning difficulties are less apparent, such as slow learners and emotionally vulnerable children. It is estimated that up to 20 per cent of school children may need special educational help at some stage in their school careers.

(DfES, 2003)

The term *special educational needs* (SEN) thus covers a variety of types of pupil, with the common feature that they experience some disadvantage in learning in ways or at the pace designed for the majority of children of their age:

- general learning difficulties;
- specific learning difficulties (most commonly dyslexia);
- emotional and behavioural difficulties;
- physical impairment;
- sensory impairment (hearing, seeing);
- speech difficulties;
- medical conditions.

(DfES, 2001b)

It has increasingly been recognised that pupils with special needs can gain from being taught alongside mainstream learners, provided that extra support is given (DfES, 2001c). This is the main principle of 'inclusion'. ICT can provide support for learning in various ways for these pupils who need extra help to participate in standard curriculum activity. This is a further extension of the principles of differentiation, and mainly involves either changing the task or changing the tools available for the task so as to increase the potential and/or structure provided. Tailoring the task for particular learning needs may involve providing special software (such as an Integrated Learning System – see Chapter 3), changing settings on the usual software so as to slow the pace, clarify the screen or reduce the expectations, or providing the opportunity for more frequent repetition of skills to be learned.

Many tools have been designed to help to compensate for the impairment and enable pupils to function at a higher level than they would otherwise be able to attain. For example, a pupil with cerebral palsy who has difficulty with writing because of poor motor control can be provided with a computer that has a special keyboard and a trackball instead of a mouse. Whilst this can be quite slow in operation, the pupil's writing can be speeded up through predictive typing software, which enables them to choose from a selection of words as soon as they have typed one or two letters. Alternatively, prepared lists or grids of possible words and phrases can be displayed on the screen for the pupil to select from by clicking (Becta, 2003d). The quality of the result is much better than could be achieved without the aid and can transform not just the pupil's achievement, but also adults' perceptions of what the child can do and the child's self-esteem (NCET, 1994). Similarly, a visually impaired pupil can be provided with text-enlarging software, voice-recognition software to enter text and a voice output device through which all the printed material made available to class-mates can be read aloud. Such tools may be less obviously related to the impairment. For instance, dyslexic learners have been found to gain particular benefit from using mind-maps to record notes and ideas (McKeown, 2000), and graphic organiser software may also be particularly helpful to dyslexic pupils.

When planning assistance for SEN pupils, you need to be aware of each pupil's Individual Education Plan (IEP) in order to make decisions concerning how you will manipulate the features of the setting in order to provide appropriate potential and structure for action. Whenever you are using ICT, you particularly need to be aware of any pupils who may have special needs in relation to the use of the equipment itself (see the section on Health and safety in Chapter 11). Many SEN pupils will have help from a Learning Support Assistant (LSA), and you should take account of this factor when planning activities for the class. The LSA may be able to advise you about what the pupil can and cannot do, and will be able to help the pupil more effectively if they are made aware in advance of what you expect.

Whilst it is often easier for slow-learning pupils to engage with an ICT task than a written one, and there is often scope for a wide range of responses to the same task, you should plan carefully to ensure that your language and presentation of ideas is accessible to all in the class. Use simplified instructions and visual presentation where possible. Voice output is valuable for many pupils who may have difficulty reading fluently the material you give them or which they find on the screen.

Also, consider where you can give options for extra challenge for the most able learners – gifted and talented – for good problem solvers, just a suggestion for an outcome will suffice and they will be able to plan how to achieve it for themselves; for the most creative pupils, there will be no need to specify an outcome, as they will generate excellent ideas of their own!

## Social inclusion

Many pupils from socially disadvantaged backgrounds are failing to participate fully in schooling. They find it hard to overcome difficulties in meeting the normal expectations of progress and, in the absence of adequate parental support, some become persistent truants or troublemakers. This disadvantage can be compounded by the lack of effective ICT support in their homes (Becta, 2001). Furthermore, when schools provide opportunities for extra access to ICT at lunchtimes and after school, the resources tend to be used by the same pupils who are already frequent users of ICT (Kennewell *et al.*, 2000). When given sufficient access, however, pupils who are disadvantaged socially and intellectually can be highly motivated by ICT (Cox, 1999; Franklin, 2001) and use it as a means of catching up on some of the learning that they have missed.

Other pupils miss school because of exclusion, long-term illness or school refusal. ICT can enable them to carry out much of the same work as their peers in school, using communications links to the school or through resources being made available on a laptop (Franklin, 2001).

| Task 9.4 | Consider whether your activities provide for the full range of needs within the class, including the most able. Identify, too, any particular |
|---|---|

pupils who may need extra support in achieving the basic objectives for the lesson or in accessing the ICT resources effectively. Discuss with your mentor, and SEN staff where appropriate, how you can provide:
- differentiated tasks and guidance for the range of abilities in the class;
- extra support for SEN pupils.

## When is it appropriate to use existing resources?

You need to keep a balance between taking advantage of good resources that have been purchased or developed within your school, and developing resources of your own that fill gaps in the school's provision or are more precisely tailored to your own teaching style.

When considering the resources available for teaching a particular unit of work, the advice of experienced teachers will be invaluable in helping to apply the principles you have learned from college tutors and books. Existing resources within the school are likely to have been selected to match the school's schemes of work and policies.

You should also seek resources such as lesson plans and pupil materials from the WWW. There are a range of sources in the UK, USA and other countries of resources which are freely downloadable for use in educational institutions (see Chapter 11 for suggestions). Many of these have no educational quality assurance associated with them other than a cursory check for contents inappropriate for children, however, and you will need to think carefully about whether they are suitable for your particular scheme of work and pupils. This is particularly essential in the case of materials from another country, where the curriculum specifications and expectations of achievement at particular ages may be quite different. You also need to check whether you are entitled to use the material – even if it is only a single image – in a document or file for distribution to pupils, as this may contravene copyright restrictions. If you do use someone else's material, even in adapted form, with permission, you should acknowledge the source. As well as being morally correct, it sets a good example for pupils.

## When should you develop new resources?

When discussing whether to design your own resources, you may be advised not to re-invent the wheel; but if there is a wheel missing, or if the wheel provided is the wrong size or shape, it may be better to construct a new one or at least adjust the one you have. Experienced teachers may not be up-to-date on the features that ICT provides, and commercial developers of educational materials may not cater for local needs or new teaching styles. Besides, you will learn more about good resource design by doing it yourself, particularly if you carry out some small-scale action research into the process (see Chapter 12).

Most schools value the fresh thinking that a student teacher can bring to teaching. However, experienced teachers and college tutors will be able to offer helpful advice based on their experience of teaching in general, even if they have not carried out the particular activity that you are planning.

### Documents

Chapter 7 considered some of the advantages and disadvantages of step-by-step handouts for pupils, and the same applies to other documents to some extent. It is therefore important to consider how pupils will use the document, and discuss this with them before they start – perhaps even before you give it out to them, so that they are not distracted by the content when you want them to think about the process.

When producing a printed document, do not try to cram too much onto a page. The alternative is not to produce several pages – photocopying budgets will probably prevent this anyway – but to cut down the detail and just make the key points clear, using images to clarify the ideas and white space to make it easier for pupils to pick out what they need. Use straightforward sentences and simple language; whilst you will need to use some specialist terminology because that is what you are teaching the pupils about, you should avoid using sophisticated terms for other aspects of what you want to say.

If you want to provide more extensive information and guidance for pupils' work, then it is sensible to use ICT and make it available through the school's network if possible. This enables you to provide several short documents for pupils to choose if they think that they will help. You could even put large amounts of detail into a single document, as long as you use hypertext rather than a linear structure (see Designing interactive learning materials below).

## Wall displays

There are two main purposes for wall displays:

- to provide information and ideas about your subject in an attractive way to help motivate and support pupils' activity;
- to show good examples of pupils' work as models for other learners and to build up the self-esteem of the pupils whose work is displayed.

The first of these is particularly valuable in an ICT classroom, as pupils who are focusing on the screen may find it easier to look up to a large display on the wall rather than trying to read a printed sheet. The second is aided by ICT, as pupils who find it difficult to present their work successfully using manual methods can produce effectively presented material with ICT.

## Artefacts

Although learning with ICT involves a lot of visual information and physical interaction through the mouse, keyboard and other devices, it will often need to be supplemented by examples of real artefacts and models of large or abstract objects, which can be seen in detail and directly handled.

## Designing interactive learning materials

As well as using existing ICT learning resources and producing printed/display materials, you should try to experiment with producing your own interactive materials. If you design and produce something yourself using generic ICT tools such as spreadsheets or web-editing tools, you will be able to adapt it for different pupils, and for other classes, and you can improve it each time you discover more about pupils' learning of the topic or about the features of the software.

Some of the purposes for which you might develop material include:

- providing information;
- explaining;
- checking understanding;
- problem posing;
- stimulating discussion.

A number of different types of software allow you to exploit ICT's feature of interactivity (see Chapter 2) so as to provide advantages over other ways of achieving these purposes. The tools you choose for this purpose should be used thoughtfully to create material for pupils that provides features which cannot easily be obtained with paper-based materials:

- choice;
- decision structure;
- contingent feedback;
- easily shared by a small group;
- links to other activities.

Suitable software includes:

- **programming languages** such as Visual Basic or C++: this is the most powerful and flexible option, but requires some serious study to learn and makes implementation hard work;
- **computer-aided learning (CAL) author tools**: these are easier to use than a general programming language, with many specific features designed to support interaction with learners, but not widely available in schools;
- **spreadsheets**: these are effective for situations such as simulations where you need formulas and graphs;
- **animation software**: this is effective for showing sequences of events visually and dynamically;
- **web editor** or **multimedia presentation** tools: these are the best compromise for teachers who have limited time to develop skills and plan sophisticated designs for interaction. They should ideally have the following features: text, images, tables, hyperlinks, frames, sound, video, animation and the ability to link in objects such as graphs created with other programs. It should be easy to incorporate images, sounds and video, and provide interactivity through the use of hyperlinks to enable the learner to make choices and give feedback.

| Task 9.5 | Produce a simple set of material for teaching a topic in your subject using one of the resources listed above. |

## Evaluating ICT resources

You may initially have little choice concerning the resources that you use for teaching a particular topic/class. As you gain more experience, however, it is important to consider in advance how effective the resources are likely to be, in order to avoid wasting time, effort and money. Time spent now reflecting on the value of the resources used for your teaching of this class/topic will be well spent.

The resources used in the classroom are just one factor of the three main influences on learning:

- the pupils;
- the teacher;
- the resources.

(Squires and McDougall, 1994)

You will therefore need to consider three sets of interactions when evaluating software and other resources:

1  resources–teacher;
2  teacher–pupil;
3  pupil–resources.

There are a number of issues to be considered for each of these sets of interactions in order to decide whether the resources will be effective. Your decision will depend on the learning objectives, on your particular teaching style, and on the particular set of pupils. Resources that are ideal in one situation may be inappropriate in another.

### Resources–teacher

- Did the content match your learning objectives?
- What teaching role were the resources designed to have:
  - demonstration;
  - providing information;
  - explanation;
  - responding to pupils' questions;
  - prompting;
  - responding to pupils' ideas;
  - questioning;
  - responding to pupils' answers;
  - assessing attainment?
- Were you able to configure the software to provide potential and structure for activity by pupils with differing ability levels?
- For each aspect, did the resources use the same approach that you might use without these resources? If so, did they add any features to what you could provide personally, or provide potential and structure to more pupils than you could deal with yourself?

- If not, did they complement your approach, or might they have confused pupils?
- Could you obtain records of pupils' work?

## Teacher–pupil

- What roles did you assume when pupils were using the resources:
  - o leader of the class, providing instructions, discussing key teaching points at planned stages of progress, and reviewing the learning at the end;
  - o coach to individuals and small groups, monitoring activity closely and intervening to help improve performance;
  - o troubleshooter, responding to problems which arise?
- Was there scope for pupils to help each other?
- You need to consider how your contribution to pupils' learning can be maximised through the use of the ICT resources, through other resources which you might provide, and through pupils sharing ideas.

## Pupil–resources

- Did the software function reliably?
- Could pupils easily see how to operate the software? Could they work independently with it?
- Did they understand the instructions for entering responses and the feedback they gained?
- Did they understand the factual and conceptual content?
- Did the pupils see a purpose for the activity, other than just 'doing ICT'?
- Was there a gap between what the pupils know already and what is expected of them in the activity?
- Did the resources help them to bridge this gap?
- Are they suitable for pair work, where pupils can discuss ideas together?
- Did they provide differentiated support for pupils with different learning needs?
- Is the structure and layout of the material effective in enabling the pupils to carry out the activity?
- Did the resources provide opportunities for pupils to try out what they have learned in different contexts?
- Could you set homework based on the resources?

If you are considering using a particular CD-ROM or other multimedia resource, you should consult the website run by the Teachers Evaluating Educational Multimedia (TEEM) project. This contains reviews of a large number of resources, carried out by teachers who have been trained in evaluation methods. You will also be able to find reviews of commercial resources in the educational press, including general magazines such as the *Times Educational Supplement*, and specific ICT journals such as *Interactive* and *Educational Computing and Technology*.

> **Task 9.6** In addition to your normal lesson evaluation, carry out an evaluation of the ICT resources in relation to the class and topic, using the prompts above. Would you use these resources again? What changes would you make to them, if possible?

## Further reading

Abbott, C. (2001) Special educational needs – becoming more inclusive, in Dillon, J. and McGuire, M. (eds) *Becoming a teacher: issues in secondary teaching* (2nd edition), Buckingham: Open University Press

Blamires, M. (ed.) (1999) *Enabling technology for inclusion*, London: Paul Chapman Publishing

Bourne, R., Davitt, J. and Wight, J. (1995) *Differentiation: taking IT forward*, Coventry: NCET

Franklin, G. and Litchfield, D. (1999) Special Educational Needs and ICT in Leask, M. and Pachler, N. (eds) *Learning to teach using ICT in the secondary school*, London: Routledge

Harrison, C. (2001) Differentiation in theory and practice, in Dillon, J. and McGuire, M. (eds) *Becoming a teacher: issues in secondary teaching* (2nd edition), Buckingham: Open University Press

McKeown, S. (2000) *Dyslexia and ICT: building on success*, Coventry: Becta

Peacey, N. (2001) An introduction to inclusion and special educational needs, in Capel, S., Leask, M. and Turner, T. (eds) *Learning to teach in the secondary school: a companion to school experience* (3rd edition), London: RoutledgeFalmer

Squires, D. and McDougall, A. (1994) *Choosing and using educational software*, London: Falmer Press

TEEM website: www.teem.org.uk

Turner, T. (2001) Pupil grouping, progression and differentiation, in Capel, S., Leask, M. and Turner, T. (eds) *Learning to teach in the secondary school: a companion to school experience* (3rd edition), London: RoutledgeFalmer

Assess
imp

# 10  Impact of ICT on Assessment

This chapter reviews assessment approaches in general and explains how ICT can help in assessment. It explores new approaches to assessment made possible by ICT, and considers the change in what is being assessed when pupils use ICT. It explains peer and self-assessment with ICT, and how this can assist learners in managing their learning. The chapter also explores the use of ICT in evaluating teaching, in producing evidence of improvements in learning, in record keeping and in reporting on pupils' progress. It also explains the legal and ethical issues involved in the gathering, recording and communication of personal data.

## How is assessment affected by ICT?

In general, there are three main purposes for assessment.

- Assessment of attainment is critical to knowing whether or not your pupils are achieving similar standards to those achieved in equivalent institutions.
- Assessment of progress is necessary if you are to judge whether or not you have succeeded in your teaching efforts.
- Assessment of pupils' performance is also necessary if they are to become effective learners.

(Stanley and Tanner, 2003)

The first of these purposes is important for the school as a community and for other stakeholders who are interested in the results of assessment such as parents, governors, employers, LEAs and governments. The second one is important for you as a teacher, both for your own satisfaction and to satisfy those to whom you are accountable: your tutors and mentors if you are a student teacher, and your Head of Department and Head teacher if you are a qualified teacher. The last of these purposes is ultimately the most important, however: pupils need to know if their work is meeting your expecta-tions and what they need to do to improve. Furthermore, if your pupils are to become independent learners, taking responsibility for their own progress, they need effective feedback to help them to set targets for themselves.

Assessment should be an integral part of teaching and learning. It should be a key element of your planning and must not be left as an afterthought, as something to be bolted-on at the end. Effective assessment is a critical feature of good learning environ-ments and implementing the best practices in assessment can result in significant gains in pupils' attainment (Stanley and Tanner, 2003).

Assessment practices can be divided into two broad categories: summative and formative. *Summative* assessments attempt to represent pupils' knowledge, skills and understanding over a broad domain at a particular point in time. Typical examples are end-of-year tests, or end of Key Stage examinations. These can be useful in making broad comparisons of performance between individual pupils within a year and course results year-on-year, but they aggregate too many quite different facets of attainment to provide pupils or teachers with information concerning how they might improve attainment.

In any case, it is difficult to evaluate the influence of ICT when learning is assessed using conventional forms of summative assessment. Indeed, it is helpful to distinguish two modes of ICT use in learning.

- Pupils learn *from* or *through* ICT – the use of ICT in studying a particular topic helps pupils to learn something that they can then *apply in a non-ICT situation*. For example, using a spreadsheet to calculate and graph population growth and economic performance in various countries may enable pupils to remember differences between developed and third world countries, which they can later write about in response to an examination question. Using a CD-ROM database may help pupils to understand the main causes, particip-ants, events and outcomes of the First World War, which they can then use to write a traditional essay.
- Pupils learn *with* ICT – they construct reports, diagrams, models and presenta-tions. As a result, they may know aspects of the subject in a way that *depends* on the use of ICT. For example, they know how to set up a model of population growth using a spreadsheet but would not be able to carry out all the calculations involved for themselves. Pupils can locate dates, locations, descriptions, documents, etc. relevant to the First World War from ICT reference sources when they need to write a report on a particular aspect, but they do not necessarily remember these details themselves.

The latter mode of use should have long-term benefits in a world where ICT use is the norm, but would not be expected to have a direct influence on performance in written tests and examinations. This may go some way to explaining the limited overall impact that ICT has had so far on standard measures of attainment, despite a widespread view by teachers that ICT is having a beneficial effect on learning (Becta, 2002a; 2002b).

*Formative* assessment, on the other hand, involves more detailed and qualitative evaluation of learners' ability and progress, and is of greater significance for day-to-day teaching and learning. An increased emphasis on formative assessment is most likely to result in improved standards of achievement. Formative assessment is assessment *for* learning as opposed to summative assessment which is assessment *of* learning. Formative assessment must happen continuously for teaching to be effective. In order to maximise learning and ensure that pupils make progress, it is necessary to provide feedback during the learning process and discuss how work could be improved (Stanley and Tanner, 2003).

Central to assessment for learning are the assumptions that it:

- is embedded in the teaching and learning process of which it is an essential part;
- shares learning goals with pupils;
- helps pupils to know and to recognise the standards to aim for;
- provides feedback, which leads pupils to identify what they should do next to improve;
- has a commitment that every pupil can improve;
- involves both teacher and pupils reviewing and reflecting on pupils' performance and progress;
- involves pupils in self-assessment.

(QCA, 2003a)

Black and Wiliam (2001) have identified some key messages concerning how to improve formative assessment:

- feedback to a pupil should be specific to their work, with advice on how to improve, avoiding comparison with other pupils;
- pupils should be trained in self-assessment, so that they can understand the purpose of their learning and what they need to do to achieve;
- teaching should provide opportunities for pupils to express their understanding, so that an interaction between teacher and pupil can take place that aids learning;
- the interaction should be thoughtful, reflective and focused on exploring understanding so that all pupils can consider and express their ideas;
- exercises must be clear and relevant to learning objectives, and feedback concerning how to improve must be followed by opportunities and support to work at improving.

The features of ICT can be helpful in various ways. The clarity of the display of pupils' work makes it easier for pupils to express their understanding and for teachers to evaluate the ideas expressed. The variety of media available – words, diagrams, images, sound and video – provide potential for alternative ways of expressing understanding and thus facilitate better feedback from the teacher. The provisionality of work provides the potential for improvement following feedback. The interactivity of

ICT often provides feedback either directly (by checking the pupils' input against the correct response to a question) or indirectly (in that the pupil realises that their response is not achieving the desired outcome). This feedback can be continual during a task, providing the structure that a pupil needs to help improve their work. If the pupil's attention is drawn to the way they are using the indirect feedback, their skills in self-assessment can be developed, ready for application in situations where they are not gaining the feedback that ICT provides.

Analysis of a range of studies concerning the effects of formative assessment has shown impressive impact on attainment, and highlighted particular value for low-attaining pupils (Black and Wiliam, 1998). It can help to break the negative loop experienced by such pupils:

> Pupils who encounter difficulties and poor results are led to believe they
> lack ability, and this belief leads them to attribute their difficulties to a
> defect in themselves about which they cannot do a great deal. So they
> 'retire hurt', avoiding investing effort in learning which could only
> result in disappointment, and try to build up esteem in other ways.
>
> (Black and Wiliam, 1998: 9)

The LEARN project found that low achieving pupils also:

- tended to be concerned with performance rather than understanding;
- had little understanding of how tasks contributed to the course as a whole;
- relied heavily on the teacher to set standards for the quality of work;
- sometimes felt that effort was not recognised;
- preferred immediate, oral feedback which was constructively critical.

(CLIO, 2000)

The use of ICT by low-achieving pupils can help to overcome problems of self-esteem, in that it is often easier for them to produce work that meets their criteria for success and gains recognition from the teacher. It can help them to shift their focus to understanding, by making it easier to express ideas rather than follow prescribed steps. It helps the teacher to be constructive by eliminating some of the minor difficulties such as poor handwriting or simple errors in calculation or spelling, which often form a barrier to seeing positive features in their work and clues concerning their developing concepts.

Assessment of progress needs comparison of current and previous attainment, and record keeping is of vital importance. Whilst much of your assessment will be ephemeral (Stanley and Tanner, 2003), unless you keep track in some way of the attainment (or lack of it) that you identify, learners' needs may go unrecognised. Furthermore, you may judge pupils on your impressions of their work and effort, rather than their actual attainment. The role that ICT plays in keeping and using records will be considered later in the chapter.

Assessment should not only inform learners; teachers, too, should seek to improve their work and information gained from assessing pupils' learning will be valuable in planning the teaching of those pupils in future, and in planning the teaching of the topic to other groups. If you are experimenting with the use of ICT, it is particularly important to consider how it is affecting pupils' learning compared with other methods.

## How can you assess pupils' attainment when ICT is used?

You may find it helpful to break down your learning objectives into categories. One popular general classification is *SACK*: skills, attitudes, concepts and knowledge (Stanley and Tanner, 2003). This combines the three main aspects of pupils' learning (knowing what, knowing how and knowing why) with an evaluation of their approach to learning, which is an important indication of their future progress. You may often need to simplify this further for school reporting purposes, making judgements under the headings *Attainment* and *Effort*. Note, however, that neither of these is represented by mere task completion, which may have been achieved with considerable help from various sources, including ICT. You will need to be clear about your learning objectives, and look more deeply into both the outcome produced, and the process through which it was produced, in order to make a useful assessment of learning achieved during a task.

When ICT is involved, there are particular issues to be considered. Pupils complete tasks using a combination of ICT's features and their own ICT capability, as well as their subject abilities, other key skills and support from the teacher and other pupils. Do you intend to assess what pupils can do with ICT, or what knowledge they can apply in a non-ICT situation? The use of ICT provides assistance with tasks, and this may need to be withdrawn in order to find out what pupils can do independently.

You should also consider whether there is a need to change what you assess. For instance, instead of merely assessing spelling itself, you will now need to assess pupils' skills in using a spellchecker as well. Instead of checking a piece of work merely for accuracy of content, you will need to assess the range and appropriateness of sources, the organisation and presentation of material, and the process of referencing sources. Instead of assessing the accuracy of a graph, you will need to ask pupils to interpret it in relation to the original data or use it for comparison with other data. In all of these cases, your assessment will shift towards higher-order skills and understanding. These aspects are traditionally the most difficult types of ability to assess, and the support for probing these aspects of attainment will be an important gain from the use of ICT.

The TAF framework for teaching can be used to aid the process of assessing subject learning rather than ICT capability when they are both involved in an activity. It indicates the importance of identifying pupils' abilities – in the subject, in ICT and in other key skills – in order to provide appropriate support, both directly and through the resources. When assessing subject learning, it is important to consider pupils' ICT capability as providing potential and structure for action. Thus, a pupil with high ICT capability may be able to achieve the task outcome more quickly and/or with higher quality than a pupil with lower ICT capability, without any greater ability in the subject matter. The ICT capability of pupils must therefore be taken into account in the same way that direct help from the teacher or peers would be in making an assessment of subject learning. This is also true if you are using peer- or self-assessment, and it is even more difficult for pupils to separate out ICT capability from subject knowledge, so it is important to discuss with pupils how both subject knowledge and ICT are used in achieving the task outcome. As suggested in Chapter 9, you will *need* to make the assessment criteria explicit, and to show examples of good work.

It is important to employ questioning effectively in order to judge how the class is progressing and how best to support individual learners. These are some common strategies, and you no doubt use others in your particular subject context:

- whole-class questioning;
- individual questioning;
- written responses to questions – if in electronic format, these can be e-mailed to you, assessed on screen and e-mailed back with comments attached;
- reports written by individuals or groups;
- creative writing, drawings or made artefacts;
- end-of-topic tests.

Your questioning needs also to be thought out in advance, who you are going to ask as well as what you are asking and how you will probe those answers. Asking mostly closed questions with just simple 'yes' or 'no' type answers will not stretch learners. More open questioning demanding higher order responses such as 'What advantages can you see in that approach?' or 'How do you think data capture ought to be organised?' will generate additional higher order thinking. You can ask other class members to add to or clarify an answer: 'Can you add anything to that?' or 'Can you explain that in more detail for us?' Try to ensure that you distribute your questioning fairly throughout the class.

Such questioning can be a valuable form of formative assessment, and it will undoubtedly inform your teaching, but you are unlikely to be able to record individual responses or attainment. However, you may occasionally note an unusually perceptive comment.

Assessment is a difficult issue in any teaching situation, and you need to look for a variety of evidence concerning pupils' attainment. The nature of the evidence will depend on the learning objectives involved and the practical constraints of the situation. When pupils are working cooperatively in a group, it will not usually be clear from the task outcome what each individual has contributed. Either oral questioning of individuals or a requirement to write an individual report is important to identifying what each has learned, as well as helping them to reflect.

The use of ICT is likely to make pupils more independent of the teacher, and it will be more difficult for you to evaluate the ways in which they are approaching a task. ICT also provides features such as spellcheckers and graph plotters that can help with successful task completion without requiring learners to know the same things as they did in the past (Pachler and Byrom, 1999). These factors can make assessment more of a challenge.

> **Task 10.1**    For your chosen class/topic, identify how you can assess the extent to which pupils have achieved the learning objectives for the lesson/ topic. Take into account the suggestions in this chapter, and discuss the matter with your mentor.

## How can ICT be used to improve assessment for learning?

If ICT appears to create an extra problem in assessing learning accurately, then it is worth considering the other side of the coin: how can ICT be used to help? The assessment process can be considered as a cycle of activity, as illustrated in Figure 10.1.

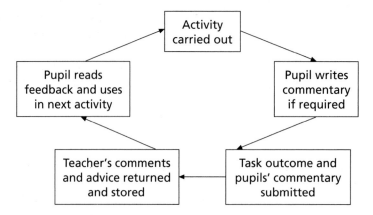

**Figure 10.1**  Cycle of assessment for learning

ICT can contribute at various stages in this cycle.

### Providing evidence for attainment

There are several types of evidence that ICT can help to produce and display, such as oral presentations, posters, concept maps, spreadsheet models, musical performance. Some evidence produced in the classroom is ephemeral, and ICT can help record and retrieve images of performances or teacher comments made on observing the evidence (for instance they could be recorded on digital audio, uploaded to a PC and voice recognition software applied). ICT facilitates the compilation and storage of a portfolio of samples or images of work. Another important aspect is the transfer of assessment information from one school to another, so that when pupils move to a new school, they are not seen as unknown quantities who must be assumed to know nothing. This issue has been identified as a particular problem for the transition from primary to secondary schools, where the 'clean slate' approach (Schagen and Kerr, 1999: 60) can lead to inadequate progress for many pupils during KS3.

## Facilitating feedback to learners

Pupils value comments rather than grades, and use them to improve their future study (Black and Wiliam, 1998). If these comments can be provided in electronic form, they are more easily communicated, stored and referred to in future by pupils. It is important, too, that there is seen to be a consequence of formative assessment (Haydn, 2001); specific, time-related targets set for pupils can more effectively be followed up by teachers if they have a computer-based record of their assessments, feedback and targets.

## Involvement of learners in the assessment process

If pupils themselves can contribute to assessment and record keeping, then not only does pupil learning benefit, but the teacher will find the administrative workload easier to manage and be able to give more attention to learning. Figure 10.2 shows an example of pupil self-assessment where an attempt has been made to capture evidence of the process as well as the final product.

With ICT, it is easier for pupils to manage a system where the teacher sets them personal targets, pupils make self-assessments against these targets, and the teacher comments on the pupils' assessments.

## Automating the assessment process

As well as helping teachers and pupils to keep records and to facilitate communication between teachers and pupils about attainment, ICT can also help by partially automating the assessment process. You can attempt to automate judgements, feedback and reporting. In order to automate judgements, the software must match a student action against predefined criteria. This usually means offering the learner a set of alternative answers to a specific question (a 'multi-choice' question), so that it is easy to specify which response is correct and what action should be taken by the software in the case of incorrect responses. This is the basis of most commercial programs that carry out assessment, and of authoring systems (see the Direct teaching section of Chapter 3, p. 51) which enable teachers to create their own quizzes and other assessment tasks. Some commercial systems are more sophisticated, however, but their content is fixed and the assessment rules complex and specific to the material and so it is not possible for the teacher to tailor them for specific purposes. Most of these programs provide feedback directly to the learner, which can be valuable in motivating and in helping pupils to manage their learning. They may additionally provide a summary report for the teacher, and some diagnostic packages, particularly in the case of learning difficulties, only provide reports for the teacher through a password system.

## Record keeping and analysis

Our three purposes for assessment, listed at the start of the section *How is assessment affected by ICT*, are assessment of attainment, progress and performance. *APP*

# PowerPoint Assessment

**Name :** ███████████_____        **Form:** ████████

| TASK | REQUIREMENTS | COMPLETED | COMMENTS |
|------|-------------|-----------|----------|
| 1 | Choose an appropriate layout for each slide | 18/1/01 | I think that I have got a good layout |
| 2 | Enter text - colour | 18/1/01 | I went all my text black |
|   | - fill | 18/1/01 | I fill the background with black and green. |
| 3 | Enter graphics – clipart, charts | 18/1/01 | I have put clipart in |
| 4 | Slide transition - effects | 18/1/01 | I have transition on my slide |
| 5 | Custom animation - effects | 18/1/01 | I have yous animation on my slid sos |
| 6 | Input, output, storage devices | 1/2/01 | I have got on input put storge it is good |
| 7 | Structure | 1/2/01 | I have change the our of the structure |

**Pupil Comment** I think that I have made a good power point and I think it is very good and also have good graphics.

**Peer Comment** I think that Andy's shoe show is good. he has chousen alot of brotons in put and out put Devises ficturs for it he has chousen merey of sounds

**Teacher Comment**
This is a good attempt Andrew You have used animation and transition to create interesting effects. Perhaps you could think about using the same format for the text and make sure you spell check.

**Figure 10.2**   Example of pupil self-assessment (from Kennewell, S., Parkinson, J. and Tanner, H. (eds) (2003) *Learning to teach ICT in the secondary school*, London: RoutledgeFalmer)

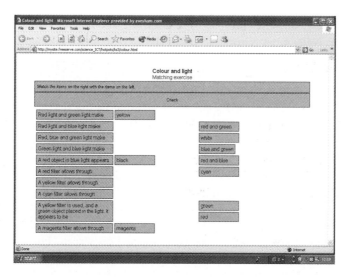

**Figure 10.3**  A matching exercise created using the Hot Potatoes system (see Chapter 3) (*Source*: Kathryn Williams, King Elizabeth VII and Queen Mary School http://www.thesciencelab.co.uk/physics/middle/light/colour.htm)

So far you have only considered attainment; in order to judge progress, you will need to compare current attainment with previous attainment. This will mean some sort of record of attainment is to be kept. For this purpose the features of capacity, speed, automation and accuracy provide considerable support for record keeping activity. Indeed, the capacity can make it tempting to record excessive information. It is important only to keep records for a particular purpose, not just for the sake of it. The main purpose is to analyse progress towards targets for attainment and provide feedback for learners; ICT can help with comparison where automatic functions in a spreadsheet, for instance, can be used to analyse the difference (using statistics or graphs) between a learner's current and past attainment, between different subjects, and between pupils.

Where progress is not being made, then you need to investigate the reasons for this more closely. The diagnostic aspect of formative assessment now comes into play, as you try to determine what precisely a learner is having difficulty with in order to help them to overcome this problem. How can ICT help with this? In general, pupils' activity with ICT is more visible because of the screen display, and misconceptions are easier to spot from their work. Furthermore, it makes it easier to talk to pupils about their work, which is also a valuable aid in identifying difficulties.

Diagnosis of difficulties is one of the most effective uses of ILS (see Chapter 3), as detailed reports of attainment by each pupil are provided for the teacher, who can then examine these to see whether the pupil's attainment in one or more particular aspects of their profile of knowledge, skills and understanding is:

- lower than in other aspects of their current profile;
- lower than that of other pupils;
- failing to improve.

Indeed, it has been suggested that teachers' learning about pupils' specific errors and misconceptions is the most valuable effect of ILS in practice (Underwood and Brown, 1997).

There are many more specific tests of literacy, numeracy and other cognitive skills, including those for diagnosing dyslexia (NCET, 1995; Keates, 2000). These are mainly used by SEN staff who have had appropriate training in the use of the tests and the remediation of learning difficulties.

Judging performance, on the other hand, involves careful observation of the way in which learners are working. A simple rating of effort does not indicate to pupils what they should do in order to improve their approach to learning, and a richer description of their approach to activity is required. Is a pupil able to follow instructions and repeat simple procedures? Do they ask questions, check their work, seek to improve, and look beyond the information given? When pupils are using ICT, these aspects may also be more visible because the work appears on screen, but again there is a danger of confusing effective learning with ICT capability, in that the pupil may be adept at manipulating information and presenting it effectively, without engaging in any thinking *about* the information or attempting to relate it to other knowledge. ICT may have caused this dilemma, but it can also help to provide the solution. For example, pupils can be asked to keep notes of how they learn, as well as what they are learning, and include this in any presentations they might give. This can help to identify what individuals have learned from group activity.

## How else can ICT help with evaluation in school?

As well as aiding record keeping, ICT can also help with reporting. This involves interpreting records of pupils' learning and performance for another audience. The value of involving pupils in the assessment process and providing targeted feedback has already been highlighted, and the reporting process usually involves re-interpreting this information for parents. Parents will require something fairly brief, and less specific to the precise topics than the feedback that pupils need. The provisionality of ICT means that information can be revised easily, so if you already have a report for a pupil, it can be adapted for the parents.

Where records are in numeric or coded form, you will need to generate text in order to interpret the results for parents. ICT is commonly used to store 'comment banks', so that the teacher merely clicks an option on screen to add a particular standard phrase or sentence to the report (see NCET, 1995). This takes advantage of the speed and automation of ICT. But ICT can also help with the collation of pupils' work itself in multimedia format on the school network, so that it can be made available to parents and others with an interest in a pupil's achievements, such as potential employers.

The role of ICT in helping to identify and analyse improvement in attainment for particular pupils has been noted. It also has value for teachers in helping to provide evidence that their classes are learning effectively (see Chapter 11) and for schools in demonstrating improvements by enabling them and their local authorities to analyse changes in pupils' performance and comparing them with other schools in a more sophisticated way than simple tables of examination results. ICT enables schools to calculate 'value added' performance: they can compare actual examination results at age 16, for instance, with the results predicted statistically by measurements of pupils' potential at age 11 (Yellis Project, 2003).

## What do you need to consider when keeping records?

This chapter has pointed out the need to ensure that assessment records are appropriate for their purpose; this is not just good practice, it is a legal requirement which will be considered further in the next chapter. You must ensure too that the records are accurate, that they are stored securely so that unauthorised access is prevented as far as possible, and that you do not reveal pupils' records to people who are not entitled to the information. And, of course, you do not want to lose the records yourself, so make sure that you have a good backup system for your files.

## Further reading

Fairbrother, B. and Harrison, C. (2001) Assessing pupils, in Dillon, J. and McGuire, M. (eds) *Becoming a teacher: issues in secondary teaching* (2nd edition), Buckingham: Open University Press

Haydn, T. (2001) Assessment and accountability, in Capel, S., Leask, M. and Turner, T. (eds) *Learning to teach in the secondary school: a companion to school experience* (3rd edition), London: RoutledgeFalmer

NCET (1995) *Using IT for assessment*, Coventry: NCET

Pachler, N. and Byrom, K. (1999) Assessment of and through ICT, in Leask, M. and Pachler, N. (eds) (1999) *Learning to teach using ICT in the secondary school*, London: Routledge

# 11 Other Professional Applications of ICT

This chapter explains how to use ICT in other aspects of teachers' professional work:

- producing, locating and evaluating lesson plans and teaching materials;
- seeking and accessing professional advice and research results;
- joining teacher networks and contributing ideas and reflections.

The use of ICT to support professional development is explored, and ideas provided concerning continuing professional development. Finally, issues concerning health and safety, and ethical and legal matters are explained.

## What other aspects of teachers' professional work can be aided by ICT?

You have developed an approach to planning, implementing and evaluating the use of ICT in teaching and learning, within the classroom and beyond. To gain full benefit from the potential of ICT, however, you should try to exploit its features in every aspect of your professional work. There may be times, as you are learning to use ICT effectively, when it seems more trouble than to use manual methods, but if you use particular hardware and software regularly, the common techniques become routine and your professional efficiency improves. The potential increase in performance and reduction in workload makes ICT as essential for teachers as it is for most other professions.

There are a number of ways in which this can be achieved, and this section presents some ideas for the tasks that may be assisted by ICT and for how the features of each type of ICT may support these tasks. These lists are not intended to exhaust the possibilities, however, and you should continually look for new opportunities to use ICT more effectively. The next chapter looks forward to new technologies which will no doubt open up more potential for the use of ICT.

For each aspect, suggestions for locating more information on the WWW will be provided. This will be in the form of useful search terms, rather than a list of websites, because web addresses (URLs) become out-of-date and it is often easier to use a search engine than type in a URL. Meanings are given in brackets where necessary; they do not have to be typed in as keywords. Where *subject* is shown, replace this with the name of your subject. In the case of general sites such as Teachernet, you may need to do a search within that site on the relevant keywords. Once you have found a useful website, you should 'bookmark' it. Be careful to organise your bookmarks into folders from the outset in the same way as you do with files.

## Lesson planning

Lesson plans serve three purposes: first, to ensure that you have thought through all aspects of teaching and learning prior to teaching a lesson; second, to serve as an aide-mémoire while you are teaching and for subsequent evaluation, and third, so that others (mentor, tutor, head of department, inspector) can see what you are planning and how you intend to go about it. ICT helps with all of these, by providing a structure in the template used for the plan (see Appendix E for an example), and through the quality of presentation that you can obtain with ICT rather than handwriting. Furthermore, the provisionality of ICT makes it easy to adapt plans in order to improve them for the next time you use them and to be appropriate for different classes. The capacity makes it possible to store systematically all your plans for later retrieval, and the range feature means that you can share your plans with other teachers. Of course, there are dangers in using someone else's plans exactly as they are, and ICT also helps you to adapt them to your own style, resources and policies.

The Internet provides communication at a distance and access to a vast range of resources. You can use websites hosted by government agencies or other educational organisations to locate carefully considered plans for lessons that you can adapt to your own circumstances. You can form or join a network of subject teachers to exchange, evaluate and collaborate on lesson plans. Other resources for teaching can come from a variety of sources on the WWW.

Useful search terms:

- TRE (Teacher Resource Exchange)
- KS3 strategy
- ICT advice
- Lesson plans *subject*.

## Access to resources

Various resources for teaching can be obtained from a range of sources using the Internet, including subject associations, museums and galleries, libraries, research centres, commercial organisations, charities, lobby groups and individual enthusiasts.

As well as lesson plans, you can obtain:

- schemes of work;
- notes on teaching approaches;
- exam board syllabuses/requirements/papers/mark schemes;
- material for pupils including specific software, learning/revision webs, web quests, work-sheets, presentations, animations, images;
- ask-an-expert services, including expert subject practitioners in science, history, RE, mathematics, and consultant teachers.

The caveat noted in Chapter 9 applies to resources obtained from the Internet: there is little quality assurance and material may not transfer well across educational systems.
Useful search terms:

- TRE
- *Subject* association
- BBC learning
- Learning
- Chalkface
- Schoolzone.

---

**Task 11.1** Use the WWW to find:
1 a site that provides teaching resources for your subject;
2 a site that provides a selected collection of links to worthwhile educational sites;
3 a site that provides information about research into the teaching and learning of your subject;
4 a site that provides inspection reports – general, subject-specific and school-specific (note: reports on schools in Wales are not generally available on the WWW).

---

## Home-school links

The traditional form of contact between schools and parents has been the regular parent-teacher meeting, usually held only once a year. The possibility of more frequent contact through ICT is clear, and many schools provide important information and regular updates for parents on the school website. Some schools use e-mail for newsletters, notice of events and reminders of items needed by pupils; they also allow, or even encourage, parents to communicate with teachers through e-mail. More formal communications, concerning serious misbehaviour, for instance, are best handled through a more formal written communication from senior staff.

This combination of web and e-mail has potential for communicating with pupils, too:

- teachers can set homework for pupils;
- reference material and interactive teaching materials can be provided on the school website or intranet;
- pupils can have access to their work stored on the school network;
- pupils can send enquiries to their teachers about the homework or about points that they did not have time to discuss during lessons;
- pupils can submit homework and teachers can give feedback on it to pupils;
- pupils who are not able to attend schools for a long time can video-conference with teachers.

(DfES, 2001b)

There is potentially a significant increase in workload for teachers, however, and its use would need to be managed carefully.

The clarity and provisionality of word processing and desktop publishing enable you to create effective letters and brochures for parents, adapt them for different occasions and tailor them to individual needs and circumstances, including different languages. Database and mail-merge facilities enable you to send the same, or even slightly different, letters to a large number of parents easily with each being individually addressed. You should, of course, make sure that you have the authority to do this before taking advantage of the potential of the technology!

Useful search terms:

- home-school links
- Becta research
- PIN (Parents' Information Network)
- Teachernet.

## Developing school ethos and image

The school website serves a wider purpose than improving communications with parents and pupils. It can help present a favourable image of the school within its community through a statement of aims, an appropriate 'house style', up-to-date details of staff, courses, pupils' achievements, examination results, inspection reports, rules and requirements, activities and events. It can help to present the school as an ICT-capable institution (Kennewell *et al.*, 2000) and provide valuable assistance in marketing the school to potential pupils and their parents. The school website can also be used to showcase pupils' work. The image may be further developed by the use of e-mail for regular communications with parents (see Home-school links above). The reputation of the school will be enhanced if all staff respond promptly to contacts from parents.

## Record keeping and the use of information for management

It is important for teachers and administrative staff to have rapid access to current records about pupils and other features of school life. A management information system (MIS) will help with this, typically allowing up-to-date records to be maintained of pupils' personal details, attendance, marks/grades, etc. together with staff records, timetabling, financial data and other information vital to the running of the school (Imison and Taylor, 2001) This is particularly important in the case of SEN pupils, where a considerable amount of detail needs to be recorded and accessed by teachers in order to provide appropriate support in the classroom (Franklin and Litchfield, 1999). Teachers commonly share opinions about appropriate methods for handling particular pupils, and this can be facilitated by e-mail. Care must be taken not to store information that is incorrect or outside the scope of what the school is registered to record (see the Legal and ethical matters below).

Information should not be stored unless you are clear about the purpose for it, however. Warner (1999) lists a number of purposes that MIS support:

- identifying trends in variables such as attendance, and highlighting where action is needed;
- seeking relationships between, for instance, attendance and examination results;
- testing the effects of possible alternative policies and procedures;
- revealing the results of changes in practice.

The MIS will have features that assist with subject-based record keeping and analysis, too. This can help with assessment and evaluation, as Chapter 10 explained. If you do not have access to appropriate features of an MIS, you can keep academic records of your pupils, either as an individual teacher or within a departmental or whole-school system and process them using a spreadsheet program, and possibly a database Program as well to provide further helpful features. This can help to monitor individual pupils' progress and identify pupils who seem to be underachieving, so that you can set them targets and provide individual support.

Useful search terms:

- assessment record keeping
- Teachernet.

---

**Task 11.2**    Find out some of the purposes of your school's ICT administrative system. If possible, use the system (or observe it in use) to find information or to enter data.

---

## Extra-curricular activities

ICT can help support a variety of activities for pupils outside the classroom. Your school may well have an ICT club, in which pupils can carry out activities that you have set using ICT, or a general homework club where pupils have access to ICT resources outside lesson time. If you are involved in organising an educational or leisure visit for pupils, ICT can help with the administration of visits, particularly the use of spreadsheets for financial modelling and a database for record keeping. And with an increasing number of museums, galleries and other visitor attractions making images, annotations and even video material available in digital form on the WWW, it is worth considering the use of the Internet or video-conferencing for a virtual visit to a key location, which is unrealistic for actual travel.

Useful search terms:

- after school activities
- Teachernet.

## Evidence of effectiveness

The culture of accountability now being experienced by teachers, particularly in England, means that you will need to continue to build up records of your work throughout your career in order to provide evidence of improving performance in teaching. ICT can help with this, as once a lesson plan has been created, you may as well keep it indefinitely, as long as you have a personal PC with a large hard disk and an effective folder system to organise your files! As well as complete sets of lesson plans, you can keep all your own resources and continually adapt and improve them. You can store all your class's results, together with statistical analysis and graphs of trends. It may also be helpful to maintain an electronic 'portfolio' of a selection of your pupils' work to showcase the quality of your results.

---

**Task 11.3**   Use a spreadsheet or database package to record assessment information about your pupils, and use it to monitor progress and produce summary data (such as totals and averages of marks or attendance).

---

## Continuing professional development (CPD)

You will be expected to work on developing your professional knowledge and skills throughout your career, starting with your induction year. ICT can help with sources of information concerning sources of professional development, including the following.

*Face-to-face courses*
Opportunities can be identified using the WWW from a wide variety of agencies, including local authorities; higher education institutions; subject associations; independent ICT centres, training organisations and consultants; examination boards and other schools or clusters.

*On-line distance learning courses*
It may be more convenient to undertake a course through the WWW itself, and opportunities for this are growing.

*Professional advice and research*
Subject associations and government advice agencies such as Becta have websites that will offer a large amount of professional advice, some of it open to all and some of it available to members only through a password system. You can also use these sources, together with university websites, to find out about the latest research on particular issues.

*Inspection reports*
These are not only valuable when seeking a job; it is beneficial to read reports on schools with similar characteristics to your own in order to identify useful ideas for improving your own practice. These are available on the WWW. Furthermore, the inspection agencies such as Ofsted in England provide a wide range of overview reports on issues such as SEN provision in mainstream schools and developing creativity in schools. They will expect the messages that they send about good practice in these reports to have been acted upon when next they inspect your school.

*Networking and professional community building*
In addition to formal courses, you can glean much useful advice from discussion lists using 'listservs' (see the section on e-mail in Chapter 3) and computer conferencing. These services may additionally be offered by local authorities, subject associations and government advice agencies. They can be more than just a source of advice or forum for opinion; they can reduce the feeling of professional isolation, enable teachers to share problems and success (Parker and Bowell, 1998), and sustain a community of teachers engaged in supporting each other's professional development through discussion of issues and sharing of research findings (Leask and Younie, 2001).

Useful search terms:

- CPD *subject*
- Inset *subject*
- Becta CPD
- Teachernet
- Schoolzone
- GTC (General Teaching Council).

**Task 11.4** If possible, join a discussion list for your subject or for your course. Use this list to seek information for teaching purposes, or find a website that can respond to requests for professional information.

## Action research

Teaching has been identified as a research-based profession, and action research is a powerful form of professional development, because teachers are involved in the process of development rather than having it done to them (Somekh, 1997). The next chapter considers the process further, but the prospective action researcher will need to consider what support they are going to need, both within and outside their institution, and ICT provides a means both of identifying such assistance and providing assistance. The WWW will enable you to make contact with Higher Education academics and many local authority advisors who will be experienced in carrying out research themselves, and may be able to acts as mentors. You will also need to find out what other research has been done on your chosen area of interest, and the Internet provides access to reports published on the WWW, to bibliographic databases that can help identify other sources, and to libraries in Higher Education Institutions that you can join. You can maintain your own database of sources for future reference using a general program or program specifically designed for bibliographic records. The WWW is an important tool in disseminating research results, too.

Useful search terms:

- action research education
- CARN (Classroom Action Research Network)
- GTC.

The final chapter discusses CPD specifically related to ICT.

## What other factors need to be taken into account when using ICT?

It is important to maintain your sense of professional values when using ICT. The technology may be neutral (although there are many who adopt a more critical stance such as that expressed by Beynon and McKay (1993), for example), but the way you use it reflects your professional values. Inappropriate organisation or application may result in direct dangers to pupils or indirect learning of poor practice from your behaviour. There are two main areas to consider: *health and safety*, and *legal and ethical matters*.

### Health and safety

You should be aware of the following points and monitor the situation each lesson, particularly in ICT rooms:

- electrical safety: equipment should be securely fixed and cables should not be hanging loose or trailing across the floor and pupils should not connect, disconnect or open up any equipment;
- dangers to sight of long exposure to screens or staring into a projector beam: pupils should have a short break from screens and keyboards every 40 minutes, and should be warned against looking towards the projector;
- dangers to particular pupils who are sensitive to computer screens: check whether any pupils in your class are required to use anti-glare screens or other safeguards;

- room lighting: this should be quite bright, and there should be means of preventing the sun shining directly onto the screen;
- poor posture: screens and seats should be positioned so that pupils' eyes are at roughly the same level as the screen, and so that they can both see the screen and use the keyboard and mouse without bending or straining;
- temperature and air: ensure that the room is ventilated and does not get too warm because computers are left switched on;
- laptops: place them firmly on tables;
- water: electrical equipment must not be used near a water supply and drinks should not be taken near PCs or other electrical equipment;
- space for working: pupils should have room to place any books or other materials needed near the PC;
- space for movement: passageways needed for general movement and rapid exit should be kept clear of bags and other clutter:
- typing: pupils should be encouraged to use more than one or two fingers in order to help avoid repetitive strain injury.

(Becta, 2003e)

---

**Task 11.5**    Find out about your school's policy concerning:

- pupils' behaviour in a computer room;
- staff supervision required for pupils using computers;
- the conditions for acceptable use of the school network and the Internet;
- the filtering software used to prohibit access to material deemed unsuitable;
- the disciplinary implications of the misuse of ICT by pupils and teachers;
- the storage and use of personal data about pupils.

---

## Legal and ethical matters

Issues to be considered include the following.

*Storing data about pupils*

Any personal data held about individuals is covered by the Data Protection Act of 1998 (Information Commissioner's Office, 2004). This is based on eight data protection principles (see Table 11.1), and requires organisations holding personal data to register the purpose for holding the data, allow individuals to check information held for accuracy, correct any inaccuracies, and use it only for the stated purpose. Your school will be registered, and you should check your school's policy to ensure that any personal data that you hold on the school or other ICT resources, and your use of it, are within the scope of the registration.

*Use of the Internet*

If pupils use the WWW under your supervision, you need to know what position to take if pupils access websites that are not within the scope of the task you have set.

**Table 11.1**  Data protection principles (Information Commissioner's Office, 2004)

Personal data must be:

- fairly and lawfully processed;
- processed for limited purposes;
- adequate, relevant and not excessive;
- accurate;
- not kept longer than necessary;
- processed in accordance with the data subject's rights;
- secure;
- not transferred to countries without adequate protection.

Personal data covers both facts and opinions about the individual.

Likely activities include games, celebrity and sports fan sites, and images that can range from the mildly racy to absolutely shocking. Minor broaches may be dealt with by means of a knowing look, but you should intervene and take disciplinary action if you see pupils accessing material which is obscene, racist, inflammatory, or otherwise inappropriate for school activity. There may be differences between merely accessing a site and purposefully downloading material to the school computer, although you need to be aware that accessing a site will usually result in some of its contents being stored in temporary files on the PC. Pupils may also use e-mail, SMS, or chat room sites, for purposes ranging from communicating with their friend sitting next to them (you should see this as an opportunity to discuss with them the choice of appropriate resources, as well as the need to stay on task!) through to arranging contact with a stranger who has taken a particular interest in them (which needs to be reported to senior management immediately).

*Storage and reproduction of material*
Copyright is an important but complex issue, and material on the WWW is subject to copyright in just the same degree as traditionally published material. You should not assume that you or your pupils can freely reproduce material that you have located on the Internet without the permission of the copyright owner. This is true whether or not there is an explicit copyright notice. Although many educational materials are made available 'free of copyright', this is usually shorthand for 'the copyright holder will allow the materials to be used for educational purposes without having to ask permission or pay a fee'. As with books, it is acceptable for small parts of works to be used by individuals for academic purposes, and it is good practice always to acknowledge the source of such material. This does not allow you to republish material, however, so check with the originator of the material before copying for a class or making it available through the intranet or WWW. Of course, the points made about obscene, racist or inflammatory content above also apply to pupils' storage of material.

> **Task 11.6**    Consider the case of a teacher who uses the school's pupil database to search for all pupils predicted to obtain low grades in mathematics. The teacher then copies the names and addresses of the parents of these pupils into a file and e-mails it to a friend who has a private tutoring business. The friend then sends out material advertising tutoring in mathematics.
>
> Which data protection principles have been broken, and by whom?
>
> What do you think the teacher's position is:
>   1  ethically;
>   2  legally?

*Measures to safeguard pupils*

It is impossible to protect pupils completely from Internet dangers, and it is inevitable that children will occasionally meet unpleasant situations in their lives. Indeed, it is important to educate them about issues of crime, sex, violence, prejudice and privacy at an appropriate age and in line with the school's Health and Safety Policy. However, you have a duty of care concerning your pupils, and must follow school policies regarding ICT use. Schools use a variety of approaches, including:

- filtering or 'nanny' software, which blocks access to inappropriate sites using either a blacklist principle (sites known to be inappropriate are blocked) or whitelist (only sites known to be appropriate are allowed), often combined with general principles for blocking based on the use of obscene or inflammatory language and proportion of naked flesh in images! This can, of course, prevent access to many valuable sites for teaching and learning, particularly in science;
- close visual monitoring by teachers and checking automatic logs of sites accessed by particular pupils;
- contracts with pupils and parents that state what Internet use is acceptable and what sanctions will be applied in cases of breach.

(NCET, 1998)

> **Task 11.7**    It has been suggested that filtering what pupils can obtain from the Internet is imposing excessive structure on pupils' activity and thereby limiting their learning. This view holds that pupils should have free access to the Internet, and be taught about the dangers involved, rather than being artificially protected from them. Use of pornography, violence, racism or bullying through the Internet would then be dealt with in the same way as with non-Internet offences of this nature.
>
> Do you agree with this argument? How would you feel if you were a Headteacher, responsible for pupils' welfare whilst in school?

These strategies will not cover all eventualities, however, and you should apply good personal judgement about what you prohibit, what you allow with caution, and what you encourage pupils to do, both in lessons and in extra-curricular activities.

## Further reading

NCET (1998) *Delivering and assessing IT through the curriculum*, Coventry: NCET

Trend, R., Davis, N. and Loveless, A. (1999) *Information and communications technology*, London: Letts Educational

Warner, G. (1999) Using ICT for professional purposes, in Leask, M. and Pachler, N. (eds) (1999) *Learning to teach using ICT in the secondary school*, London: Routledge

# 12 The Future – Developments in Technology and Improvements in Pedagogy

There are important technological developments on the horizon and their potential impact on education is considered in this chapter, which explains the need for continuing professional development to build on existing skills and incorporate new technology. It explores the development of new teaching methods and discusses how the professional role may be adapted in order to make the most of e-learning in school and beyond. It explains how teachers can contribute to a whole-school approach to developing ICT in teaching and learning and the role of ICT in contributing to school improvement, explaining the principles and providing examples.

## What new technological developments are likely to impact on education shortly?

A number of aspects of ICT have been changing constantly over the past 50 years and are likely to do so. These are primarily physical size, processing (and communications) speed, storage capacity and cost. It is likely that these will continue to develop in the same way over the next few years. In addition, there are aspects that have developed in quality, such as visual displays, speech input and output, and the software applications we use.

At the time of writing, the most significant development for education would seem to be in four areas:

- smaller devices;
- rapid information transfer (particularly video);
- wireless communications between devices;
- human-computer interfaces.

Handheld devices, for instance, are likely to be much more widely used. Whilst 'laptop' PCs are now being used very widely in schools by teachers and pupils, 'palmtop' devices such as the increasingly powerful personal digital assistants (PDA), pocket PCs and the more specialised graphic calculators have not been exploited to the extent that they might be. This is likely to change, as costs decrease, the processing and memory power available in small devices improves, standard software becomes available, hand-writing recognition improves and networking capability develops. Fully functional, handheld computers are likely to become as common as mobile phones and simple calculators in due course. They need some practice in operation for users to become confident, but they generate a strong sense of ownership for those who achieve an adequate level of competence and a high degree of motivation for pupils (Perry, 2003).

Wireless network communications are being used increasingly widely, and as their range and reliability grow, this is likely to continue. This technology allows a computer with a wireless interface (usually a laptop or PDA) to connect to the network whenever it is in range of an access point. Giving network features to portable devices will make a tremendous difference to classroom layout and organisation, particularly when com-bined with the keyboardless tablet PC. There is no need to decide whether to have one, a few or a lot of PCs in a room: as many as needed can be brought in for each lesson – and soon most pupils will be able to bring their own. With access points spread around the whole local community, the opportunities for e-learning outside school will increase tremendously (Perry, 2002).

Flat-screen display technology enables screens to be installed in innovative ways which save space and facilitate new ways of working. Combined with the stylus (developed as a means of operation for handheld devices) to produce the tablet PC, the screen can function as the main input device as well as output display. These devices provide many of the best features of laptop and handheld PCs, and may be more effective than either for many educational applications. For too long, the so called QWERTY keyboard has dominated the input of data by humans. It was developed in the early days of typewriter technology in order to prevent hammers sticking together during rapid typing, yet it is still the norm today when most users are not touch typists. It is perhaps the single most influential factor in slowing the spread of ICT use in schools, acting as a repressive counterweight to the emancipatory effect of the mouse/pointer system. Increasingly, the electronic stylus with handwriting recognition software is reducing the need for keyboard input, and this is having a beneficial effect on pupils' motivation to take notes in lessons where tablet PCs are available (RM, 2003). And how much greater would be the effect on learning for those who experience difficulties in writing, if voice input were routinely available?

The impact of broad-band Internet technology has probably been oversold by government and industry alike, but there is no doubt that the speed and capacity brought to communications by this technology is turning many of the best features of the Internet from slow, unreliable disappointments into almost immediate, routine yet impressive events. Video-conferencing has been exploited in a limited way for many years now, but the infrastructure is now in place to enable it to become a much more widespread way of teachers and learners communicating as though face-to-face, but actually a distance apart.

| Task 12.1 | Extend your mind-map from Task 3.9 (p. 49) to incorporate these and any other examples of ICT which you feel should be added. |
|---|---|

## How can new technologies be exploited in your work?

You should not generally assume that a new resource has to be used just for the sake of it. It is important to consider what its benefits might be; these could include the following.

- It has the potential to increase the effectiveness of teaching and learning, as with the IWB, for instance.
- It can enable new curriculum or learner needs to be met; voice recognition, for instance.
- The technology is pervading society, and its educational value needs to be evaluated, as in the case of the mobile phone.
- It may have a special function in education, such as a virtual reality simulation of a desert landscape or a Tudor house.

So rather than focusing on the technology itself, you should identify its features and analyse the potential and structure for action that they provide in the teaching and learning environment.

The value of *personal laptop computers* is well established. For pupils, they stimulate a degree of motivation and enthusiasm that translates into more study time and improved learning. They provide a high degree of independence for pupils, and interdependence between pupils, that enables pupils to assume ownership of activities and take more responsibility for their learning. They also facilitate the greater involvement of parents in their children's school activities (NCET, 1994). Teachers with personal portable PCs also gain from the continual availability and sense of ownership. Portables enable skills to be developed at any time that is convenient to the teacher, and can provide a seamless transition from preparation and administration carried out at home to use in the classroom for teaching. This makes it more likely that teachers will use ICT in the classroom, and although the time taken to plan ICT-based lessons and prepare resources increases the workload in the short term, it can save time in the long term because of re-use of resources and exchange of files (Kennewell and Beauchamp, 2003).

The great value in the *handheld device* is that it can be carried around by an individual easily and has constant availability (subject to occasional recharging); you have seen the revolution in phone communication brought about by this feature. With very small screens, handheld devices are less easy to share when working collaboratively, and the amount that can be displayed clearly is always going to be limited, but it is easy to pass files between handhelds. When every pupil has one in the classroom, however, it may be better to attach large screens and other peripheral devices when needed than to switch to desktop devices. This will have radical implications for classroom layout and management, and suggests that any further proliferation of desktop PCs in schools would be inappropriate. With the integration of cell-phone technology and video image capture, collaboration will be able to develop in whole new directions. The widespread availability of e-books provides the potential for radical change in the way pupils access course texts and other published material. The potential for pupils with special needs and for those not attending school is yet to be evaluated at the time of writing (Perry, 2003).

The *flat-screen visual display* need take up no space in a room; a large one can be set vertically into the wall for group or class viewing, whilst a small one can be set horizontally into a table. A computer room therefore has the same working surface as an ordinary classroom, and provides the potential for easy transition between ICT and non-ICT activity and between whole-class interaction and individual work.

The *wireless network* provides the potential for seamless access to ICT resources though an intranet and the Internet: wherever teachers and pupils go, they can access the software and files they want to work on. This means that the current physical boundaries between school and outside, between different schools, and between classrooms in the school, become less significant (Perry, 2002). It may affect the traditional boundaries and competition between subjects that are currently a feature of secondary schools (Kennewell *et al.*, 2000), as perhaps a scientific environment can be created in the mathematics classroom, and a French environment in the history classroom, when appropriate to pupils' learning.

*Voice input* provides massive potential for the drafting and developing of ideas, and may have its greatest initial effect in handheld devices which only need to respond to one voice. The stimulus for creation of text will be great, but the distinction in style between spoken and written text may become increasingly blurred.

*Video-conferencing* provides much of the potential of the ordinary classroom – but without the need for the teacher and the learners to be together in one room. It adds structure to the activity by requiring the people involved to remain where the camera can point at them and the microphone can pick up their voices clearly, which limits the tasks that can be carried out. There is potential for new types of activity however, such as virtual visits to other schools, work places, museums, laboratories, historical sites, geographical locations or subject experts.

The main impact of the new features is to increase the potential for action. Their effect on structure for action is generally to remove structure that was imposed by 'old' technology – structure that constrained learners in time, space and operating procedures that were unhelpful in stimulating learning. However, increasing potential and reducing structure in a setting can create chaotic activity unless the people involved have the ability to impose their own structure when necessary to constrain action along fruitful pathways. Consequently, teachers will need to extend their skills in designing ICT materials to provide structure on a flexible basis for those pupils who need it.

| Task 12.2 | Choose a particular ICT activity in your subject, and consider whether and how it could be improved using new forms of technology discussed above. |

There is another factor to consider when contemplating investment in new technology. Commercial equipment manufacturers have a vested interest in making ICT users feel that their old equipment is inadequate, and making it 'essential' to purchase the latest version. Schools need to consider this point very carefully; if they are to take a leading role in education for global citizenship and sustainable development, the impact of continuing equipment renewal needs to be considered (see the ICT subject section of Chapter 4, pp. 83–5).

| | |
|---|---|
| **Task 12.3** | Choose a particular example of the newest technology and consider how it could be exploited to improve the teaching and learning in your subject. |

## How can you continue to improve your use of ICT and take advantage of new technologies and ideas which arise?

For the General Teaching Council for Wales, 'CPD encompasses all formal and informal learning which enables teachers to improve their own practice' (GTCW, 2002). It is important to identify opportunities for professional learning throughout your career, to recognise improvements in your practice, and to disseminate your ideas to others who may also be able to benefit.

Most professional development activities in the UK take place outside the school day, and involve some sacrifice of leisure time or postponement of other work. You should look for opportunities that will be worthwhile investments of your time. According to Owen (1992), effective professional development for ICT should:

- maintain a constant focus on classroom practice;
- take into account the radical effects that IT can have on the teaching environment;
- take account of the organisational structure of the school climate;
- take into account the personal and professional aspirations and long-term interests of the teacher;
- address issues of progression of skills, competency and attitude;
- encourage self and professional reflection.

(Owen, 1992: 134)

Professional learning arises from various activities, and there are many ways that can contribute to the development of your personal and professional ICT capability.

### External courses

You will find courses provided by your Local Education Authority, higher education institutions and independent consultants. You should ensure that any course that you commit yourself to is well thought through and relevant to your needs. The available options will cover various types of content and level, ranging from skills in using a new piece of software to a doctorate in effective ICT pedagogy. In between these extremes, look for opportunities to gain higher degree accreditation for advanced study concerning the teaching and management of your subject, and for school-based modules of study that can be tailored to developing your practical and professional skills in ICT.

## Internal courses

This is the most common form of professional development. Kennewell *et al.* (2000) recommend that it should be based on teaching and learning needs rather than being technology-driven. Furthermore, it should be planned as part of a whole-school programme rather than responding to ad hoc requirements, so that it can:

- be based on a needs analysis;
- motivate teachers to learn;
- challenge the teacher as to the effectiveness of current practice.

NCET (1995) recommend that secondary schools should:

- target specific departments in a rolling programme;
- target specific individuals within departments, who then act as disseminators;
- target specific applications or programs that have relevance to a number of departments.

The school's ICT coordinator, together with contributions from specialist ICT teachers and teachers in departments which have carried out successful ICT developments, can often provide an effective programme that is carefully designed to meet teachers' needs and school priorities. However, if a programme of professional development is provided only by staff within the school, there is a danger of stagnation, and Kennewell *et al.* (2000) recommend considering the involvement of external consultants, perhaps from the LEA, higher education or an independent organisation. An external input should be more than a quick, flashy presentation, however; the consultant needs to work with staff in the school over a period of time, and aim to leave staff in a position to sustain the momentum.

## Self-study and distance learning

It is unlikely that internal provision will cover everything that you want to achieve in professional development, and external courses may not meet your needs in terms of content, approach, location or timing. You may be able to find distance learning or self-study courses; these normally involve the Internet for provision of material and communication with tutors (see Chapter 11 for ideas concerning locating these).

## Incidental and planned learning from colleagues

Much of teachers' professional learning is achieved more informally, through conversations within and across departments about issues that arise in classrooms, and through colleagues sharing materials. When working in a school, you will become aware of which teachers are the best sources of advice on different aspects of using ICT. You may well be asked for advice yourself as you will be seen as more likely to have had effective training in the use of ICT in the classroom.

This may be formalised into a peer-coaching approach (Joyce et al., 1999), whereby groups of colleagues agree to share in a development of practice, plan together, observe each others' lessons, and reflect jointly on the experiences. Feedback from colleagues can help you to appreciate issues that you would not have noticed as a key participant in the classroom activity. Prior planning is essential, however, to ensure that the roles of the two teachers during the lesson are clear concerning both class management and teaching, and to ensure that the class/subject teacher conveys an understanding of the learning outcomes of the lesson to the observer. Following the lesson, the resulting discussion can:

- identify gaps in competence in using the computers;
- help the subject teacher analyse what has happened and why it has happened (ways in which pupils' ICT capability has been enhanced or how the use of ICT has helped the pupils to learn the subject matter);
- assist the class/subject teacher to think about how they could improve on what has been taught (whether the methodology used was the most appropriate with this class or for this topic).

(Kennewell et al., 2000: 164)

## Personal exploration and reflection

Whilst it is valuable to share reflection with colleagues, many developments in your teaching will be initiated personally as you explore new resources, evaluate their potential, try them in your classroom, and reflect on their impact on pupils' learning. You will not always be successful, but just as pupils learn eagerly from trying things out and making mistakes, so can you. This approach has been characterised as *bricolage* by Papert (1996). Of course, you should plan carefully to avoid making too many errors or too large a blunder in front of pupils, but if you have a good relationship with a class, if you explain to them that you want them to work with you on something new, and if you are prepared to accept help from them, then it is unlikely to be a failure in terms of learning. Following the lesson, your immediate feelings will concern your own performance, and it is helpful to have a list of prompts to help reflect on pupils' learning.

- To what extent am I catering for the abilities of all the pupils in the class?
- Are pupils able to build on prior learning?
- Have I considered common misconceptions associated with this topic?

- Are the pupils able to use what they have learnt in new situations?
- Did the pupils appreciate that they were making progress?
- Did the pupils improve their confidence in the subject and the image they have of themselves as learners of the subject?
- Did the pupils develop good habits of work, including perseverance and a concern for correctness?
- Did the pupils use their initiative, exercise imagination and think for themselves?

(Kennewell *et al.*, 2000: 166)

## Action research

This is potentially the most powerful form of professional development, as it is focused on an issue of interest and under the full control of the person carrying it out. The process involves identifying an issue, finding out what others have learned about the issue, proposing a change in practice, deciding how to study the change, characterising the situation before, implementing the change with records of activity and reflections on activities, characterising the situation afterwards, analysing the effects of the change, refining the proposals for change in the light of the effects, and starting the process again on a second cycle. Indeed, the cycle of planning, acting, observing, reflecting and change may be repeated indefinitely (see, for example, Hitchcock and Hughes (1995)).

It is best if carried out collaboratively, where a group of teachers work on similar issues and provide each other with ideas and support, or at least with help of a mentor with research experience. It should be rigorous, but is less constrained by issues of sampling, experimental design, or objectivity in interpretation than a research study carried out by an independent body. Much of its value lies in its identification with the individual who is learning from the process, and generalisations should be considered only very cautiously and conditionally.

| **Task 12.4** | Look back to the section in Chapter 3 concerning your specialist subject. Draw on your own experience of teaching with ICT, your knowledge of recent developments in technology, and the TTA list of potential ICT uses, to suggest ways in which the activity described in the case study could be improved or extended. |
|---|---|

## How can you help develop the ICT-capable school?

The *ICT capable school* is characterised by:

- pupils with a positive attitude towards ICT, and a disposition to apply ICT to relevant curriculum tasks and to evaluate the outcomes of their use of ICT;
- pupils planning and applying ICT to tasks, describing and evaluating their work with ICT, with a high level of knowledge, skill and understanding in relation to their age;

- a strong role for ICT in the teaching and learning culture of the school, so that frequent opportunities are planned and provided for pupils to develop their skills in applying ICT to worthwhile tasks;
- teachers helping pupils to develop their ICT capability whenever there is an opportunity to do so, and provision for pupils to work on purposeful ICT tasks beyond the standard teaching times.

(Kennewell *et al.*, 2000: 13)

This idea was echoed by NAACE (2003) who characterise the *ICT-enabling school* as one that develops pupils who are:

- *autonomous* in their use of ICT;
- *capable* with ICT;
- *creative* in their use of ICT;
- using ICT to produce work of *quality*;
- adding value to their learning through the *scope* of ICT.

These abilities are the ones that characterise good quality teaching and learning with ICT: 'as a result, teaching is more effective, learning is more dynamic and demanding, and standards are rising' (NAACE, 2003: 21).

Kennewell *et al.* (2000) recommended schools to develop ICT-capable thinking right through the school, and stressed the importance of:

- having high expectations of pupils in their use of ICT, in and out of school, and providing opportunities for disadvantaged pupils to spend as much time using up-to-date ICT resources as their more fortunate peers;
- focusing on teaching and learning higher order aspects of all Key Skills, throughout the curriculum, with a reduction in emphasis on low-level techniques and routines;
- purposeful assessment of attainment and use of assessment information to provide feedback to pupils and inform teacher planning;
- leadership from management and a cycle of ICT development within a culture of school improvement;
- supporting teachers in changing their teaching approaches to accommodate the potential of ICT as an educational tool;
- collaborating in response to challenge – management and staff, different subjects and age groups, teaching and support staff, teachers and pupils, school and home;
- a shared vision of what it means to be ICT capable, and a recognition that the process of developing ICT capability can never be complete.

(Kennewell *et al.*, 2000: 3)

*ICT-capable pupils* are encouraged to develop their work in as many lessons as possible and outside lessons. They are given structured teaching on ICT concepts by specialists when appropriate, together with opportunities to use these concepts in constructive ICT activities in all subjects. They are given challenging tasks that give them opportunities to explore and make decisions. They are supported in developing higher order skills.

*ICT-capable teachers* are prepared to experiment with ICT in teaching and learning in order to gain the experience required to evaluate its effectiveness. They are prepared to attend courses, participate in school-based professional development, and try new software out for themselves in order to develop skills to the level where they can apply them in the classroom. They will use ICT policies effectively and form good relationships with the ICT coordinator (see below) and ICT specialist staff.

*ICT-capable classrooms* are formed from a combination of ICT-capable pupils and teachers, and also the appropriate resources to exploit the features of ICT effectively in the subject, including at least one Internet-linked PC. Each room maintains the culture of the subject mainly taught there, and encourages effective ICT application rather than 'doing ICT'.

*ICT-capable subjects* have a head of department who is ICT capable and provides appropriate leadership in the use of ICT. There will often be a junior member of the department who has a greater specialist knowledge of ICT in the subject, and represents the department on the school ICT Committee. The subject schemes of work incorporate specific requirements for ICT use in particular topics in order to promote continuity and progression in the use of ICT, and suggest other topics where ICT will be helpful in teaching and learning.

The ICT-capable school will also have effective staff in the following roles:

- ICT coordinator, who plans, monitors and supports pupils' ICT capability development across the curriculum;
- e-learning coordinator, who plans, monitors and supports the use of ICT for learning;
- head of ICT, who leads the team of staff who teach ICT as a subject;
- network manager, who ensures that appropriate resources are available to pupils and staff according to policies and procedures agreed by the coordinators.

These roles may be combined, and carried out by, perhaps, two members of staff in smaller schools.

Ancillary staff will also be willing and able to use ICT where appropriate.

## The future role of ICT and the teacher in schools

The combination of developments in ICT itself, and in teachers' skills in using it, mean that a time can be envisaged when schools will be able to realise all the potential that Bowring-Carr and West-Burnham (1997: 114) suggest ICT has to offer;

- information on the learner's terms (not the teacher's);
- individualised access and control;
- structured progression at the learner's own pace;

- ability to repeat;
- the possibility of error-free work;
- individual interaction;
- absence of problems in that interaction;
- the opportunity for an individual to work alone or in a small group;
- enhancement of creativity;
- learning free of time limitation;
- learning free of geographical limitations;
- learning free of assumptions about limitations.

Do you want this vision to come about? Will you be able to adapt as a teacher, in order to make the vision work?

| Task 12.5 | Add to your ICT profile to incorporate your new abilities gained from reflection on experience and reading. |
|---|---|

## Further reading

Bowring-Carr, C. and West-Burnham, J. (1997) *Effective learning in schools*, London: Pitman.

Davis, N. (1997) 'Strategies for staff and institutional development for IT in education: an integrated approach', in Somekh, B. and Davis, N. (eds) (1997) *Using information technology effectively in teaching and learning*, London: Routledge, 167–80.

Imison, T. and Taylor, P. (2001) *Managing ICT in the secondary school*, Oxford: Heinemann.

Kennewell, S., Parkinson, J. and Tanner, H. (2000) *Developing the ICT capable school*, London: RoutledgeFalmer.

Perry, D. (2002) *Wireless networking in schools*, Coventry: Becta.

Perry, D. (2003) *Handheld computers (PDAs) in schools*, Coventry: Becta.

Somekh, B. (1997) Classroom investigations: exploring and evaluating how IT can support learning, in Somekh, B. and Davis, N. (1997) *Using information technology effectively in teaching and learning*, London: Routledge, 114–26.

The Anglia Polytechnic University *Ultralab* website http://194.83.41.152/flash/default.html

The National Endowment for Science, Technology and the Arts (nesta) *futurelab* website http://www.nestafuturelab.org/

# Appendix A
## Extracts relating to ICT from *Qualifying to Teach: Professional Standards for Qualified Teacher Status and Requirements for Initial Teacher Training (TTA, 2002)*

Those awarded Qualified Teacher Status must demonstrate that:

**2.5**  They know how to use ICT effectively, both to teach their subject and to support their wider professional role.

## Scope

Information and Communications Technology (ICT) has an important role to play in most aspects of teachers' work in schools: in teaching and learning for individuals, small groups and whole classes; and in planning, assessment, evaluation, administration and management.

This Standard sets out two aspects of ICT competence which trainees can be expected to develop and demonstrate: how best to use ICT to teach the subject(s) they are trained to teach, and their own ICT skills, which will allow them to, for example, complete pupils' records of progress, prepare resources for pupils and keep to a minimum their administrative tasks. In each of these two aspects, trainees' expertise should be such that they can easily identify opportunities to use ICT and know how to do so confidently and independently. This standard does not require trainees to be ICT experts, or ICT coordinators.

ICT includes Internet-aware computers and the relevant peripherals, e.g. CD-ROM, subject and professional software, projectors, interactive whiteboards, digital cameras, scanners, video, control and sensing technology and calculators.

## Evidence relevant to meeting the Standard

Trainees will be able to demonstrate that they have met this Standard in a number of ways, mainly during their school-based training. Trainees' opportunities will be dependent on school software, hardware and access to the Internet, and these may be limited for some trainees. Trainees' explanations of why they would have selected particular software (or hardware), how they planned to use ICT as part of their subject teaching, and how they prepared to respond to pupils' different levels of confidence and expertise, could all provide opportunities for trainees to demonstrate that they have met this Standard. Evidence of knowledge could also be gathered from, for example, the ways in which trainees record pupils' progress and show how ICT has enhanced pupils' learning, their ability to access resources and information in remote databases such as the National Grid for Learning (NGfL), and their ability to select, customise and use these materials with pupils.

In considering whether trainee teachers know how to use ICT in their wider professional role, and are sufficiently secure in their ability to do this, assessors may wish to consider how well trainees use, for example, electronic mail, the Internet, digital cameras and electronic whiteboards, and how they select materials for pupils of different abilities. Trainees' ability to transfer ICT expertise between software packages and media could provide further evidence of their confidence as users of ICT.

> Those awarded Qualified Teacher Status must demonstrate that:
> **3.3.10** They use ICT effectively in their teaching.

## Scope

Information and communications technology (ICT) provides teachers with opportunities to increase the effectiveness of their teaching. Trainees will need to be able to use ICT with discrimination, knowing where and how it can be used to have the greatest effect on pupils' learning. This Standard requires trainees to use ICT to teach the subject(s) they are trained to teach and is closely related to Standard 2.5 on knowledge about ICT. This Standard does not require trainees to teach National Curriculum ICT or ICT Key Skills.

ICT includes Internet-aware computers and the relevant peripherals, e.g. CD-ROM, subject and professional software, projectors, interactive whiteboards, digital cameras, scanners, video, control and sensing technology and calculators.

## Evidence relevant to meeting the Standard

Trainees' opportunities to demonstrate that they have met this Standard will be dependent on school software, hardware and access to the Internet, and these may be limited for some trainees. Some evidence will come from their work in the classroom but other evidence may come from out-of-school contexts.

When judging trainees' teaching, assessors might wish to consider: is the trainee able to select and use software to support the teaching of subjects? Can the trainee access interactive on-line database content using, for example, the National Grid for Learning (NGfL) or the Teacher Resource Exchange (TRE) and select, customise and use these materials with pupils? Can the trainee provide opportunities for pupils to use ICT to find things out, try things out and make things happen? Does the trainee use ICT terminology accurately? Can the trainee make use of ICT with individuals, groups and the whole class? Does the trainee take account of copyright, reliability, privacy and confidentiality issues when preparing materials for pupils or collecting data? Can the trainee identify opportunities to use ICT with confidence without the assistance of others?

# Appendix B
# Programmes of Study for the National Curriculum for ICT in England

## Knowledge, skills and understanding

**During Key Stage 3** pupils become increasingly independent users of ICT tools and information sources. They have a better understanding of how ICT can help their work in other subjects and develop their ability to judge when and how to use ICT and where it has limitations. They think about the quality and reliability of information, and access and combine increasing amounts of information. They become more focused, efficient and rigorous in their use of ICT, and carry out a range of increasingly complex tasks.

## Finding things out

(1) Pupils should be taught:
   (a) to be systematic in considering the information they need and to discuss how it will be used;
   (b) how to obtain information well matched to purpose by selecting appropriate sources, using and refining search methods and questioning the plausibility and value of the information found;
   (c) how to collect, enter, analyse and evaluate quantitative and qualitative information, checking its accuracy (for example, carrying out a survey of local traffic, analysing data gathered in fieldwork).

## Developing ideas and making things happen

(2) Pupils should be taught:
   (a) to develop and explore information, solve problems and derive new information for particular purposes (for example, deriving totals from raw data, reaching conclusions by exploring information);

(b)   how to use ICT to measure, record, respond to and control events by planning, testing and modifying sequences of instructions (for example, using automatic weather stations, data logging in fieldwork and experiments, using feedback to control devices);

(c)   how to use ICT to test predictions and discover patterns and relationships, by exploring, evaluating and developing models and changing their rules and values;

(d)   to recognise where groups of instructions need repeating and to automate frequently used processes by constructing efficient procedures that are fit for purpose (for example, templates and macros, control procedures, formulae and calculations in spreadsheets).

## Exchanging and sharing information

(3)   Pupils should be taught:

(a)   how to interpret information and to reorganise and present it in a variety of forms that are fit for purpose (for example, information about a charitable cause presented in a leaflet for a school fundraising event);

(b)   to use a range of ICT tools efficiently to draft, bring together and refine information and create good quality presentations in a form that is sensitive to the needs of particular audiences and suits the information content;

(c)   how to use ICT, including e-mail, to share and exchange information effectively (for example, web publishing, video-conferencing).

## Reviewing, modifying and evaluating work as it progresses

(4)   Pupils should be taught to:

(a)   reflect critically on their own and others' uses of ICT to help them develop and improve their ideas and the quality of their work;

(b)   share their views and experiences of ICT, considering the range of its uses and talking about its significance to individuals, communities and society;

(c)   discuss how they might use ICT in future work and how they would judge its effectiveness, using relevant technical terms;

(d)   be independent and discriminating when using ICT.

## Breadth of study

(5)   During the key stage, pupils should be taught the **knowledge, skills and understanding** through:

(a)   working with a range of information to consider its characteristics, structure, organisation and purposes (for example, using database, spreadsheet and presentation software to manage membership and finances of a club and present the annual report);

(b)    working with others to explore a variety of information sources and ICT tools in a variety of contexts;

(c)    designing information systems and evaluating and suggesting improvements to existing systems (for example, evaluating a website or researching, designing and producing a multimedia presentation for a science topic);

(d)    comparing their use of ICT with its use in the wider world.

(DfEE/QCA, 1999: 20–21)

# Appendix C
# Suggested Answers
# to Tasks

## Task 1.1

| Resource | Type |
|---|---|
| CAD (computer-aided design) | Software |
| Calculator | Hardware |
| CD-ROM | Media |
| CD writer | Hardware |
| Data logging | Software and hardware |
| Database | Software |
| Desktop PC | Hardware |
| Digital camera | Hardware |
| Digital video | Media |
| DTP (desktop publishing) | Software |
| E-commerce | Service |
| E-mail | Service |
| Encyclopaedia | Software |
| Graphic organiser | Software |
| Internet | Service |
| Intranet | Service |
| Laptop PC | Hardware |
| MIS (management information system) | Software |
| Mobile phone | Hardware |
| PDA (personal data assistant) | Hardware |
| Playstation | Hardware |
| Process control | Software |
| SMS (text messaging) | Service |
| Spreadsheet | Software |
| Video game | Software |
| VLE (virtual learning environment) | Software |
| WWW (World Wide Web) | Service |

## Task 2.1

1   Mobile phone with voice and text messaging (ordinary telephone) – Automation.
2   Simple calculator (pencil and paper) – Speed, Automation, Provisionality.
3   Notebook PC (briefcase) – Automation, Capacity, Range, Provisionality, Interactivity.
4   Video-conferencing (face-to-face meeting) – Range.
5   Digital camera (film camera) – Capacity, Provisionality.
6   Automated Teller Machine or ATM (bank cashier) – Automation.
7   Email (postal service) – Speed, Automation, Interactivity.
8   Playstation (playground) – Automation, Interactivity.

## Task 2.4

|                | 1.1 | 1.2 | 1.3 | 1.4 | 1.5 | 1.6 | 1.7 | 1.8 | 1.9 |
|----------------|-----|-----|-----|-----|-----|-----|-----|-----|-----|
| Capacity       | Y   |     | Y   |     | Y   | Y   | Y   | Y   | Y   |
| Range          | Y   |     | Y   |     |     |     |     | Y   | Y   |
| Speed          | Y   | Y   | Y   | Y   | Y   | Y   | Y   | Y   | Y   |
| Automation     | Y   | Y   | Y   | Y   | Y   | Y   | Y   | Y   | Y   |
| Provisionality | Y   | Y   |     | Y   | Y   |     | Y   |     |     |
| Interactivity  |     | Y   |     | Y   |     | Y   |     | Y   |     |
| Clarity        |     | Y   | Y   | Y   | Y   | Y   | Y   | Y   |     |
| Authenticity   | Y   | Y   | Y   | Y   | Y   |     |     | Y   |     |
| Focusability   |     |     | Y   | Y   | Y   |     | Y   |     | Y   |
| Multimodality  |     |     | Y   | Y   |     | Y   |     |     |     |
| Availability   |     |     | Y   |     |     |     |     | Y   | Y   |

## Task 2.5

- Showing video clips – instructive.
- Word processing key points – constructive.
- Mapping data – constructive.
- Discussing printout – instructive.

## Task 9.3

- Task – some groups of pupils could be allocated faiths that were more familiar or easier to research than others.
- Response – the task can be completed with quite a simple report, but there is scope for very sophisticated analysis.
- Support – the teacher can help some pupils considerably in finding material and deciding how to use it, but leave others to manage this for themselves.
- Resources – the teacher can provide specific websites, other materials, and locations, or can let pupils find sources for themselves.

# Appendix D
# ICT and Subject Teaching: Self-assessment and Record of Progress

Name: _____ Subject: _____

Please indicate your level of confidence with the following skills and techniques as follows:

0    I have no experience of this
1    I have done this, but I'm not confident with it
2    I am fairly confident with this when using a familiar computer and software package
3    I am very confident with this and could adapt my skills to a different computer/software.

## 1    General system operation

|  | Personal computer | Network computer |
|---|---|---|
| 1.1  Start up computer and log on if required | | |
| 1.2  Use a mouse | | |
| 1.3  Choose from menus | | |
| 1.4  Load a program | | |
| 1.5  Manipulate windows and switch between applications | | |
| 1.6  Save and reload files (hard disk and floppy) | | |

| 1.7  Copy/move/delete files | | |
|---|---|---|
| 1.8  Cut/copy and paste, drag and drop material | | |
| 1.9  Print | | |
| 1.10 Scan documents/images | | |
| 1.11 Connect devices (e.g. printer) | | |
| 1.12 Take screenshots and paste into documents, etc. | | |
| 1.13 Install/run CD-ROM | | |
| 1.14 Select devices for input and output (e.g. scanner, printer) | | |
| 1.15 Use a virus checker | | |
| 1.16 Set appropriate security options for PC and Internet use | | |

## 2    Developing, presenting and exchanging ideas

Using word processing, slide presentation and/or DTP software:

| 2.1  Enter and revise text | |
|---|---|
| 2.2  Select/delete/move text | |
| 2.3  Change size/font/attributes of text | |
| 2.4  Centre/justify/indent text | |
| 2.5  Check spelling | |
| 2.6  Use tables | |
| 2.7  Use bullets and numbered lists | |
| 2.8  Use boxes/frames to position items on the page | |
| 2.9  Import files | |
| 2.10 Add images | |
| 2.11 Use page numbers, running headers/footers | |

Using e-mail/conferencing software:

| | |
|---|---|
| 2.12  Send and read e-mails | |
| 2.13  Reply to and forward e-mails | |
| 2.14  Send and read attachments | |
| 2.15  Manage stored e-mails and e-mail address lists | |
| 2.16  Join and use list/newsgroup/conference | |

Using a graphics package, or drawing tools within another generic package:

| | |
|---|---|
| 2.17  Draw 'freehand' | |
| 2.18  Produce straight lines | |
| 2.19  Produce shapes | |
| 2.20  Change line/fill attributes | |
| 2.21  Move/copy/resize objects | |
| 2.22  Crop images | |

## 3    Structuring, processing and finding information

Using CD-ROM/WWW:

| | |
|---|---|
| 3.1    Find information using menus/links/indexes | |
| 3.2    Find information using simple keyword searches | |
| 3.3    Find information using search engine with complex keyword searches | |
| 3.4    Use bookmarks and 'history' features to retrieve pages | |
| 3.5    Create simple set of linked hypertext/web pages | |

Using a database package:

| | |
|---|---|
| 3.6    Find information using field criteria | |
| 3.7    Sort data into order | |
| 3.8    Produce reports | |
| 3.9    Design data capture forms (e.g. questionnaires) | |

| 3.10 | Create database with record/field structure | |
| 3.11 | Enter data into record/field structure | |
| 3.12 | Amend incorrect data | |

## 4    Exploring and creating models of relationships

Using a spreadsheet package or similar modelling program:

| 4.1 | Enter text and numbers into cells | |
| 4.2 | Edit cell contents and draw conclusions from changes | |
| 4.3 | Enter formulas | |
| 4.4 | Format cells, e.g. changing borders, text size, font, number type | |
| 4.5 | Hide and protect cell contents | |
| 4.6 | Produce graphs | |

## 5    General task control strategies for using ICT

| 5.1 | Identify the objectives of the work | |
| 5.2 | Decide on software/techniques to be used | |
| 5.3 | Plan the work | |
| 5.4 | Evaluate and develop the work | |
| 5.5 | Refer to help when needed | |
| 5.6 | Use 'wizards' when appropriate | |
| 5.7 | Identify and rectify simple faults and safety hazards | |
| 5.8 | Backup work | |
| 5.9 | Consider the legal and ethical implications of any action involving the communication, storage or processing of information | |

## 6    Using an interactive whiteboard

| | | |
|---|---|---|
| 6.1 | Start system and calibrate board | |
| 6.2 | Write notes in 'electronic handwriting' | |
| 6.3 | Store and retrieve notes | |
| 6.4 | Convert handwriting to text | |
| 6.5 | Use resource libraries | |
| 6.6 | Create prepared files of visual material in 'flipchart' or 'notebook' form | |
| 6.7 | Use on-screen keyboard to enter data | |

## 7    Planning to teach with ICT and evaluating the effectiveness of ICT

| | | |
|---|---|---|
| 7.1 | Identify when ICT is likely to be effective in helping pupils to learn | |
| 7.2 | Use the Internet to identify appropriate resources for teaching and learning | |
| 7.3 | Select appropriate resources in relation to particular learning objectives | |
| 7.4 | Use ICT to support differentiated activity | |
| 7.5 | Structure pupil tasks to minimise potential frustration and off-task activity | |
| 7.6 | Recognise the ICT skills needed by pupils to carry out set tasks | |
| 7.7 | Evaluate the contribution of ICT resources to teaching and learning | |
| 7.8 | Use ICT to identify and access relevant research and inspection findings | |

## 8    Teaching with ICT

| | |  |
|---|---|---|
| 8.1 | Use a single computer in the classroom effectively, either with the whole class or by organising its use by pupils/groups | |
| 8.2 | Manage pupils' use of an ICT room effectively | |
| 8.3 | Use ICT to focus pupils' attention and aid them in responding to questions | |
| 8.4 | Monitor pupils' progress with ICT tasks | |
| 8.5 | Recognise when to intervene in pupils' use of ICT and when to encourage independent exploration | |
| 8.6 | Support pupils in developing ICT skills when necessary | |
| 8.7 | Assess subject attainment, taking account of the use of ICT | |
| 8.8 | Use ICT to help support pupils with special educational needs | |

As you gain experience, you should update your record. You may be asked to discuss your experience or provide evidence of your activity.

# Appendix E
# Lesson Plan Template

| DATE | | CLASS | | NUMBER OF PUPILS | | ABILITY | |
|------|--|-------|--|------------------|--|---------|--|

| LENGTH | | TOPIC AND CONTEXT | | NC REF. | |
|--------|--|-------------------|--|---------|--|

**AIMS**

**LEARNING OBJECTIVES**

**TASK OUTCOMES AND EXPECT-ATIONS**

ROLE OF ICT

PRIOR
KNOWLEDGE

POSSIBLE
PROBLEMS

EQUIPMENT
REQUIRED

ASSESSMENT
OPPORTUN-
ITIES

LESSON STRUCTURE

| TIMING | TEACHER ACTIVITY | PUPIL ACTIVITY | RESOURCE |
|---|---|---|---|
|  |  |  |  |

# Bibliography

Abbott, C. (2001) 'Special educational needs – becoming more inclusive', in Dillon, J. and McGuire, M. (eds) *Becoming a teacher: issues in secondary teaching* (2nd edition), Buckingham: Open University Press.

Adey, P. and Shayer, M. (1994) *Really Raising Standards*, London: Routledge.

Adey, P. *et al.* (1999) *Learning styles and strategies: a review of research*, London: King's College.

BCS (2002) *A glossary of computing terms* (10th edition), Harlow: Addison Wesley and British Computer Society.

Becta (2001) *The 'Digital Divide': a discussion paper*, Coventry: Becta.

Becta (2002a) *The impact of ICT on pupil learning and attainment*, Coventry: Becta.

Becta (2002b) *Pupils' and teachers' perceptions of ICT in the home, school and community*, Coventry: Becta.

Becta (2002c) *Learning at home and school: case studies*, Coventry: Becta.

Becta (2003a) *What is a Virtual Learning Environment?* On-line at http://www.ictadvice.org.uk/index.php?section=te&rid=77 (accessed 17th November 2003).

Becta (2003b) *What the research says about Virtual Learning environments in teaching and learning.* On-line at http://www.becta.org.uk/page_documents/research/wtrs_vles.pdf (accessed 17th November 2003).

Becta (2003c) *Differentiation* On-line at http://www.becta.org.uk/teachers/teachers.cfm?section=1_6_2&id=948 (accessed 17th November 2003).

Becta (2003d) *How to use software to support pupils with special educational needs.* On-line at http://www.ictadvice.org.uk (accessed 1st November 2003).

Becta (2003e) *How to ensure the safe use of ICT in schools.* On-line at http://www.ictadvice.org.uk/index.php?section=ap&rid=151&country=eng (accessed 17th November 2003).

Beynon, J. and McKay, H. (1993) *Computers into classrooms: more questions than answers*, London: Falmer Press.

Birnbaum, I. (1989) *IT and the National Curriculum: some fundamental issues*, Doncaster: Resource.

Birnbaum, I. (1990) 'The assessment of IT capability', *Journal of Computer Assisted Learning*, 6: 88–97.

Black, P. and Wiliam, D. (1998) Assessment and Classroom Learning. *Assessment in education*, **5**(1): 7–71. (accessed 17th November 2003).

Blamires, M. (ed.) (1999) *Enabling technology for inclusion*, London: Paul Chapman Publishing.

Bliss, J., Askew, M. and Macrae, S. (1996) 'Effective teaching and learning: scaffolding revisited', *Oxford Review of Education*, 22: 37–61.

Bourne, R., Davitt, J. and Wight, J. (1995) *Differentiation: taking IT forward*, Coventry: NCET.

Bowell, B., France, S. and Redfern, S. (1994) *Portable computers in action*, Coventry: NCET.

Bowring-Carr, C. and West-Burnham, J. (1997) *Effective learning in schools*, London: Pitman.

Bransford, J., Brown, A. and Cocking, R. (1999) *How people learn*, Washington, DC: National Academy Press.

Brown, S. and McIntyre, D. (1993) *Making sense of teaching*, Buckingham: Open University Press.

Capel, S., Leask, M. and Turner, T. (eds) (2001) *Learning to teach in the secondary school: a companion to school experience* (3rd edition), London: RoutledgeFalmer.

CCEA (2003) *Skills and capabilities framework*. On-line at http://www.ccea.org.uk/ks3/pdf/teacher_pack/skills+capabilities_fwk.pdf (accessed 17th November 2003).

CLIO (2000) *'Could try harder' – The LEARN Project guidance for schools on assessment for learning*, Bristol: CLIO.

Collin, S. (2002) *Dictionary of information technology* (3rd edition), London: Peter Collin Publishing.

Conlon, T. (2002) 'Information mapping as support for learning and teaching', *Computer Education*, 102: 2–12.

Cornu (2003) 'The teaching profession: a networked profession in new networked environments', in Dowling, C. and Lai, K. (eds) (2003) *ICT and the teacher of the future*, Dordrecht: Kluwer Academic.

Cox, M. (1999) 'Motivating pupils', in Leask, M. and Pachler, N. (eds) (1999) *Learning to teach using ICT in the secondary school*, London: Routledge.

Crook, C. (1994) *Computers and the collaborative experience of learning*, London: Routledge.

Deadman, G. (2003) 'KS3 strategy, ICT strand: additional materials to support schools in challenging circumstances', *Computer Education*, 104: 23–4.

DFE (1995b) *Value Added in Education: A Briefing Paper from the Department for Education*, London: DFE.

DfEE/QCA (1999) *Information and Communications Technology: the National Curriculum for England*, London: Department for Education and Employment and Qualifications and Curriculum Authority.

DfES (2001a) *What are the key skills?* On-line at http://www.dfes.gov.uk/keyskills/what.shtml (accessed 17th November 2003).

DfES (2001b) *SEN Code of Practice*, London: Department for Education and Employment.

DfES (2001c) *Inclusive Schooling – Children With Special Educational Needs*, London: DfES.

DfES (2002a) *KS3 National Strategy: Key messages from the ICT launch*. Online at http://www.standards.dfes.gov.uk/midbins/keystage3/launch_key_messages.pdf (accessed 17th November 2003).

DfES (2003) *Special Educational Needs*. On-line at http://www.dfes.gov.uk/sen/index.cfm (accessed 17th November 2003).

Dodge, B. (1995) *Some thoughts about web quests*. On-line at web quest.sdsu.edu/about_webquests.html (accessed 17th November 2003).

Ellis, V. (2002) *Learning and teaching in secondary schools*. Exeter: Learning Matters.

Fairbrother, B. and Harrison, C. (2001) 'Assessing pupils', in Dillon, J. and McGuire, M. (eds) *Becoming a teacher: issues in secondary teaching* (2nd edition), Buckingham: Open University Press.

Flavell, J. H. (1976) 'Metacognitive aspects of problem solving', in Resnick L. B. (ed.), *The nature of intelligence*, Hillsdale, NJ: Lawrence Erlbaum.

Franklin, G. (2001) 'Special educational needs issues and ICT', in Leask, M. (ed.) *Issues in learning using ICT*, London: RoutledgeFalmer.

Franklin, G. and Litchfield, D. (1999) 'Special Educational Needs and ICT', in Leask, M. and Pachler, N. (eds) *Learning to teach using ICT in the secondary school*, London: Routledge.

Gardner, H. (1993 2nd edition) *Frames of mind: the theory of multiple intelligences*, London: Fontana.

Glover, D. and Law, S. (2002) *Improving learning: professional practice in secondary schools*, Buckingham: Open University Press.

Goldstein, G. (1997) *Information Technology in English Schools – a commentary on inspection findings 1995–6*, London: Office for Standards in Education.

GTCW (2002) *Continuing Professional Development: an entitlement for all*, Cardiff: General Teaching Council for Wales.

Harrison, C. (2001) 'Differentiation in theory and practice', in Dillon, J. and McGuire, M. (eds) *Becoming a teacher: issues in secondary teaching* (2nd edition), Buckingham: Open University Press.

Hassell, D. and Warner, H. (1995) *Using ICT to enhance geography: case studies at KS3 and KS4*, Coventry: NCET and the Geographical Association.

Haydn, T. (2001) 'Assessment and accountability', in Capel, S., Leask, M. and Turner, T. (eds) *Learning to teach in the secondary school: a companion to school experience* (3rd edition), London: RoutledgeFalmer.

Hitchcock, G. and Hughes, G. (1995 2nd edition) *Research and the teacher*, London: Routledge.

Hughes, I. and Kennewell, S. (2003) 'Organising learning and monitoring progress', in Kennewell, S., Parkinson, J. and Tanner, H. (eds) (2003) *Learning to teach ICT in the secondary school*, London: RoutledgeFalmer.

Hughes, M. and Vass, A. (2001) *Strategies for closing the learning gap*, Stafford: Network Educational Press.

Imison, T. and Taylor, P. (2001) *Managing ICT in the secondary school*, Oxford: Heinemann.

Information Commissioner's Office (2004) *Principles of data protection*. On-line at http://www.informationcommissioner.gov.uk/eventual.aspx?id=302 (accessed 3rd February 2004).

Inspiration Software Inc. (2002) *Inspiration getting started guide*, Portland, Oregon: Inspiration Software.

ISTE (2003a) *National Educational Technology Standards for Students*. On-line at http://cnets.iste.org/students/s_stands.html (accessed 17th November 2003).

ISTE (2003b) *National Educational Technology Standards for Teachers*. On-line at http://cnets.iste.org/teachers/t_stands.html (accessed 17th November 2003).

Joyce, B., Calhoun, E. and Hopkins, D. (1999) *New structure of school improvement: inquiring schools and achieving students*, Buckingham: Open University Press.

Keates, A. (2000) *Dyslexia and ICT: a guide for teachers and parents*, London: David Fulton.

Kennewell, S. (2001) 'Using affordances and constraints to evaluate the use of ICT in teaching and learning', *Journal of IT and Teacher Education*, **10**, 101–16.

Kennewell, S. (2002) 'Developing an ICT capability for learning', in Marshall, G. and Katz, Y. (eds) (2002) *Learning in School, Home and Community: ICT in Early and Elementary Education*, Boston: Kluwer Academic Press.

Kennewell, S. (2003) 'The nature of ICT as subject', in Kennewell, S., Parkinson, J. and Tanner, H. (eds) (2003) *Learning to teach ICT in the secondary school*, London: RoutledgeFalmer.

Kennewell, S. and Beauchamp, G. (2003) 'The influence of a technology-rich classroom environment on elementary teachers' pedagogy and children's learning', in Wright, J., McDougall, A., Murnane, J. and Lowe, J. (eds) (2003) *Young children and learning technologies*, Sydney: Australian Computer Society.

Kennewell, S., Parkinson, J. and Tanner, H. (2000) *Developing the ICT-capable school*, London: RoutledgeFalmer.

Kennewell, S., Parkinson, J. and Tanner, H. (eds) (2003) *Learning to teach ICT in the secondary school*, London: RoutledgeFalmer.

Knowsley LEA (2003) *The impact of e-learning on GCSE results in Knowsley, 2002*, Knowsley: Knowsley Council.

Lave, J. and Wenger, E. (1991) *Situated learning: legitimate peripheral participation*, Cambridge: Cambridge University Press.

Leask, M. and Pachler, N. (eds) (1999) *Learning to teach using ICT in the secondary school*, London: Routledge.

Leask, M. and Younie, S. (2001) 'Building on-line communities for teachers', in Leask, M. (ed.) *Issues in learning using ICT*, London: RoutledgeFalmer.

McKeown, S. (2000) *Dyslexia and ICT: building on success*, Coventry: Becta.

Macrae, S. and Quintrell, M. (2001) 'Managing effective classrooms', in Dillon, J. and McGuire, M. (eds) *Becoming a teacher: issues in secondary teaching* (2nd edition), Buckingham: Open University Press.

March, T. (1997) *The web quest design process*. On-line at www.ozeline.com/webquests/design.html (accessed 17th November 2003).

Martin, D. and Walsh, B. (1998) *History using IT: searching for patterns in the past using spreadsheets and databases*, Coventry: NCET and the Historical Association.

Mellar, H., Bliss, J., Boohan, R. Ogborn, J. and Tompsett, C. (eds) (1994) *Learning with artificial worlds: computer-based modelling in the curriculum*, London: Falmer Press.

Muijs, D. and Reynolds, D. (2001) *Effective teaching: evidence and practice*, London: Paul Chapman.

NAACE (2003) 'Key characteristics of good quality teaching and learning with ICT' *Computer Education*, 104: 10–21.

NCC (1990) *Non-statutory Guidance: Information Technology Capability*, York: National Curriculum Council.

NCET (1994) *IT works*, Coventry: National Council for Educational Technology.

NCET (1995) *Using IT for assessment*, Coventry: National Council for Educational Technology.

NCET (1997) *IT in English: case studies and materials*, Coventry: National Council for Educational Technology.

NCET (1998) *Delivering and assessing IT through the curriculum*, Coventry: National Council for Educational Technology.

Newton, L. and Rogers, L. (2001) *Teaching Science with ICT*, London: Continuum Press.

Ofsted (2004) Standards and Quality 2002–03: Annual Report of Her Majesty's Chief Inspector of Schools, London: The Stationery Office.

Owen, M. (1992) 'A teacher-centred model of development in the educational use of computers', *Journal of Information Technology for Teacher Education*, 1: 127–38.

Pachler, N. and Byrom, K. (1999) 'Assessment of and through ICT', in Leask, M. and Pachler, N. (ed.) (1999) *Learning to teach using ICT in the secondary school*, London: Routledge.

Papert, S. (1996) *Connected family: bridging the digital generation gap*, Atlanta: Longstreet Press.

Parker, B. and Bowell, B. (1998) 'Exploiting computer-mediated communications to support in-service professional development', *Journal of Information Technology and Teacher Education*, 7: 229–62.

Perry, D. (2002) *Wireless networking in schools*, Coventry: Becta.

Perry, D. (2003) *Handheld computers (PDAs) in schools*, Coventry: Becta.

Poole, P. (1998) *Talking about ICT in subject teaching*, Canterbury: Canterbury. Christchurch University College.

Preston, C. (1999) 'Bulding on-line professional development communities for schools, professional associations or LEAs', in Leask, M. and Pachler, N. (eds) (1999) *Learning to teach using ICT in the secondary school*, London: Routledge.

QCA (2003a) *Assessment for learning*. On-line at http://www.qca.org.uk/ca/5-14/afl/ characteristics.asp (accessed 17th November 2003).

QCA (2003b) *ICT: a scheme of work for Key Stages 1 and 2* (2ⁿᵈ edition), London: Qualifications and Curriculum Authority.

Riding, R. and Rayner, S. (1998) *Cognitive styles and learning strategies*, London: David Fulton.

RM (2003) *Using RM tablet PC at the Cornwallis School*. Online at http://www.rm.com/ Secondary/CaseStudies/CaseStudyDetail.asp?cref=CS113293 (accessed 17ᵗʰ November 2003).

SBOLP (1999) Using *ICT in teaching secondary mathematics: case study 3*, Swansea: Swansea Bay Online Learning Partnership.

Schagen, S. and Kerr, D. (1999) *Bridging the gap?: the National Curriculum and progression from primary to secondary school*, Slough: National Foundation for Educational Research.

Schön, D. (1987) *Educating the Reflective Practitioner*, San Francisco: Jossey Bass.

Scottish Executive (2000) *The 5–14 Curriculum (Scotland) Guidelines*, Edinburgh: Scottish Executive and Learning and Teaching Scotland.

Skinner, B. (1968) *The Technology of Teaching*, New York: Appleton-Century-Crofts.

Smith, A. (1997) *Accelerated learning in the classroom*, Stafford: Network Educational Press.

Somekh, B. (1997) 'Classroom investigations: exploring and evaluating how IT can support learning', in Somekh, B. and Davis, N. (1997) *Using information technology effectively in teaching and learning*, London: Routledge.

Somekh, B. and Davis, N. (1997) *Using information technology effectively in teaching and learning*, London: Routledge.

Somekh, B. and Davies, R. (1991) 'Towards a pedagogy for information technology', *The Curriculum Journal*, 2, 153–70.

Squires, D. and McDougall, A. (1994) *Choosing and using educational software*, London: Falmer Press.

Stanley, N. and Tanner, H. (2003) 'Assessing attainment', in Kennewell, S., Parkinson, J. and Tanner, H. (eds) (2003) *Learning to teach ICT in the secondary school*, London: RoutledgeFalmer.

Stevenson, D. (1997) *Information and communications technology: an independent inquiry*, London: Independent ICT in Schools Commission.

Tanner, H. (2003) 'The place of ICT in secondary education', in Kennewell, S., Parkinson, J. and Tanner, H. (eds) (2003) *Learning to teach ICT in the secondary school*, London: RoutledgeFalmer.

Tanner, H. and Jones, S. (2000) *Becoming a successful teacher of mathematics*, London: RoutledgeFalmer.

Trend, R., Davis, N. and Loveless, A. (1999) *Information and communications technology*, London: Letts Educational.

TTA (1998) *The Use of ICT in Subject Teaching: expected outcomes for teachers*, London: Teacher Training Agency and the Departments of Education.

TTA (1999a) ICT: *Identification of your training needs* [CD-ROM], London: Teacher Training Agency.

TTA (1999b) *Using ICT to meet teaching objectives in secondary geography*, London: Teacher Training Agency.

TTA (2002) *Qualifying to Teach: Professional Standards for Qualified Teacher Status and Requirements for Initial Teacher Training*, London: Teacher Traning Agency.

Underwood, J. (1994) *Computer based learning: potential into practice*, London: David Fulton.

Underwood, J. and Brown, J. (1997) *Integrated Learning Systems: potential into practice*, Oxford: Heinemann.

Virtual Teachers' Centre (2003) *Case study: Travellers' Tales*, On-line at http://vtc.ngfl.gov.uk/ docserver.php?docid=3706 (accessed 17ᵗʰ November 2003).

Vygotsky, L. (1978) *Mind in society: the development of higher psychological processes*, Cambridge, MA: Harvard University Press.

Warner, G. (1999) 'Using ICT for professional purposes', in Leask, M. and Pachler, N. (eds) (1999) *Learning to teach using ICT in the secondary school*, London: Routledge.

Watkins, C. *et al.* (2000) *Learning about learning: resources for supporting effective learning*, London: RoutledgeFalmer.

Wood, D. (1988) *How children think and learn: the social context of cognitive development*, Oxford: Blackwell.

Yellis Project (2003) *What is Value-added?* On-line at http://www.yellisproject.org/Handbook/whatisva.asp (accessed 17th November 2003).

# Index